# Abbé Groulx

Issues in Canadian History
General Editor: J.L. Granatstein

# Abbé Groulx

## VARIATIONS ON A
## NATIONALIST THEME

Edited by Susan Mann Trofimenkoff

Copp Clark Publishing

A Division of Copp Clark Limited
Vancouver   Calgary   Toronto   Montreal

This book was published with the assistance of a grant
from the Canadian Horizons Program of the Canada
Council.


Translation by Joanne L'Heureux and Susan Mann
Trofimenkoff

ISBN 0-7730-3119-7

Printed and bound in Canada
Copp Clark Publishing
517 Wellington Street West, Toronto M5V 1G1

# Contents

INTRODUCTION  7

LITERARY GROULX  23

A Lesson From the Maple Trees  23
How I Came to Leave Politics  24
To Erle Bartlett  31
A Peerless Old Bachelor  34
The Call of the Race  35
To Cape Blomidon  44

VOCAL GROULX  55

The Tradition of French Literature in Canada  55
Duties of the University Community  62
*L'Action française*  68
*L'Action nationale*  83
French Canadian Nationalism  87

HISTORICAL GROULX  97

The Teaching of History in Our Colleges  97
The Role and Traditions of the French Canadian Family  100
The British Regime in Canada  120
The Explosion  126
French Canadians and Confederation  134
History as a Guardian of Living Traditions  146

DOCTRINAL GROULX  163

Our French Canadian and Catholic Youth  163
The Clergy and Social Action  170
The Economic Problem  172
Our Political Future  176

To *L'Echo*, Collège d'Edmonton                                186
The National Problem                                           189
Mr. Bourassa's Lecture Series                                  191
To Pierre Chaloult                                             195

GROULX ON GROULX                                               198

My Childhood                                                   198
The Vicarage at Mile End                                       204
*L'Action française*: An Appraisal                             208
On the Fiftieth Anniversary of my Priesthood                  211
In Defense of the Nationalism of my Generation                216
My Concept of History                                         223
Last Will and Testament                                       233

QUÉBÉCOIS ON GROULX                                            234

A Narrow Little Sect                                           234
    *Le Soleil*

Blind Prejudice                                                234
    *Le Soleil*

Mr. Lionel Groulx, Prime Minister                              235
    *Le Jour*

The Spiritual Father of Modern Quebec                          237
    CLAUDE RYAN, *Le Devoir*

In Memoriam                                                    240
    JEAN-PIERRE WALLOT, *Le Progrès de Valleyfield*

Lionel Groulx                                                  242
    JEAN HAMELIN

Lionel Groulx, National Historian                              244
    MICHEL BRUNET

Lionel Groulx                                                  253
    ANDRÉ LAURENDEAU

SUGGESTED READING                                              256

# Introduction

Lionel Groulx was a nationalist priest. Imitating the celebrated aphorism of Michelet lecturing on England, one might add that that is all one needs to know about Groulx. Groulx was, in fact, and remains, a favourite subject for labels. Early critics, both English and French Canadian, came close to dubbing him a traitor for his querying of imperialism and of Confederation. Later critics, mostly English Canadian, attached a fascist tag to Groulx for his unashamed admiration of certain European leaders. Still later commentators, from both solitudes this time, tarred Groulx with an unrealistic brush, feathered him with conservatism, agriculturalism, traditionalism. By the time of his death in 1967, Groulx had become for some the "spiritual father of modern Quebec," a label no less debatable for all its sympathetic largesse.

Is it really fair, is it actually possible to encompass in a word or phrase the hyperactive, octogenarian Groulx? Groulx was peasant, priest and professor; he dabbled in poetry, philosophy, pamphleteering, politics and prophecy. And he wore all of his guises simultaneously. Possibly, therefore, Groulx's organic view of society stemmed in part from his unwillingness to shed any of his earlier skins. One can find, for example, traces of his peasant origin throughout his life: rural metaphors abound in speeches and articles; organic analogies constitute some of his more felicitous phrases. Perhaps even the battle imagery, the most striking of Groulx's colourful prose, developed in the subconscious of a peasant lad: the struggle for survival was very tangible to large rural families in the last quarter of the nineteenth century.

Groulx in fact seemed to thrive, not just on imagery, but on the struggle itself. Almost every aspect of his life involved serious obstacles for him. He battled disease in childhood, poor health throughout his life. He battled poverty, loneliness and homesickness to acquire an education. He battled an outmoded and uninspiring curriculum in his teaching. He battled some of his ecclesiastical colleagues over his notions of catholic action. He battled university and government establishments in his history lessons and his political programmes. He battled the lethargy of his compatriots. By the 1950's he was having to do battle with the indifference, often the open hostility, of a new generation of self-styled spokesmen for French Canada. Struggle was an essential part of Groulx's character.

Through all his battles Groulx maintained an extraordinary sense of optimism. Undoubtedly his faith, his religious profession, had much to do with the buoyancy of character, even of appearance, of the diminutive abbé Groulx. He had, in fact, a double faith, in God and in his fellow man. God, Groulx insisted, would never wish the death of a Catholic people. And that very people, Groulx fervently believed, had the will to take its destiny into its own hands.

That belief may have sustained Groulx's optimism; in no way did it restrain his proselytizing. Groulx had to act upon that belief. He had to convey it. He had to convince the doubting; he had to convert the apathetic; he had to arouse the lazy. French Canadians had to will their survival and they had to act upon that will. Neither God's presence nor Groulx's faith could do the job alone. Groulx was then essentially a teacher of the will. All his lessons, literary, religious, historical, polemical, taught pride, determination, resolution. From the meanest poem to the loftiest sermon, from the academic podium to the public platform, Groulx never once forgot his purpose – steeling the French Canadian will to survive.

Groulx's talents matched his self-imposed task. He was a devoted teacher, an inspiring friend, an encourager of young people, an indefatigable worker. He turned to history only in his late thirties, trained himself and undertook the Canadian History course at the Université Laval (Montreal); he even taught a course in the history of commerce at the Ecole des Hautes Etudes Commerciales. During the 1920's he added administrative and diplomatic skills to his professorial and priestly functions; his was the guiding hand behind the Action Française movement.[1] By the early 1930's a biographical sketch portrayed Groulx in the forefront of the Canadian intellectual scene: a prolific thinker, an introducer of new ideas, an historian-sociologist, a daring essayist.[2] And through it all – he had another thirty-six years to live – Groulx displayed a warm, generous, often humorous manner.

Lest such a personality appear super-human, Groulx had other characteristics. He basked in the adoration of groups of young people at the Collège de Valleyfield. He obviously enjoyed the notoriety he acquired during his years with the Action Française. Any doubts he professed about the compatibility of the priestly and the profane were strictly ex-post-facto. Possibly associated with the notoriety was Groulx's doctrinaire manner of thinking and acting. Much later, Groulx recognized these features as bordering on dogmatism and absolutism. Yet he seldom revised and never repented his former utterances. Indeed, he resented, to the point of taking personally, much criticism that was levelled only indirectly at him. His memoirs, for instance, are a lengthy rebuttal to the young people of the 1950's, struggling for a secular definition of French Canada. Then again, Groulx's penchant for moralizing often became overbearing; how long could people take the message that theirs was an endless watch through a potentially endless night?

Perhaps the most intriguing of Groulx's traits was his ambivalence. Was he a priest or a politician? Was he Ramsay Cook's frustrated man of action[3] or was he more secure in the priestly prohibition of active participation in politics? Where exactly did he put the emphasis – on his faith or on his nation? The concealed quarrel with Bourassa[4] during the 1920's and 1930's would seem to indicate the latter. However, Groulx the priest may have been just as scandalized as Groulx the nationalist by Bourassa's supposedly odd behaviour. Then too, was Groulx a separatist or was he not? He tended to deny separatism as fast as he proclaimed it. When a worried Westerner queried the implication of Our Political Future, Groulx replied that he was simply advocating preparation for the inevitable.[5] When an overtly separatist newspaper sought Groulx's sanction, he insisted that a spiritual renaissance precede any political innovation.[6] When wildly cheering crowds greeted his exclamation "We shall have our French state", Groulx dampened their ardour in a preface to that and other speeches: "Why can't people understand an autonomous state within a federation?"[7] The answer was simple. No one could understand because Groulx never elaborated. He obviously feared the revolutionary import of the very term separatism, yet he relished its revolutionary fervour. During the 1950's, in the privacy of his memoirs, Groulx confided that he had proposed the ideal of a French state to his students as long ago as 1904. But the French state was just that, an ideal, a state of mind, not a state of law.

Adding to the ambiguity over separatism was Groulx's attitude to French Canadian minorities outside Quebec. Were they part of the stumbling block to his openly declaring separatism? Groulx seemed unable to reconcile his desire for a strong Quebec as the national home of French Canada and the old dream of a French Canada from sea to sea. Groulx could not, and did not, ignore the minorities, yet he was well aware that Quebec had been able to do precious little for them in the past. On occasion he speculated about the superior sustenance an independent French state might provide. But more often Groulx seemed to invoke the minorities for their symbolic value. Like Bourassa, he saw them as a first line of defence. As they go, so go we. For Groulx, their presence served to remind French-speaking Québécois of their own minority status. The minorities outside Quebec became, therefore, essential to Groulx's entire task of awakening and alerting. Had they not existed, Groulx might well have invented them.

In all Groulx appears to be an equivocal combination of excessive modesty and innovative boldness. The latter realm embraced most of his actions and a fair number of his ideas; the former encompassed all of his explanations, recollections and rationalizations. Groulx was always seeking sanction for his undertakings. The annotated books in his library attest to the delight he felt when a known French author expressed views similar to his own. In the 1920's, for example, Groulx cited Charles Maurras[8] and the other writers of the French Action Française;[9] in the 1930's he lauded the work of Mussolini (one should have Groulx's pre-Mussolini experience of Rome before admonishing him), Salazar, Dolfuss and De Valera; in the 1950's, how happy he was to don the cloak of Marshal Pétain's authority; in the 1960's he insisted that his historical views coincided with those of Henri Marrou, Lucien Febvre and Marc Bloch.[10] Groulx's designated authorities reveal less about his political views than about his need for sanction. Indeed this may well be the origin of Groulx's cry for a *chef*, a leader. From Dollard to Duplessis, Groulx unceasingly invoked the ideal figure of *le chef*. Dollard he could and did embellish;[11] of Duplessis, after a fleeting hope, he despaired. Groulx never would, never could, recognize the fact that for some people, *he* was *le chef*. For in spite of his antipathy to partisan politics, Groulx portrayed the ideal *chef* in a political role. From such a role, Groulx was barred by the cloth.

The bar, the ambivalence, the equivocation, the almost split personality tempts one to make of Groulx a microcosm of French Canadian society. Just as Frank Underhill has described Mackenzie King as "the typical Canadian ... the Canadian as he exists in the mind of God",[12] so might one portray Groulx as the typical French Canadian. Until the 1960's, that is. Then is the modesty tossed aside – a modesty that may well have inhibited French Canada from following Groulx's directives. The need and search for authority – in the guise of Groulx's closest love, the Church – is similarly discarded. Groulx and his *petit peuple* went their separate ways.

And yet that very divergence may have been a result of Groulx's efforts. He taught collective pride. He taught it from the traditional vantage, and hence advantage, points of the podium and the pulpit. The geometric progression of such an idea from such a post was bound to culminate in something like the 'no' to the Victoria constitutional charter or like the movement for a unilingual Quebec. Groulx also taught independence, however vaguely and with whatever moralistic overtones. The power of that idea in contemporary French Canada requires little proof. Groulx taught the potential of an *état national* and hence weaned his compatriots from federal politics and federal politicians. Groulx thus provided much of the ideological framework for the Quiet Revolution. But given the nature of those very teachings – Groulx was always lean on practicalities – it is no surprise that a different generation would construe the application of those teachings differently.

But what of Groulx's own generation? How many people really listened to him? What kind of weight did he pull? What kind of power did he exercise?

The accepted view implies positive answers to those questions. It is a view shared, curiously enough, by the most conservative of nationalists and the most liberal of academics. The two differ only in their attitude to contemporary Quebec society: the first regret it as a rejection of the good of the past; the second welcome it as a rejection of the bad of the past. On the past itself they both agree. Dominating that past – at least since about 1850 – they posit a monolithic, unitary, conservative, ruralistic, élitist, clerical ideology. They point to aberrations like the Institut Canadien[13] and to misfits like Arthur Buies[14] as proof of the strength of the ideology. They wonder about the economic inferiority of French Canadians and look for the reasons within the ideology. They look for class consciousness in French Canada's past; finding none, they once again point the finger at the ideology. They project, in fact, in nationalistic or academic jargon, the very view that uninformed English Canadians have always harboured about French Canada: a static, unenlightened, unprogressive, priest-ridden, backward (albeit quaint) society. Into that society and its ideology, Groulx would fit as the epitome, the last and loudest spokesman.

A number of facts flaw this analysis. The battle between the Bishop of Montreal and the Institut Canadien, for instance, was long and protracted. The outcome was by no means predetermined. The fact that one can find so few individuals of the stamp of Arthur Buies probably says less about a particular ideology than about the élitist views of historians, of whatever origin or training. Few societies produce their "characters" among their generals, politicians or priests. Then too, this well-trussed, immobile society produced millions of migrants. Whether heading for the United States or the cities, these people calmly ignored the Official Ideology of perdition among the factories and the furnaces. And again, French Canada's post-Confederation generation of businessmen lagged little (except in sheer luck of the geographical draw) behind their English Canadian counterparts. They lost out, in the first decade of the twentieth century, less to ideology (a good many English and English Canadian businessmen had classical educations; Latin and Greek did not deplete *their* pockets) than to American capital. One might even speculate that the post-Second World War generation of French Canadian businessmen owes something to Groulx's unceasing lessons of collective pride and autonomous development. Finally, the lack of an ideological expression of class consciousness hardly proves that classes themselves did not exist in nineteenth and twentieth century French Canada.

The foregoing suggests that ideologies may not be very important in the life of the ordinary citizen. How many students, for instance, took up Groulx's call to a kind of lay priesthood? How many shopkeepers, at Groulx's request, put pressure on suppliers for goods labelled in French? How many parents considered withdrawing their children from schools where mathematics and science were taught in English? How many politicians paid much attention to the rantings of abbé Groulx? How many youngsters avoided the Sunday, English language, cinema? How many mothers refrained from working outside the home in order to follow Groulx's strictures? How many children could resist Santa Claus? Ideologies may be the very stuff of nationalists and of academics – the latter earn their living thereby, the former their notoriety – but their relevance to the common man has yet to be proven.

Abbé Groulx of course believed that he could speak to and of most of the people. His peasant origin, he felt, accorded him a kind of *passe-partout* to every level of society. But his education and his profession elevated him far beyond the ordinary man. His was a class apart. Trained for, and used to, an élitist conception of society, was Groulx the last of the line? Can an urban industrial society accept clerical leadership? Were Groulx's cries a swan song? Or was much of his stridency, his repetitiveness, indicative of his inability to reach his *petit peuple*?

What exactly does one make of this man Groulx harking back and harking forward while seemingly crying in a contemporary wilderness? He appears to be less the epitome of the old religio-nationalism (of which Jules-Paul Tardivel[15] and Henri Bourassa are perhaps the true spokesmen) than a bridge to the new secular nationalism of the 1960's. Groulx's cassock prevented him from being more than the transition. Yet, just as he could not take the final step, so too he refused to stumble back to the earlier stage.

Groulx's quarrel with Bourassa illustrates the dilemma. During the 1920's, Bourassa began to look askance at the younger group of nationalists surrounding abbé Groulx and the

Montreal periodical *L'Action française*. Progressively he accused them of being ungrateful separatists, preferring their language to their faith, advocating immoderate nationalism, abetting revolt against Catholic authority. Bourassa misunderstood the essentially poetic nature of Groulx's separatism; he also regretted the loss of previously devoted followers. Because he was perfectly capable of making a rational distinction between his faith and his nationalism – Catholicism surpassed all – he could not conceive of a Groulx emotionally insisting that no distinction be made. And so upset was Groulx over what he considered to be Bourassa's deviation that he too engaged in some surreptitious speculation. Bourassa, he claimed, had fallen victim to religious scruples. Bourassa was mad.

The vehemence of Groulx's accusation was undoubtedly indicative of the importance of Bourassa to Groulx. More than the electrifying orator, more than the esteemed mentor, more than the revered *chef*, Bourassa may have represented a kind of religious *alter ego* to Groulx. For all his external aplomb in the face of the Papal condemnation of the French Action Française and the Sentinelle movement in Rhode Island,[16] Groulx could not conceal his fear. Papal displeasure with nationalistic assertiveness appeared to be closing in on the Montreal Action Française. When a rumour suggested the possibility of Papal censure of the Montreal publication, Groulx was thrown into a fearful flurry. Contributing to the uneasiness was Groulx's total conviction of the righteousness of his cause: the spiritual revival that he so ardently preached surely could not be foreign to Catholicism. But there was that outspoken and pesky Bourassa, a layman at that, attempting to read religious lessons to an ordained priest! Groulx could take neither the irony nor the insult. He therefore flailed Bourassa almost as part of himself. Did he exorcise some personal ghost by lashing out at Bourassa?

Groulx was very much of a transition. He had gone beyond Bourassa. His was not a clearly defined hierarchy with Catholicism at the top but rather a vague synthesis with a pervading Catholicism. Just as Bourassa did not understand him, so too Groulx did not appreciate a later generation. In a manner reminiscent of Bourassa's quarrel with his younger disciples, Groulx scorned those young students, writers, journalists, and trade union leaders of the 1950's and 1960's who attempted to discard the religious side of their nationalist heritage. But participation in a generation gap did not render Groulx any more sympathetic to earlier situations. He saw no good in a bifurcated nationalism, whether religious or secular. Similar to the Bloc Populaire[17] in the political field (wavering between a movement and a party, between a federal and a provincial orientation), Groulx was the transition, necessarily ambiguous, inevitably equivocal, between the two.

Groulx's nationalism, probably like all nationalisms, becomes then a highly personal thing. The very lack of satisfactory explanations of nationalism, in spite of many erudite attempts, suggests that the phenomenon may have no meaning beyond the individual or group expressing it and the moment of expression. Groulx we have seen; the context remains.


Abbé Groulx emerged from rural Quebec in the late nineteenth century, studied in Europe, and spent most of his life in Canada's burgeoning metropolis. Into that setting he brought many of the characteristics of rural Victorian Canada: the doctrine of work, duty, thrift, frugality, prudence and otherworldly rewards. With those characteristics and against that backdrop, Groulx watched, sometimes guiding, often chiding, his *petit peuple* through industrialization, urbanization, anglicization, war, emigration to the cities and to the United States, depression (economic, political and moral), war again and conscription again, boom times, reform times, secularization of Quebec society in general and of education in particular, quiet and not-so-quiet revolutions, even Expo. Groulx witnessed them all, participating in some, pronouncing on most.

Only a few of Groulx's numerous pronouncements appear in this book. Groulx's bibliography alone, published in 1964, is longer than most of the books in this series; this one must necessarily be a selection. The pieces chosen fall roughly into five periods: pre-World War One; the war; the 1920's; the 1930's; post-World War Two.[18]

Prior to the First World War, abbé Groulx devoted his time to perfecting his own education and that of his young students at Valleyfield. He spent three years in Europe, acquiring doctorates in philosophy and theology in Rome and commencing yet another – a philological study of French in Canada – in Switzerland. The state of his health and his finances forced him to abandon the latter course and return to Canada. There he revived the minuscule *Action catholique*, a group he had inspired in 1902. Indeed, thanks largely to Groulx's initiative, the provincewide organization, L'Association catholique de la jeunesse canadienne-française (ACJC), was established in 1904. Groulx encouraged his young people to live their faith ardently. Whether or not they were headed for the priesthood, they must mould their characters on their belief and carry that belief into everyday life. Groulx presented the pattern; his closest students followed it: a life of Christian perfection, disciplined, deter-

14

mined and ascetic, a constant exercise of the will. Such characters, Groulx was convinced, would face the world with boldness, even nobility.

The Quebec world of the 1900's certainly provided scope for such individuals. An economic surge washed the first waves of affluence over the entire country. Early stages of industrialization and urbanization caused wonderment and worry. Groulx was even speaking and writing of socialism in that first decade of the twentieth century. The predominance of the English language in industry and commerce caused concern. Groulx participated in all the early organizations combatting such usage: La Société du parler français, Le Congrès de la langue française, La Ligue des droits du français.[19] Groulx was very much part of a period that looked askance at a rapidly secularizing France, that debated separatism (in the pages of the first newspaper that Groulx subscribed to, Jules-Paul Tardivel's *La Vérité*), that pondered the political and economic system (in the Ligue nationaliste[20] and the writings of Errol Bouchette[21]), that denounced imperialism in whatever guise – a South African War, a French Canadian Prime Minister, a British Admiralty or an English Catholic Archbishop. In those early days, Groulx hung on every word uttered by Henri Bourassa. He heard Bourassa's censure of the Federal Government over the North West schools issue. He listened spellbound in the cathedral of Notre Dame to Bourassa's impassioned plea for the French language. He attributed much of the cultural and moral revival of French Canada in that pre-war period to Henri Bourassa.

Bourassa came even closer to Groulx during the First World War. It was Bourassa who urged the creation of a chair in Canadian History at the Université Laval in Montreal. And it was Groulx whom the Archbishop of Montreal invited to assume the chair. In Montreal, Groulx stayed in the presbytery of abbé Perrier[22], one of whose more prominent parishioners was Henri Bourassa. Bourassa's weekly visits would last far into the night as the powerful orator and journalist entertained his priestly hosts with erudite monologues on Canadian and world history and politics. In many ways Bourassa initiated Groulx into the Canadian political scene.

For French Canadians that scene was a black one indeed. The Ontario schools question, the war, conscription, and the bitterness of the federal elections of 1917 all threatened French Canada. Abbé Groulx reacted in anguish to the domestic repercussions of the First World War. Would French Canada survive the combined assault on its language, its education, its traditions and its loyalty? Lacking any pre-war political experience, Groulx tended to define the fundamental reality of Canada in terms of the war. The real enemy was not in Europe but in the Anglo-Saxon fanatics that appeared in every government, every newspaper and every recruiting station. Because of the war, Groulx refused to see Canada as anything but a purveyor of pain and humiliation to French Canada.

That attitude Groulx carried into the 1920's. The nation in danger became his rallying cry. And since a minority nation cannot simply count heads and expect to win the democratic game, Groulx had to make of his *petit peuple* more than the sum of its parts. Hence the stress on history lessons with their glorious tales and their envigorating examples. Hence the call for *le chef* who would illustrate, in one supreme individual, the qualities so lacking in the group. Hence the urgent need for a doctrine to provide a coherent pattern for national behaviour. Hence the call for a separate state as an integrating and exhilarating ideal. And thus was born the Action Française movement.

The movement had an arduous task. It had to face political, economic and social disintegration not only on the Canadian but also on the world scene. Much of this it accepted, even welcomed. The decline of the British Empire, for instance, presaged a break-up of Confederation. And the federal elections of 1921 with the dramatic appearance of the western Progressives emphasized the absurdity, the crumbling of the country. The post-war depression gave birth to novel critiques of the economic system, stressing thereby the disparities within Confederation. On the home front too, a second phase of urbanization threatened much of the social fabric of French Canada. The inescapable facts of large cities were appalling: overcrowding, poor housing, infantile mortality, tuberculosis, alcoholism, drug addiction, venereal disease, police corruption and a declining birth rate. All of this the Action Française, encompassed, often moralising, sometimes counselling, occasionally shrieking, but never shirking. By the late 1920's however, Confederation was obviously not disintegrating. And the Action Française, whose earlier notes of separatism had sounded like variations on a Canadian theme (played in the Maritimes and in the West) began to sound the note of "better terms." By 1927 Groulx would give Confederation another chance. Bilingual stamps and bilingual cheques were not too little and too late in the 1920's.

The 1930's found Groulx writing his most heated critique of economic liberalism. And with some justification. Unhappily he had witnessed what he believed to be the over-industrialization of the 1920's. Worriedly he had watched the balance between agriculture and industry swing in favour of the latter. Angrily he had denounced the alienation of Quebec's natural resources to the Foreigner, particularly the American. Now came the depression, long and bitter, confirming, he felt, his analysis of the 1920's. He could even trace a line of causality from the dire social conditions to an industrial system largely financed with foreign capital and abetted by a Liberal provincial government. Groulx attacked them all.

Groulx's reaction cannot easily be dubbed conservative or traditionalist. For in that decade, people *did* return to the land, people *did* take up the old ways of farming and of transport, people *did* question the validity of the capitalist regime, people *did* form new political parties and *did* defeat established governments. The kind of economic autarky that Groulx implied was practised by most countries of the western world. Still another very typical reaction: Groulx, like so many Canadians, was brought up on the doctrine of work; to such people, unemployment was a scandal, even a sin. Groulx's priestly clucking was a mere straw in the wind that was returning the whole world to the jungle.

Only in the period following the Second World War did some light appear through the jungle. And abbé Groulx was not at all sure that he liked what he saw. He had followed the fortunes and the misfortunes of the Bloc Populaire very closely. Was there then to be no hope of political renovation in Quebec? He had lauded the spokesmen of provincial autonomy but he could not alter his antipathy to partisan politicians. He had encouraged young people to live boldly but he scowled when that boldness turned on him. He must have relished the growing opposition to the Duplessis regime but he was shaken to think that he too was considered a dispensable relic of the past. Abbé Groulx was in his seventies; some unkindly tongues wished his silence.

Groulx jumped rather into the fray. He was too old? He would begin something new: the *Revue d'histoire de l'Amérique française*, inspired and directed by him, began publication in 1947. He was irrelevant? He would justify his work and his nationalism all over the province, in speeches, in memoirs, on radio, on television. He would show these croaking young upstarts in *Cité Libre* and in *Le Devoir* that the world had not begun with them. He would repeat his contention that only at great peril did a people discard its past. He scoffed at the "internationalists" of the 1950's floating about on airy dreams; he had seen their kind in the heyday of *bonne entente*[23]: they were the sweetness before the poison of assimilation. And with Quebec in the final fling of industrialization, how could assimilation to this North American English-speaking Leviathan be avoided? The questions grew bitter and so, occasionally, did abbé Groulx.

The format of this book is designed to stress the versatility of Groulx. If he was not quite a man for all seasons, he used every seasoning to savour his message. As a propagandist, Groulx was probably unmatched in French Canadian history. He turned his hand to every literary and oratorical technique: he lauded nature in poems and scolded politicians in novels; he read moral lessons in sermons and history lessons on the radio; he told tall tales and gave long lectures. He prodded and pummelled and pleaded with his *petit peuple*.

Part One offers a glimpse into Groulx's literary ventures. Groulx always claimed that such ventures were pure escapism. Poetry, novels, short stories (even memoirs) were, he insisted, mere diversions while holidaying or recovering from illness. Strange interludes! For although he may have temporarily left the city, the podium and the pulpit, Groulx left nothing else behind. One can find, in his literary escapism, all the elements of his more weighty tomes: the romantic attachment to the land, the moral lessons from the past, the hostility to party politics, the faith in young people, the sense of struggle and of mission, the pervading Catholicism. Had Groulx engaged in nothing but literary activities, he would have been a force to be reckoned with in French Canada.

Part Two listens in to Groulx the orator. An inveterate speaker, Groulx delivered hundreds of speeches and sermons (without even counting his lectures). From a youngster playing politics in the school yard in Vaudreuil to an octogenarian revealing memoirs on television in Montreal, Groulx travelled all over Quebec, into Ontario and into the States, talking all the way. A rather select audience was his: students, religious personnel and devout lay people, intellectuals, members of nationalist organizations. Fertile ground, no doubt. Yet Groulx later wondered about the efficacy of so much talk. Unable and unwilling to turn off the verbal torrent himself, he occasionally worried about others' ability to do so. They might hang on his words but would they practise his precepts?

Part Three peeks at Groulx the historian. History, Groulx felt, was the prerequisite of any true patriotism. Pride in, love for, and devotion to, a particular people developed only through knowledge. History was the key. But it was more. History provided the moral continuity between ancestors and descendants. History was a cohesive force for a people. As a key and as a force, history thus had a very present purpose for Groulx. His historical vision tended, therefore, to contain as many lessons to the present as revelations of the past: the qualities he spotted in French Canadians of the past, for example, – strength, independence, morality, integrity and resistance – were qualities he desperately wanted to evoke in his contemporaries. Like most histories written in Canada, in English or in French, Groulx's had as the ultimate aim the survival of his nation.

Part Four sketches Groulx the doctrinaire teacher of the will. The selections come primarily from the 1920's and 1930's. These were the years of Groulx's greatest concern for the way in which French Canadians would confront economic, social and political novelties. Groulx had to face, in these years, the agonizing question of the compatibility of a French and Catholic ideal with North American civilization. Groulx would have his people united, determined, brave and aggressive instead of scattered, vague, fearful and submissive. Hence the boldness of his idea of a separate state. The future too, like the past, was to provide a cohesive force for French Canadians. Groulx undoutedly engaged in some wishful thinking about the nature of society's novelties: he tended to assume that they were imposed upon French Canada from the Outside, by the Other, that they therefore constituted one more hurdle in the obstacle race of French Canadian survival. Quite the contrary. The phenomena were world wide. Every burgeoning city of the 1920's and every hollow metropolis of the 1930's faced similar problems. Groulx's insistence on confronting these problems in a French Canadian way and for French Canadian purposes was one response, but by no means a peculiar one.

Part Five pictures Groulx the explainer and the justifier. All of the selections correspond to the period in which Groulx faced his most serious criticism. He had to rationalize French Canadian nationalism, to demonstrate that other peoples (notably Anglo-Saxons) practised the same thing without the name, to prove that nationalism did not entail enclosing oneself in a ghetto. He had to satisfy not only the scepticism of others but also perhaps his own wondering about the import of his fervent and full life. Certainly Groulx had no intention of permitting himself or his *petit peuple*, if he could help it, to become T. S. Eliot's Hollow Men, ending "Not with a bang but a whimper."

Part Six is the merest of sneak previews. So many people have said so much, for and against Groulx, that a volume of their comments alone would not suffice. In general, Groulx did not enjoy the favour of politicians – *Le Soleil* was the official organ of the provincial Liberal party. He was too outspoken, too challenging, too much of a thorn in public men's sides. Various political manoeuvres to silence him came to naught. Groulx of course heartily reciprocated their disdain. With his fellow ecclesiastics, Groulx found more, although by no means unanimous favour. It was of journalists, former students and younger history teachers, particularly in the Montreal area in the latter half of the 1960's, that Groulx became the darling. As the death notices testify, all of these people acknowledged one of Groulx's basic tenets: that great men of the past have something to say to the present.

Groulx therefore, should have the final word. Any book organized around the media rather than the message is bound to harbour repetitions. Groulx himself was the first to admit to, even to justify, echoing so many of his dicta. He was also amusedly aware that re-editions of his work only emphasized that characteristic. Tucked into yet another reprint of one of his collections of speeches was a comment in Groulx's writing fitting for this book: *Pour bien rappeler que les vieillards se répètent on les ré-édite.* Another re-edition, a reminder that old men repeat themselves.

1. The Action Française movement harboured a small group of men – priests, lawyers, doctors, journalists – in Montreal in the 1920's. Through a monthly periodical, *L'Action française* (1917-1928), study sessions, lectures, speeches, a publishing house and a book shop, the group attempted to awaken French Canadians to the national plight posed by the post-war world.

2. R. Ouimet, *Biographies canadiennes-françaises* (Montreal, 1931), p. 339.

3. Ramsay Cook, review of J.-P. Gaboury, *Le nationalisme de Lionel Groulx* in *Histoire Sociale/Social History* 6 (1971), p. 138.

4. Henri Bourassa (1868-1952), the grandson of Louis-Joseph Papineau, was a journalist and politician. Founder of *Le Devoir* (1910), Bourassa devoted most of his energies to the campaign for Canadian autonomy. With a fiery tongue and a vitriolic pen, Bourassa lashed his contemporaries about the folly of imperialist wars abroad, the danger of racial, religious and linguistic bigotry at home. Bourassa never sanctioned separatism for French Canada.

5. Fondation Lionel Groulx, Groulx papers, undated draft of a letter from Groulx to the *Echo* of the Collège d'Edmonton.

6. Open letter from Groulx to Pierre Chaloult in *La Nation*, 22 February 1936.

7. "Pour ceux-là seulement qui savent lire" (Only for those who know how to read), *Directives* (Montreal, Les Editions du Zodiaque, 1937), p. 13.

8. Charles Maurras (1868-1952) was a French writer, political commentator and journalist for the royalist cause. Maurras saw only decadence in the political mores of France of the Third Republic; he convinced himself – by logic he always claimed – that the monarchy was the solution to France's political, social, economic and even moral ills.

9. The French Action Française, sparked by hostility to the Dreyfus affair, dates from 1899. Although the movement began in a reformist-republican vein, it soon – thanks to Charles Maurras – embraced the royalist cause. Its most prominent feature was the Parisian daily newspaper *L'Action française* (1908-1944) with acerbic comments on political and international affairs from the pens of Maurras, Léon Daudet and Jacques Bainville. The similarity of names between the Action Française in Paris and in Montreal, is, I believe, less a sign of political or spiritual influence or affinity than an indication of the Montreal group's anxiety to don some of the prestige of an internationally acclaimed group of writers.

10. Henri-Irenée Marrou (1904-   ), Lucien Febvre (1878-1956) and Marc Bloch (1886-1944) are among the most noted of French historians in the twentieth century. Although each has his field of specialization (history of Christianity, sixteenth century France and medieval Europe respectively), they have all turned their interest and their pens to the nature of history and historical writing: *De la connaissance historique*, *Combats pour l'histoire* and *Apologie pour l'histoire* respectively. Febvre and Bloch are particularly associated with early attempts to broaden history from a purely political study to a comprehensive view of man in society.

11. E.g. *Si Dollard revenait ...* (Montreal, Bibliothèque de L'Action française, 1919). The speech is not in this volume since it appears as "If Dollard were alive today" in R. Cook (ed.) *French Canadian Nationalism* (Toronto, Macmillan, 1969), pp. 188-201.

Also L. Groulx, *Le Dossier de Dollard* (Montreal, L'Imprimerie populaire, 1932) and *Dollard est-il un mythe?* (Montreal, Les Editions Fides, 1960).

See also André Vachon, "Dollard" in *Dictionary of Canadian Biography* (Toronto, University of Toronto Press, 1966), vol. 1, pp. 266-274 and Groulx's review of the volume in *Revue d'histoire de l'Amérique française*, XIX (March 1966) pp. 637-640.

12. F. H. Underhill, *In Search of Canadian Liberalism* (Toronto, Macmillan, 1961), p. 127.

13. The Institut Canadien was established in Montreal in 1844 as a centre for discussion and study of political, literary, economic, social and philosophical topics. The two hundred young founders were all enamoured of liberal and revolutionary ideas emanating from Europe. Such ideas – strict separation of Church and State, an end to the temporal power of the Pope, popular government, progress for the people, secular education – led to an inevitable clash with the Bishop of Montreal, Mgr. Ignace Bourget. A twenty-five year struggle ensued: French Canada's version of the nineteenth century western world conflict between liberty and authority. The Institut Canadien petered out in the 1870's.

14. Arthur Buies (1840-1901) was a journalist of mordant wit and unstable character. He edited a series of short-lived newspapers in which he delighted in poking fun and throwing barbs at Authority, be it clerical or political.

15. Jules-Paul Tardivel (1851-1905) was an ultramontane journalist, founder in 1881 and editor until his death of the Quebec City weekly newspaper *La Vérité*. His separatism began as the providential destiny of French Canada in the mid 1880's, was confirmed by the Manitoba Schools question, found expression in an apocryphal novel *Pour la Patrie* (1895) and formed the substance of a heated exchange with Bourassa in 1904.

16. The Sentinelle movement embraced a number of French-speaking citizens of Woonsocket, Rhode Island. Using the newspaper *La Sentinelle* (1924-28), the group contested the right of the Bishop to tax his French-speaking parishioners to aid English language diocesan high schools. The question dragged through civil and ecclesiastical courts until 1928 when the Pope condemned the newspaper.

17. The Bloc Populaire was a political movement in Quebec during the Second World War. Growing out of the anti-conscription campaign in 1942, the Bloc advocated political and economic reforms. Although it captured four seats in the provincial election of 1944, it was unable to enhance its electoral support, its leadership or its programme. By the mid 1940's, the Bloc had all but disintegrated.

18. A notable omission from this book is Groulx's war-time speech *Why we are divided*. The speech was published in pamphlet form in English in 1943 and is reproduced in R. Cook (ed.), *French Canadian Nationalism*, pp. 237-256.

19. La Société du parler français was founded under the auspices of the Université Laval

in Quebec City in 1902 to foster the study, purification, perfection and defence of the French language.

Le Congrès de la langue française was organized by the Société du parler français for June 1912. Attracting people from all over North America and from France, the congress served as a stocktaking of cultural resources.

La Ligue des droits du français was one of the many results of the congress. Founded in Montreal in 1913, the Ligue intended to give practical import to the resolutions of the congress. It therefore acted as a watchdog for the French language, particularly in the burgeoning realms of commerce and industry.

20. The Ligue nationaliste began in Montreal in 1903. Strongly influenced by Henri Bourassa, the programme of the Ligue reflected Canadian anxiety about imperialism, French Canadian anxiety about federalism and a novel interest in social and economic questions.

21. Errol Bouchette (1863-1912) was a lawyer, journalist and civil servant, an early advocate of industrial and technical education in Quebec. Like other Canadians he caught the spirit of the boom years of the first decade of the twentieth century, realized that the path of the future was an industrial one and urged his compatriots' preparation for it.

22. Abbé Philippe Perrier (1870-1947) was the curé of the parish of Saint-Enfant-Jésus du Mile End in Montreal. Like Groulx he abounded in energy and zeal for the numerous organizations and undertakings of a nationalist hue that dotted the French Canadian landscape. During the 1920's he was president of the Action Française movement.

23. The *bonne entente* ("good will" or "cordial co-operation") movement attempted just after the First World War and through the 1920's to heal some of the widening fissures between English and French Canadians. The movement harboured business men and politicians whose vested interests were fairly obvious in innumerable after-dinner speeches of good will. The term became, and has remained, one of derision in nationalist circles in Quebec.

# Literary Groulx

## A Lesson From the Maple Trees

L. Groulx, "La leçon des érables," 1912, *Les Rapaillages* (Montreal, Editions Albert Lévesque, 1935), pp. 11-13. Reprinted by permission of Mme J. Rémillard.

I walked in flowered groves among the trees
And heard, while pondering verses yesterday
The stir and hum of growing life around me
And saw the tall green maples bend to say:

"We lift proud foreheads to the light of day;
Our limbs rise straight and strong into the air;
Our roots plunge deeply into native clay
To draw our strength from dead trees lying there.

Our verdure rises like a mighty crown
In sign of tribute, to perpetuate
(Despite an age which lets all fires die down)
The glory of our epic forebears great.

Among our leaves there sometimes stirs a breeze
Singing tunes of an old and vanished age;
Listen: it sings the soul of former trees
Surviving still in our strong foliage.

At times the solemn notes of our grave hymn
Like organ music ring out epic sound:
We bow our heads as sighing with the wind
To God we breathe the prayer of the ground.

Our duties are to pray and daily sing
The soul of nature and of days gone by:
Remember, never cease remembering;
Thus do we grow to tower in the sky."

\*   \*   \*

'Twas so that in the forest's rosy wilderness
I heard one day the tall green maples whisper;
And musing, recognized the price of greatness
Which makes a nation overcome disaster.

The future shall be theirs, who keep the past
Who keep their unremorseful memories whole
And stay near tombs of glory to the last
To mingle with the dead their living soul.

The future shall be theirs whose proudest goal
Is the retention of their mother tongue:
This epic music where their father's soul
Vibrates in prayer as though a hymn were sung.

Keep the words that give us love and faith:
Those syllables are richer than mere sighs;
Each noble word of France a record of our race
And each abandoned is a soul that dies.

To speak our tongue well is to keep our soul:
And we shall speak the language of our sires
As long as flames immortal at the pole
Are lit each evening in unmoving fires;

As long as toss the virile seas of wheat
As long as bells ring out from steeples high
As long as proud in the immortal breeze
The maple trees rise to the sky.


# How I Came to Leave Politics

L. Groulx, "Comment j'ai quitté la politique," *Les Rapaillages* (Montreal, Editions Albert Lévesque, 1935), pp. 71-80. Reprinted by permission of Mme J. Rémillard.

I must have been about twelve years old. The winter of 1891 was just drawing to a close. Our village of Saint Michel awoke one fine morning to find itself rocked by a high fever of excitement. It was an entirely new kind of political campaign that was raging: the local schoolboys had decided to stage a mock election. The annals of history have not, somehow, condescended to record the great event. Still, it did have its repercussions and was indeed mentioned in *La Presse* – which, to young rustics such as we were then, constituted the very summits of glory.

How easy it is to be carried away by the excitement of politics, even the merest suggestion of politics! The old folks themselves were drawn into the game, arguing and quarrelling around our hustings. Pipes and checker boards lay idle in the stores while the elders joined the debate. As for the children! Twenty times a day you could have heard shouts ringing in the village streets: "Hurrah for the *Bleus!*" And each time some boy's voice would retort: "Hurrah for the *Rouges!* Down with the *Bleus!*" Historians must find it a revealing characteristic, this passion for politics which has filtered right down into the children. I have read in learned books that the soul and culture of a nation can be detected in the quality of its popular heroes. When the history of our generation is written, it will have to be remembered that our childhood heroes were politicians.

In every election, we had been told, there must be two candidates. And so we had two, clearly marked by distinct colours, one red and one blue. No Independents for us: they would have seemed almost as wicked as atheists. With a maturity of instinct belying our years, we also took care not to choose our candidates among those boys who were considered the local school's best. No one, for example, gave a thought to my good friend Henri Desrosiers, the future Vice-President of Imperial Tobacco, a witty and brilliant student of whom the smallest boys whispered in awe: "He's the one who stood up to Brother Michael about the proper use of the pronoun *one*; but he's done more: they say that on some days he teaches the class instead of the Brother!" Our Conventions – we had to have Conventions; indeed we had two – selected two sturdy lads renowned for their quick tongue and quicker fists. Our own candidate had distinguished himself in the midst of a fierce electoral battle by seizing and tearing to bits a scarlet cap which one little monster had been so rash as to wave aloft, shouting: "Hurrah for Laurier!" Each one of us thought to himself, at the time, that anyone who could carry off such an exploit was bound to go far . . . at least as far as Parliament.

So the campaign got under way. It was a time of hard politicking in Saint Michel, with plots and intrigues in every corner, much to *Monsieur le Curé*'s annoyance. Not only men, but things, were pressed into the service of one party or the other. There were red ties and blue ties; red caps and blue caps; red carriages and blue carriages. The colours were brandished proudly, like flags. To match red carriages there were, needless to say, bay horses; and this plunged some of our worthy citizens into despair, for how could they contrive a blue horse? Furious at losing a county which they had held almost as a birthright since the time of Confederation, grown-up *Bleus* replied to *Rouges* victories by repeated confrontations. One election followed another: it was a time of chronic electioneering! In the evenings, after school, we would quickly make our way to the clubs – for of course there were clubs – where, whatever the time of day, speakers could be heard spouting their inspired slogans. Their faces were purple, their fists clenched, their mouths and eyes glistened like a cannibal's. "Oh, those *Rouges*!" the one group seemed to be saying, "If only we could seize them, fry them and devour them!" "Oh, those *Bleus*!" the others seemed to be saying, "How we would love to chop them up and fling them into our stewing pot!" Out we would come, our minds filled, and our pockets even more so: crammed with newspapers, pamphlets, and political cartoons. Of these, I especially remember one coloured poster which we young *Bleus* found particularly humiliating. It portrayed an enormous, emaciated pig, its ribs sticking out, grazing disconsolately in a field as bald as an egg. Two feet away rippled a meadow of luxuriant green grass. But alas! a very high, forbidding, insolent fence stood between that grass and the noble animal, who was further burdened by a heavy yoke inscribed with the word: *Protection*. I can hardly tell you what damage was done to our cause in the village by that melancholy pig!

In this atmosphere it did not take long for me to complete my political education. I soon had a head stuffed with election clichés: ample, stirring phrases which I found completely intoxicating. I soon learned, also, to pronounce with suitable unction the ritualistic incantation: "My fellow constituents of this fair county of Vaudreuil ... " Protectionism; tariffs; unrestricted reciprocity; annexation: all these I managed to explain to my schoolmates one lunch-time, with a school bench as my platform. I even mustered that self-assurance with which club speakers gave the impression of always knowing exactly what they were talking about. Such learning, such eloquence were greeted by general stupefaction. "He will surely grow up to become an M.P. ... " everyone thought. I became, on the spot, the beacon and main pillar of the *Bleu* Party. Our candidate hastened to retain my services. And, as in those days there were Chief Judges, Chief Lawyers, and even Chief Foremen, so it was decided that I should thenceforth be Chief Speaker for the *Bleus*.

\* \* \*

26

The day of the nominating assembly arrived: a Thursday, school holiday. I will never forget the look of astonishment on my father's face when, after lunch, he saw me quite mysteriously preparing to leave for the village, my pockets bulging with electoral ammunition.

"And where do you think you're going?" he asked.

"Down to the village."

"To the village? Is that so? Do you realize there is wood to be brought in, my boy? And hens and the calf to be cleaned?"

My face fell. To be harassed about such mundane matters, when one has become a political personality, a Chief Speaker! Explanations were obviously in order. My mother came to the rescue. She was proud of having a son who was so popular, so eloquent on the hustings, just like any lawyer or "M.P.". I was released. Still, I must confess it had been a bad moment, with my entire political career hanging in the balance.

In the village, everything had been set in readiness for the full-scale debate which was to follow the nominations. A most memorable scene! Among the crowd were some adults, and, naturally, many children: children from within the village and children from without, swelling the ranks. A hundred of them, packed into a back room, cold, muddy, apprentice voters already gesturing and shouting like professionals. We entered with our candidates. Caps flew off, and prolonged, tumultuous applause filled the room.

"The meeting is with us," whispered my honourable Leader.

With great solemnity, the Chairman rose to announce the opening of the meeting. The speeches began. Historical accuracy prompts me to describe the platform we were using that day: it was a simple barrel, as rotund as a successful politician, and from it had poured forth, long before our streams of rhetoric, no less honourable streams of Barbados molasses. The *Rouge* candidate was the first to climb up. The crowd listened to him coldly. He had a slight stammer and, for some obscure reason, was not a very popular person. In a thin high voice he set about reciting a page of Chapleau which he had memorized, yet managed to pass it off coolly as sound Liberal doctrine.

My candidate was straining at the bit, like a nervous animal impatient to reach the starting gate. I was meanwhile wrestling with a horrible apprehension. Of my candidate's fists I had the highest opinion; I was less sure about the power of his oratory. His beautiful self-confidence, however, did much to dispel my fears. At last it was his turn to climb upon the barrel. But no sooner had he started off with: "My fellow constituents of this fair county of Vaudreuil ... " than he was drowned in applause. "Gentlemen ... ," he continued, "I ... I ... Gentlemen ... eh ... I ... " A great silence descended upon the hall. The speaker twisted his cap, stared at his shoes, then launched out again, this time very loudly, as though to shake the rafters: "MY FELLOW CONSTITUENTS OF THIS FAIR COUNTY OF VAUDREUIL ... " Alas, the rest of the speech simply would not come. Standing behind him, I tried to whisper the sacramental phrases: "I have been selected ... " He repeated: "I have been suspected ... " Bad luck! Undaunted, I pursued: "As a symbol of high purpose ... " "As a symbol of high surplus ... " Hoots of laughter rang out in the hall. Furious, the speaker leaped from his platform, pummelled his way through the crowd to the door, and disappeared.

It was a critical moment. Everyone turned to the Chief Speaker for the *Bleu* Party. What would he do? Realizing that the fate of the battle had been placed in his hands, he decided on a final assault to rally the troops. He sprang to the tribune, his heart beating beneath his homespun coat, his cap – a blue cap – pushed back from his forehead. He attacked, he defended, he made emotional appeals to the "free and independent voters". At one point there was a flurry behind him: a door opened, a ripple passed over the audience. He did not turn to look, but dashed on, more strongly than ever. At last, summoning all his strength and waving his fists, he plunged into a final tirade, which he had discovered in some pamphlet and was to use many times in the course of the campaign: "We are the heirs of honesty and tolerance: we shall not fear the heirs of falsehood and bigotry. We are the heirs of Sir John A. Macdonald and Sir George-Etienne Cartier. We shall not fear the heirs of Dorion and George Brown!"

The Speaker for the *Bleu* Party, out of breath, turned from the mingled cheers of his fans and jeers of his foes; he stepped down from the platform. What a surprise! There he was, face to face with the former deputy and *Seigneur* of the village, the eminent Colonel Antoine Chartier de Lotbinière-Harwood. The unexpected entrance of this famous personality had produced the audience movement noted above. I can still see the tall, handsome old man, standing very erect like the soldier he was, with his long cane, his monocle, and a flowing beard like Charlemagne's.

"Shake hands with me, my friend," he said in a voice filled with kindness and contentment. "You did well, to stand up for the right principles. You must go on to college, my boy, and become a man."

This incident was worth more to us than a hundred speeches. There was talk of little else in the village that night. And my mother, when she heard, became quite convinced that I was to grow up to be a Member of Parliament, or something of the sort.

During the days that remained before the election, our cause went forward, with its ups and its downs. Our wretched candidate almost spoiled everything once again. This happened one evening, when we were all coming out of school. One brash boy took it upon himself to wave a large handkerchief, the colour of which had the effect of sending my honourable Leader into paroxysms of belligerence. With two strides he was upon the insolent lad:

"Tear that up!"

"Never", came the cool reply.

An interested circle immediately began to form: no one wanted to miss the fight.

"Do you hear?" our Leader returned to the charge, "Tear that up, or I'll ... "

"You had better not touch me," retorted the flag-waver, "I'll tell the Principal!"

"Do you think I'm afraid of the Principal? I'll ... "

He was not given time to finish. The shout went up:

"Here comes the Principal!"

Whereupon our honourable Leader took to his heels and vanished down the first lane he could find. As you can well imagine, it was all a hoax, and we were left without the Principal, admittedly, but without a candidate as well. This unfortunate adventure did us incalculable harm. Things were definitely beginning to look grim, very grim. On top of it all, the *Rouges* launched into a wholesale campaign to corrupt the "free and independent voters".

We, meanwhile, continued the good fight. Every evening without fail, I left the house at seven to go to the village. It was a walk of almost a mile, in the bitterest cold. Sometimes we held our meetings in a hayloft, sometimes in a woodshed. They were a sight to see: in a circle of smoky lantern light, our earnest young speakers would be holding forth to an audience of about twenty youngsters, surrounded by four or five old men of the village puffing on their pipes, with a certain look, an undefinable smile on their faces. I would come back home at ten, often at eleven, conscious of having lent a hand in a great undertaking. On my way home, I would look up to the stars in the dark sky, thinking they promised victory. And while she was tucking me in, my mother would speak to me of my future life as an M.P.

\*   \*   \*

The election had been set for the following Sunday. By that day we were fully convinced of our victory. During the last twenty-four hours, our opponents' faces grew steadily longer. The Liberal store was rife with cabals. I wonder if any of the older inhabitants of the village can still remember as I do the very unusual atmosphere of that Sunday in 1891? The afternoon drew on; it was time for vespers. In the streets, there was an extraordinary bustle: the entire parish seemed to have turned out. Crowds of people pressed into the church square; the place was soon filled with wagons and with enormous carriages overflowing with young voters. From Saint-Lazare they had come, and from Ile-Perrot, from the most remote concessions. Our election, starting off as a parish concern, had so stirred popular enthusiasm that it had become a county election. According to Monsieur le Curé's dictate, everyone was obliged to attend the service first. Never had that old church been so packed with the faithful!

Voting began at three o'clock. The place was teeming with people. Excitement ran even higher among the adults, it seemed, than among the young. By four o'clock, it was all over. There followed an anxious lull, while the votes were being counted. Then the solemn moment arrived; the election secretary came forward on the club balcony. Not a rustle, not a sound in the whole assembly.

"Mister X ... ," he proclaimed in a slightly affected tone, "Mister X, the Liberal candidate, is elected by 30 votes."

The blow could not have been more brutal: I was thunderstruck. "Beaten ... crushed ... " I muttered repeatedly. All my new-found political expertise deserted me: I became simply a child again, weeping bitterly. All around me young Rouges were celebrating their triumph. Their speakers were suddenly very eloquent in their mockery of our affliction. Our fans were pressing me to speak. I was dragged most reluctantly to the balcony. With eyes still reddened, the Chief Speaker of the Bleu Party was forced to face this little world gone mad. I cannot tell you everything he said. He thanked his Leader's faithful followers. He spoke, naturally enough, of "moral victory"; he rebuked the Rouges for the shameless, corrupt means to which they had stooped in order to buy victory. He poured scorn over their intrigues, and especially over that big Léandre who had, so rumour went, gone so far as to offer little Arthur Lefebvre and others whole packets of cigarettes. He denounced, as was fitting, the scandalous bribes of candies and nuts that had been distributed right and left throughout the village, in broad daylight.

What more did the Chief Speaker for the Bleu Party find to say? Looking back from a distance of forty-five years, I can hardly remember. What I do know is that on that particular evening the Chief Speaker for the Bleu Party did not leave his house at seven; he did not address a meeting in the village; he did not wait for the stroke of midnight to go to bed; and I am assured that his mother never spoke another word about his life as a Member of Parliament.

# To Erle Bartlett

L. Groulx, manuscript letter to Erle Bartlett, July 20, 1904. From Groulx papers, Fondation Lionel Groulx, Montreal. Reprinted by permission.

My dearest Erle,

Do you know, the letter you wrote me the other day was the most delightful one I could ever hope to receive or keep? In it I found the real you, with that affectionate nature you some-times conceal beneath your British phlegm, with your special affinity for great and beautiful things, with your courage just beginning to assert itself amidst the first serious difficulties to arise along your way. At last you have written me a letter after my own heart, a letter of the kind I would expect from you, my beloved friend. You conjure up a host of memories from a now distant past, memories which I cherish as much as you do, or perhaps even more, because as we see the future dwindling before us, we come to derive more pleasure from our remem-brances. I too have turned to the past, perhaps at the very same moment as you. It is an *annual* habit of mine – a kind of tradi-tion which I respect and scrupulously uphold because I find it so completely enchanting – always to sort out my corre-spondence when I get back from the College. And then, when I discover at the bottom of my drawers the old bundles of letters so redolent of past years – the best years of my life – I find their seductive appeal impossible to resist. I have to leaf through the old pages, revive those bygone things, relive the old and cherished days, even if it means reading through hundreds of pages of correspondence. I am drawn by preference to your letters, to those of my young friends. There I find such enthusi-asm, such vigorous, idealistic flights of thought, such a promise of future fecundity! Then too, they remind me of the time I felt younger myself, when I was just beginning to devote myself to young people, with such an absolute, ardent and strong devotion. Reviving this period is beneficial to me, for it repre-sents much more than simply a time of dreams or enthusiastic words and letters. It is a fountain of youth in which I can reach back to the springtime of my own life and in which I, who would never wish to grow old but be always young in order to serve the young, can recover the zeal and ardour of my twenty-second year. May God, who loves you even more than I do, bless all of you young men, and especially you, Erle, to whom I owe whatever is best in my past; and let me add my own blessings, those of the young priest who first revealed to you the celestial regions of idealism, and whose greatest wish is to see your gaze turned constantly to those empyreal heights.

Would you like to know what I think about, when I am outside strolling, or meditating, or in my long hours of day-dreaming? You are surely entitled to look into the innermost folds of my life; do you know that I am still dreaming and making plans? Yes, I have the dream of writing a book for young people, which would be called "Youth's Apostle". I have it all here in my head. Already I have jotted down the various chapters in a notebook in which I intend to gather all my material. Should my "Youth's Apostle" never see the light of day, you will find among the intimate papers I shall leave to you these sketchy outlines of a project I have long mulled over. Mine would be a small book destined for young college students, with the purpose of disseminating the ideas of "Catholic Action". An older friend in whom I have confided encourages me and assures me that young people now lack such a book. Apostles are hard to find among the young; and yet am I wrong in believing and wishing to say to them that a true Catholic life can never be anything other than an apostolate, "the highest form of life"? Why should that great wealth of energy stored within young people be left dormant, unproductive, sterile, when they ask for nothing better than to be given a cause to devote themselves to? What is required to induce them to join the Crusade? What was missing for you before you decided to become apostles? Simply the revelation that there are indeed these supremely beautiful truths in life. A life of apostleship has a certain fascination which becomes irresistible after such a revelation. What we need today are new generations: we must prevent those who are now growing up as well as those who are about to grow up from poisoning themselves at the same source as the former generation. Well then: let us seize upon the newest, youngest souls. Let us make use of the best influence upon the young, that of the young themselves. If we wish our young people to be concerned about their social duties, we must not allow them to believe that such duties begin at thirty; let us initiate them early into a life of devotion, give them the conviction that life must be useful, and persuade them that the first victory to be won is that over one's own selfishness.

There, my beloved friend, you have everything that I would like my book to say, and that it will say if only God will grant me the knowledge, the power, and the capacity for work which I shall need to get to the end of the 250 or 300 pages such a book must have. I admit, not everything in my "Youth's Apostle" will be my own. All the young people I have loved will be writing it with me. I have stored up a great fund of beautiful things I have heard, or read, or had written to me since I started living among you, my dear friends. Moreover, you young people have been my inspiration: it is your soul rather than mine which will find its expression on my future pages. If only I had the leisure, I could begin at once. The passing of time will not bring me what I need to write a book of this nature. I must write it while I am still young, or abandon it like so many other projects which were sprouting in my mind when I was twenty. The young will not read or understand me unless I can speak to them in their language, and in my preface – I must have a *preface*, of course – I should like to be able to present my book as one written almost by a colleague of theirs. Time alone, which is capital for genius and dunce alike, time alone is lacking. . . .

Forgive me for chatting on at such length about a project which totally absorbs me at the moment, and about which I felt a rather pressing need to let off steam. I am sorry that you had to be my captive audience. Still, I would ask you as a youth's apostle yourself to remember my book in your prayers. If it could be instrumental in calling forth such noble young men as I have known in my life as a priest, then I should indeed presume to ask God to let me write my "Youth's Apostle". If not, if my pen drops before I have had time to realize my dream, I leave it to you as my legacy, my dearest Erle. And I shall inspire you from heaven, I shall be writing it with you. For this book must be written; and it will be written, I am convinced, though I know not by whom – perhaps by one of today's young men who has been more fortunate than we in not having to wait until the age of twenty to be initiated into real life . . . But I have written enough: here I must stop, and no doubt you will be quite relieved! . . .

And so goodbye, my dearest Erle. Write me many more splendid letters. They are so good for me. Remember that you appeared in my life partly to sustain me with the warmth of your disciple's affection. I have now written eight pages. You hold the record. That is as it should be, since you are the more *American* of the two. Furthermore, I shall let you keep the record, if only to encourage you to retain it always.

I press you to my heart.


Yours, in Christ,


L.A. Groulx, priest.

# A Peerless Old Bachelor

L. Groulx, "Un vieux garçon dépareillé," *L'Almanach de la langue française*, 1917, pp. 28-29. Reprinted by permission of Mme J. Rémillard.

Old Jacquot the notary has a tendency to be long-winded and solemn, not to say sanctimonious, when he gets going on one of his stories. But never mind: he does sometimes come up with a good one.

"You know," he said to me one day when I was teasing him about his reluctance to consider matrimony, "You know they're not all bad, those people." By "those people" he meant, of course, seasoned bachelors like himself.

"I know one in particular," he went on, "although you realize there's a whole crew of them – but this one would really suit you. You'll see: he's just the kind of person who should be put into books . . . "

"And did your old bachelor fall in love?" I queried. "That would be just the thing!"

Whereupon the old notary set his spectacles upon his forehead, and, with many expressive gestures or subtle winks to accompany his flowery phrases, he launched into his tale.

"I tell you, that bachelor is a *peerless* man. His younger brother – the family favourite who went to college – informed the poor old man one day that to use the English word "shed" when you are speaking French is nothing short of barbarous: "shed" being a foreign intruder that has unnaturally supplanted a perfectly good native word, a word of the most authentic and noble stock. Now this old bachelor, the best of men, has a sweetheart who is the queen of his thoughts – they all have, no matter what they say – and that sweetheart is his mother tongue, a language which he loves with all the passion of a heart forever young. Well, he immediately formed a colossal resolution, which was never, ever to allow the Anglo-Saxon sound to pass his lips again. Of course he had not reckoned upon the force of habit, which can be pretty stubborn in hardened bachelors like us. Time and time again, the refractory word came slipping out. Either it was the "shed" door he had forgotten to shut, or it was the wood he was fetching from the "shed", or again the car that had to be put away in the "shed". No matter how hard he tried, the terrible "shed" kept cropping up everywhere, until it became a real nuisance, a thorn in the flesh. Determined to conquer it, he finally hit, as we all do sometimes, upon a heroic stratagem: he decided there was nothing for it but to fight fire with fire. And so one morning, fortified no doubt with the previous night's dreams about his sweetheart, he armed himself with a poker, heated it in the stove, and, on the "shed" door, in the maple that seemed created especially to receive such French inscriptions, with all the solemnity of a Phidias carving immortal phrases in marble or granite, he traced in large and beautiful letters the famous word of his maternal tongue as a visible symbol of its victory over the alien invader."

*   *   *

Let me add one final comment to Jacquot's story. I would say, to anyone who belongs to the Société du parler français, or to the Ligue des droits du français, or to the Société Saint-Jean-Baptiste: try to discover the name of this *peerless* old man, so that when the day comes for distributing prizes for devotion to the cause, you may begin by rewarding true virtue in bachelors.

# The Call of the Race

L.Groulx, *L'Appel de la race*, 1922, 5th edition (Montreal, Les Editions Fides, 1956), pp.97-101; pp.106-109; pp.234-236. Reprinted by permission.

Jules was the first one of the family to be sent to college. He was only ten years old when he set off for the Seminary at X ... A precociously intelligent yet sensible child, he did well in his studies. In only one respect was his education deficient, and that was in its woeful lack of any kind of patriotic training. Such was, alas, the atmosphere prevailing in the province of Quebec at the time.

For later historians, there can hardly be anything more puzzling and more disturbing than that period of lethargy the French-Canadian nation underwent during the last thirty years of the nineteenth century. This was the rapid and fatal result of a doctrine which succeeded in influencing an entire nation, even though it had to overcome the strongest atavistic instincts to do so. It is, indeed, difficult to see how the embattled vigilance of the small nation of Quebec, so highly developed over two centuries of struggle, could so suddenly have been transformed into a morbid desire for rest! All that had been required were a few speeches, a few political intrigues. To ensure the success of their plans for Confederation, politicians in 1867 presented the federal union as a panacea for all the nation's ills. Party men devoted to furthering their political platform, they had used and abused their power of persuasion. The false security generated and widely diffused by these rash speeches soon produced a generation of pacifists. A strange state of mind immediately became apparent. It was like a sudden slackening in all the coiled springs of a nation's energies, a weakening of its moral muscle: the relaxing of a knight who has borne his coat of armour too long and at last unbuckles it to slumber in the sun. After less than a quarter of a century within a federation that it had accepted with superstitious good faith, French Quebec was left in a state of the most depressing languor. Politicians came to be considered the most authoritative leaders; the exigencies of party alliances and their own desire to conciliate the English majority led them to abandon their traditional positions. Gradually, Quebec's French patriotism was weakened, without being replaced by an equally strong Canadian patriotism. In 1867 politicians tried to fashion a country by joining various parts of a large body, leaving to their successors the task of infusing that body with some form of organic life. Unfortunately, such a supreme task was beyond the powers of those petty men who were totally lacking in creative genius. With the decline of parliamentary forms, what had been merely a party line gradually became a sentimental tradition, and finally a doctrine. Around 1885, at the time of the Riel affair, and around 1890, at the time of the school question in Manitoba, there were rumblings which seemed to indicate a gathering storm. The slumbering nation was seen to shake itself and yawn. But the same old soporifics were still at work. And how could an awakening of the national conscience be expected when all the leaders elevated slumber to the rank of a foremost political necessity?

Such was the poisoned atmosphere in which young Lamontagne's generation had grown up. One day Father Fabien said to him with a sigh: "Isn't it mystifying, my friend, to see this aberration of patriotic instinct in all the young people of your generation?"

That day, Lantagnac, nettled, had retorted: "But Father, you are forgetting something: I graduated from college around 1890. Do you realize what I heard, first as a schoolboy and then as a college student, on national holidays and on Saint-Jean-Baptiste Day? Ask the young people of my generation. Ask them what patriotic sentiments were expressed in those long speeches we listened to. Was it love of Canada, or praise for its beauty, do you think? Was it a tribute to the nobility of our race, the pride in our history, the military or political glory of our ancestors, the greatness of our future? Not at all: but rather the advantages of British institutions; the liberality of Anglo-Saxon traditions; the faithfulness of our fathers to the Crown of England. That last one above all: our first and highest national virtue! As to a more rational and objective kind of patriotism based on our actual land and on our history, a patriotism full of luminous conviction and revitalizing energy, well that was entirely unknown! Our homeland! a concept bandied about on those nights only to vanish into thin air afterwards like so many other concepts ... Oh! you should be more indulgent towards us," pleaded Lantagnac finally. "It is unfair to forget what sad times we lived through in our youth. Do you realize how strongly the attitudes and state of mind befitting a vanquished and perpetually resigned nation were preached to us as our duty in those days? Do you know that simply to mention the possibility of uniting French Canadians for their political or economic defense was considered an immoral presumption?"

Lantagnac was right. When he had left college, chance and the need to earn money had led him to the study of the famous English lawyer George Blackwell. This in turn led him to study law at McGill University. In that atmosphere the young man soon lost what little patriotism he had left. He was soon convinced that superiority lay on the side of greater numbers and wealth; he abandoned his Latin ideals and his French culture; he acquired the arrogance of the newly Anglicized. Contempt for his compatriots had not yet found its way into his heart, but he did pity them as one pities the poor who will not be cured of their poverty. Having become a lawyer and feeling ill at ease among his own people, he set out for Ottawa. There, with his brilliant mind, his devotion to work and his gifted tongue, he soon built up a large practice. Lantagnac – he no longer called himself anything but Lantagnac – became the most popular lawyer in the capital, and a consultant for several powerful English companies, among them the famous construction firm, Aitkens Brothers. Meanwhile, he married a young Englishwoman, a convert to Catholicism. To the couple were born four children, two sons and two daughters. The boys studied at Loyola College in Montreal – the youngest was there still – and the girls were sent to Loretto Abbey.

Everything went smoothly for the Anglicized lawyer until one day he was suddenly seized by a desire to play a more important role in life. He was then approaching the age of forty-three. All the wealth and fame he had gained in his legal practice were no longer enough to satisfy his ambitions. A man of valiant and generous disposition, he longed to devote himself to a greater cause, to broaden his outlook and his life. He was not so frivolous as to approach politics without preparation, and resolved therefore to return to his studies. Convinced that in the context of Canadian politics success could only belong to a man fluent in both official languages, he first decided to brush up on his mother tongue. To achieve this he began by reading some of the French authors who were well known for their political writings. He read Le Play, the Abbé de Tourville, la Tour du Pin, Charles Périn, Charles Gide, Charles Antoine, Count Albert de Mun and a few others. That was when he received the first shock to his system: his reading left him dazzled. Coming into contact again with such lucidity, such order, such spiritual distinction was a completely enchanting experience. At that moment a man entered his life who was to have a profound influence upon him: he began to see Father Fabien. For some time now the lawyer had been aware of a vague, uneasy feeling stirring deep within him, a kind of nostalgia for the past which he had previously thought dead for ever. He wondered whether it was not simply an illusion. But the loss of his love for his nation had indeed left a corner of his heart arid and barren, like a desert. It suddenly seemed to him that the Anglo-Saxon ideology he had adopted was melting away and leaving his whole being unbalanced. At the same time he discovered that his own principles were being terribly undermined by Protestant infiltration. Although he had always been a devout Catholic, he now felt his most sacred beliefs daily shaken by insidious attacks. Where would these new disorders lead him? He realized that "free thought" was pushing him to create his own rules of conduct, and that this was leading to a disintegration of his moral fibre which both worried and distressed him.

Father Fabien lost no time in diagnosing his new penitent's state of mind. "The old dilemma!" he said to himself. Very early in his interviews with the famous lawyer, the priest became convinced that Lantagnac's strength of character would save him, if anything could; Lantagnac had a certain basic integrity which was like an absolute and unassailable virtue within him. It was not through lack of sincerity that as a student he had abandoned his culture. In all good faith, he had persuaded himself that for anyone in his position, intellectual enrichment and Anglicization must be synonymous.

"If I can only reveal the truth behind that mirage," thought Father Fabien, "the illusion should simply fade away."

He accordingly directed his new protégé to the study of French civilization, and particularly to the study of its great classical literature. René Johannet once wrote: "The French Classics being what they are, one should never despair of a cultured man, any more than one should despair of French culture itself." In Lantagnac's case the intellectual tonic worked beautifully. Every fortnight, as he opened his brief case to return the borrowed volumes to Father Fabien, he spoke enthusiastically of his reading, and of the prodigious effect it was having upon him. One day, more deeply moved than ever, he said to the priest: "It's strange, but ever since I started immersing myself in French culture, I have felt all of a piece again, in harmony with my own being, like a newly-tuned musical instrument. But at other times I must say I am overcome by some sort of nostalgia, by an indescribable melancholy. I cannot hide it from you: something half-dead within me is stirring into life again. I am homesick for my village, for my father's house which I have not seen for twenty years and which I thought I had forgotten entirely."

"Well, there is a simple solution," commented Father Fabien. "You must go back and see them again." ...

"Father, you are really a child of the land, like me. You must have savoured those wonderful periods of quiet meditation in the fields at the end of the day – the time when the stillness of night begins to steal over the land, intensifying the scent of the new-mown hay; the humming of the mills dies down; the countryside lies hushed as it awaits the evensong bells ... the very best time and place for fruitful musings ... do you remember? Nearly every day, just before six o'clock, I would set out as I did when I was a child, and sit on the fence at the very end of the last field. I gazed and gazed at the long black furrows and the green shrubbery, without ever tiring of it. There before my eyes lay the battlefield upon which my ancestors had fought to clear the land and conquer the virgin forests. It was a task which required their most determined, their most violent efforts and which absorbed the lives of five generations. Yet these people, leading such harsh lives, managed somehow, by some miracle, to retain serene and cheerful faces. I could never look down those long, narrow fields without noticing some cottage with its smoke curling upwards like a visible symbol of peace and happiness. How evocative those scenes were, and how much I learned from them ... "

"And what about the church steeple? I am sure you did not forget that!"

"No, I often found my eyes turning to it, for the steeple is truly the centre and magnetic pole of our villages. I may as well tell you straight away, Father Fabien, since I know you are dying to find out: in that little corner of my homeland I discovered a great and joyful truth."

He went on in a lyrical vein: "Nor was it simply the reflection of my own thoughts upon surrounding things. No, I saw that truth, I felt it everywhere: in the clear laughter of women and girls, in the songs children sang as they brought the cows home at night, in the greetings the country folk would call out to me along my way; and I saw it too in their faces as they came to Mass on Sunday. To such a scene, the church bells could hardly add a transcendental note at all."

The pilgrim paused for a moment after these words, but he soon concluded, with happy and heartfelt conviction: "I tell you Father, everywhere I came into contact with the very soul of a fine and sensitive race, governed by spiritual values and drawn by higher things."

Father Fabien applauded: "Lantagnac, I was sure you would come to that conclusion eventually!"

Then, pushing aside a few books on his table as though to repress a criticism he was about to make, the priest continued: "If only people knew how to interpret our customs and our landscape! But alas they don't, or they attempt to do so in a distracted way or from an unsympathetic, foreign point of view."

Lantagnac had become graver and more pensive.

"Was there anything else, my friend?" asked the priest.

"Yes, there was one more thing," replied Lantagnac in a more subdued voice. "My pilgrimage took me as far as the cemetery ..."

"I can just visualize it; tell me about it ... "

"Do you remember it – the old cemetery at Saint-Michel? It is really a very ancient cemetery; it was the first and is still the only one in the parish. You can still see old oaken tombstones, weatherbeaten and half covered in grass, with their old lettering all worn away. It is touching to see some of them nestling right up to the church walls. Further on there is a picturesque point where the Little River flows alongside the cemetery between two rows of trees, and on its banks can still be seen the rather mysterious and romantic ruins of two manor houses which belonged to my family. In this impressive scene, within sight of those feudal ruins, I who had been in exile for twenty years rediscovered my forefathers and renewed my allegiance to them. I can truly say, Father, that it was on my family's tombs that I finally arrived at the culminating point of my intellectual and spiritual development. In that old cemetery I completely recovered my French soul."

Lantagnac's voice faltered as he uttered the last words in a moved and solemn tone. Then he went on in a firmer voice: "Thanks to your guidance, Father Fabien, my intellectual being had been made whole again by my contact with the great masters of French thought; now my emotional being was fulfilled by the countryside around Saint-Michel, the people, the things, the sweep of the horizon, the memories of my paternal house. On the Lantagnac tombs I was reconciled with my ancestors and my race. I realized then, indeed I felt it as a palpable reality, that the Lantagnac I had become was a doomed and anarchic force. I could not help thinking, as I strolled among the tombs, that here on this earth whatever value we have can only be achieved through tradition and continuity. One generation must rise on the shoulders of the previous one. Just as great works of art cannot be created with isolated sentences or disjointed fragments so too great races cannot be created with disconnected families. I could hear the voice of my dead ancestors whispering to me: 'A long time ago Gailhard de Lantagnac inherited the second farm on Chenaux Lane in Saint-Michel from Roland de Lantagnac, then later Roland de Lantagnac called Lamontagne inherited it from Salaberry de Lantagnac, then Guillaume Lamontagne inherited it from Paul Lamontagne; because of them all, because of the successive and cumulative work of all these generations, a corner of the homeland was cleared and made habitable; proficiency in agriculture was gradually learned; successive generations of Lamontagnes took possession of a large portion of the parish of Saint-Michel and in their homes was preserved the moral force which has brought you back to your original integrity.'"

The priest's face increasingly radiated happiness: "Your words are pure gold, my friend."

Lantagnac got up. His hands resting lightly on his hips, his shoulders squared, he stood erect in an attitude which he often adopted when strongly moved: "That is not all, Father. There, in the cemetery at Saint-Michel, upon my family's tombs, I made a solemn resolution. Shall I tell you what it was?"

"Yes, do," quickly replied Father Fabien, hoping to hear the ultimate decision.

"I promised my ancestors that I would restore my children to them."

"Good for you!"

"My sons and daughters," Lantagnac continued, "have some English blood in their veins because of their mother; but through me they have inherited above all the ancient blood of the Lantagnacs, of our Canadian ancestors to begin with, and of the French Lantagnacs from Monteil and Grignan – forty generations. I have vowed that this is the side to which they must turn."

"Good for you!" repeated Father Fabien.

"I might add, the Christian future of my children worries me above all else. If my recent studies have shown me anything, it is surely the profound affinity that exists between the French race and Catholicism. Perhaps that is why the French race is so often termed universal. Rivarol has written that the French language 'has integrity incorporated into its genius'. And I would add that this integrity comes from whatever is best in Latin and Christian thought. I have therefore decided: my children will return to their first education. If they are willing, I shall place them once more in the direct line of their ancestors."

Father Fabien was exultant. Rising to seize his pupil's hands and pressing them affectionately, he exclaimed: "God be praised, you have arrived at last! If only you knew how I have been waiting for you! Lantagnac, I shall say something which may astonish you: but today is a great day for the French minority in Ontario! A Leader has been given to it!" . . .


. . . At the last moment, something had acted mysteriously upon him. He thought he recognized one of those extraordinary shocks Father Fabien had once mentioned, a flash of enlightenment from the Holy Spirit raising the human will beyond its own powers. In less than a second the man was on his feet; he asked permission to speak and immediately began.

His speech showed none of the effects of its sudden improvisation. The preliminary work which had been going on below the surface of his mind was yielding fruit. He spoke with ease, developing his points with orderly and harmonious precision, like a classical composition. As a speaker he could draw strength from his conscience and his naturally candid honesty. He possessed the very qualities which please both Parliament and the public. To the coldly logical, knowledgeable, moderate style of the English debater, he allied the controlled emotional power of French lyricism which, when expressed with such conviction, still exercises a kind of magnetic sway even over old and jaded members of Parliament.

Lantagnac, unlike all the other speakers, did not repeat the history of the school question in Ontario, nor argue the rights of bilingualism. The natural loftiness of his mind carried him directly to the heart of the matter. His was a speech on general themes where his mind could work at ease. Returning to his favourite ideas, he showed forcefully how struggles such as the present one constituted a danger to peace in the country and to the continued existence of Confederation.

"What can be the aim of those who persecute French in Canada?" he cried, turning to the row of Ministers. "Do they wish to undermine the very foundations of that structure so painfully erected fifty years ago? I would like to recall for their benefit some of the realities of our situation: along the entire border which separates us from our neighbours to the South, we lack any kind of natural frontier. Geographically the two countries occupy the same territory from ocean to ocean. The only boundaries that exist are within our country, and they divide it into three distinct and separate zones. Unfortunately, these are not the only divisive elements present in the country! Western Canada favours free trade while Eastern Canada is protectionist. You Anglo-Saxons are imperialists while we who are sons of Canada are above all Canadian. How blind our politicians must be if, to all these possibilities of rupture, they deliberately add the threat of religious and national conflict!"

"Yes," continued the Member of Parliament for Russell, "these persecutors may well destroy the Canadian Confederation, by killing my compatriots' faith in federal institutions and by sabotaging the principle of absolute equality between associates, which is the principle at the very basis of our political alliance. For I must warn this House: our nation is too proud to go on accepting insults from people implied by the constitution to be our equals. I also warn those ambitious men who may be harbouring even more sinister plans; I warn them to banish all futile hopes from their minds. Our race is too strong to succumb beneath their blows. We are no longer, thank God, the handful of vanquished people we were in 1760. We are a nation of three million people and have uncontested mastery over a province of the Dominion which is four times as large as the British Isles. We constitute the largest and strongest nationality within the entire North American continent. No other human group above the forty-fifth parallel has a greater homogeneity; none has so well adapted itself to the atmosphere of the New World; none has stronger traditions or more vigorous social institutions. More than a century and a half after the Conquest, the people of Quebec remain as French as they were in the days of New France. Since even amorphous fragments of the German or Polish nations have triumphed over the efforts of their formidable neighbours to assimilate them, how could a few thousand oppressors manage to crush a race whose roots plunge as deeply into Canadian soil as the maple tree which is its emblem?"

And then, resorting to a strategy particularly calculated to impress the Cabinet and the persecutors from Ontario, the speaker directed an appeal to all moderate men and to all Catholics of other nationalities. To the former, law-abiding and conservative men, he represented the traditional and Catholic province of Quebec as an invincible fortress against the onslaught of anti-social propaganda; he stressed the role which groups of French people might play in the maintenance of a

Canadian spirit, since these groups were not given to annexationist tendencies. Then, appealing to all Catholics of Canada, he demonstrated that the war against bilingual schools was merely a first step in the campaign against all Catholic separate schools. In the name of the fellowship that arises from similar beliefs and misfortunes, he especially pleaded with Irish Catholics to abandon the struggle which was now setting brother against brother: "I see only too well what we both stand to lose in this painful conflict; but I cannot yet see what benefit our fellow Catholics could possibly reap from the ruins of our schools."

For over an hour the speaker developed these themes with a loftiness of purpose, a perfection of rhetorical form, and a vehemence of language which he had never achieved before.

Emerson has said that there are occasionally moments when the soul of our forefathers can be seen in the clear mirror of our eyes. The very soul of his nation was vibrating in the speaker's voice and in his whole person. Witnesses who could understand the significance of the debate saw the parliamentary arena expanding to become the battlefield upon which, ever since Sainte-Foy, two civilizations have perpetually confronted each other.

# To Cape Blomidon

L.Groulx, *Au Cap Blomidon* (Montreal, n.p.,1932), pp.9-20; pp.218-226. Reprinted by permission of Mme J.Rémillard.

It was a June evening in the Park of Memories at Grand'Prée.

Jean Bérubé was strolling along a deeply shaded walk between two rows of willow trees, immersed in thought. He was reliving the moment when, one Sunday afternoon, he had told Lucienne Bellefleur about the irrevocable decision he had made. It had happened in Saint-Donat de Montcalm, until so recently his home . . .

That day, he and his cousin Paul Comeau had set off on a fishing expedition to Lake Lajoie. Behind them an immense landscape stretched from the fields of water lilies carpeting Lake Tire to the distant mountains of Lake Archambault with their jagged pine trees clinging to rocky peaks. The two men paddled their canoe into the Pembina, a narrow river which bears the same name as the lake from which it rises.

The canoe sped smoothly on. With his cocked rifle by his side, Paul kept a lookout in the bow, hoping to raise a flight of ducks or perhaps even get a shot at some deer coming down to drink or nibble the rushes at the river's edge. Jean gazed at the scenery with a look of deepest melancholy, as though to imprint it forever on his mind. He was reflecting on that voyage to Acadia which had so unexpectedly changed the entire course of his life. The trip had begun innocently enough as a pilgrimage to Grand'Prée with his Uncle Norbert. But once there the young Acadian had fallen under the spell of his ancestral land, which beckoned to him, tugging at his heartstrings and drawing him back.

How beautiful it seemed, this little river, under the autumn sky! It may be that Jean coloured it with a projection of his own feeling, for he found it as charming, as enticing as a fiancée on the eve of some great separation. In places it ran deep and dark, enveloping itself in the mystery of the great forest which crept down steep mountain slopes almost to the water's edge, almost within reach of the paddles. At other spots it widened into a shimmering expanse rippling over a gravelly bed. There skeletons of trees enshrouded in silt lay motionless on the bottom like sleeping reptiles. Then, like a young girl pirouetting to display her frock, the Pembina indulged in gracious curves and sudden bends; in order to skirt her islands the canoe had to twist and turn in narrow channels. Bending loftily over the moving mirror, birches shook down upon the travellers the fine gold flakes of their doomed foliage; the sedge brushed by their hands; and beneath their knees they could feel the harsh and grating impact of sunken trees against the hull. Suddenly they heard a distant murmur, the sound of rapids; the water began to rush more swiftly past the bow, tugging fiercely at the paddles; and looking down they saw long grasses bending and waving like loosened hair in the strong current. They were drawing near the outlet of the Pembina.

"Look," said Paul, "there are people here already. Look at all the boats near the mill."

"That yellow one belongs to the Lavoies," commented Jean.

"And what about that white boat, with the strawberry trim?" asked Paul in a teasing voice.

"Have the Bellefleurs come here as well?" his cousin exclaimed, sincerely puzzled. "All the way from the other side of the lake?"

"Come, come," said Paul, a bit sceptical about Jean's surprise, "we aren't children any more!"

"But I tell you I really am surprised!"

"And I tell you the Bellefleurs have come, and Lucienne Bellefleur as well, I'd be willing to bet!"

"You'd lose your shirt," was the off-hand reply.

There was a crunch as the stem of the canoe came up against the gravel shore. They had arrived at the sandy inlet near the mouth of the river. Below the rapids stood the gaunt wooden structure of the mill, enveloped in Sunday stillness. Through the open gables its motionless gears and chains could be seen, and not a whiff of smoke issued from the rusty chimney upon which perched a metal bonnet almost like a cardinal's hat. While Jean pulled the canoe up the beach, Paul, with his gun tucked under his arm, crossed over to the mill, where he could hear the sound of voices. Suddenly he turned to his cousin, with a meaningful look. Sure enough, the Bellefleurs were there, and Lucienne as well. Jean saw her glance round to her father and then wave timidly. For the fishing trip she had worn a grey skirt, blue woollen sweater, and brown rubber boots. A straw hat, secured with ribbons beneath her chin, framed the lightly tanned features of this mountain girl, her dark eyes alive with candour and intelligence.

"How lovely you look in that outfit, Lucienne!" said Jean Bérubé to her.

"I suppose you think it makes me look like Evangéline!" pouted the young girl.

"Shh! . . . " said Jean, a finger on his lips, "Don't you start now . . . "

A few minutes later, Lucienne and Jean were sitting on a rock, supposedly fishing for red trout. The proposed expedition to Lake Lajoie had somehow been forgotten. Lucienne had made a seat of a large, rounded spruce root, and Jean was standing beside her. Paul had vanished into the woods in search of game. Fifty feet away Lucienne's father and his old friend Lavoie sat hunched in a rowboat, quietly fishing as they smoked their pipes. Like all seasoned fishermen, they hardly spoke. The only time the silence was broken was when Bellefleur lost his catch and Lavoie, who loved to tease, cried out: "Was that ever a beauty that got away!"

Bellefleur, his features stern, went on baiting his line with a firm and rapid gesture.

The two lovers, meanwhile, were not taking their fishing quite so seriously.

"Look, you've lost the worm," said Jean to Lucienne, who simply continued to dangle her line.

"And what about your bait?" Jean's hook was hardly in a better state than Lucienne's.

"What a stroke of luck that you were able to come here this afternoon!" said Jean.

"Yes, it was very lucky," replied the young girl, "especially since everything has turned out so well." Then, struggling to control her emotion, she added: "Since you spoke to me about your departure, Jean, you've no idea how miserable I've been when I'm alone. And so, when I heard Father saying, after lunch: 'Guess I'll go up to Pembina; they say the little trout are biting, just like in the old days.' I said, 'I'll come with you.'"

"I don't suppose you expected to find such poor fishing?" ventured Jean. She turned to him with a look of tender reproach: "Do you think I haven't caught much? Or that I shan't be able to keep what I have caught? Oh Jean," she cried out, suddenly deciding to speak her mind, "is it really true that you are going away?" And she dipped the end of her pole into the water, to show that she was no longer interested in fishing.

Jean answered: "You know that I have to. It is all because of my Uncle Norbert and that promise I made him when we came back from Acadia. I had been reading Acadian history to him for a couple of years, and the poor old man must have taken it all very seriously. Anyway, you know, he suddenly developed an irresistible urge to see the land where his forefathers had lived. And when I finally gave in and went with him to attend the unveiling of the statue of Evangéline, he was simply overwhelmed. I, of course, had memorized the map of Grand'Prée down to the last square inch, and it was child's play to find the land that had belonged to the Pellerins, who were later called Bérubé – not the complete property, because all those old holdings have since been subdivided by English surveyors, but a portion of it at least, which I am sure belonged to our ancestors. I can still see the look on my uncle's face, when I took him to the spot, a few acres from the church, and told him: 'This is it. To your left lies the land of the Cormier family, to your right that of old Basile Landry, and in between, the land of the Pellerins.' My uncle did not utter a word. His hands clasped behind his back, he simply stood and looked at the lovely green meadows, the beautiful apple trees upon the hill; then his eyes fell upon a prosperous looking cottage with white gables and brown shutters: the home of the new owners. With tears streaming down his face he turned and said, 'Let us go.'"

Jean Bérubé became pensive as he remembered the scene. Lucienne, who had been listening with mixed feelings of interest and anxiety, asked: "So it was there he extracted that terrible promise from you?"

"No, not there. He attended all the ceremonies, without saying a word. But the next day, when we went to Cape Blomidon, a high cliff at the head of the Bay of Mines, he asked me whether I knew who owned our ancestral land. I had found out, and was able to tell him:

'Mr. Hugh Finlay.'

'Is he young, or old?'

'He's an old man.'

'Has he any children?'

'He has a son, who has apparently gone off to other parts of the world, and has not been heard of for many years.'

"That was all. But on our way back, in the train, he looked me straight in the eye and said: 'There's a wonderful land to be taken, there, my boy. I'm too old now, and anyway I'm a bachelor, without any children. But you're free, you haven't any family ties. If you'll keep an eye open for a chance to buy that land, I'll make provision for it in my will.'

"Well you can imagine, Lucienne, how moved I was to find my old uncle so strongly bent on buying back his ancestral land, and prepared to put all his worldly wealth into it. In fact I could hardly believe my ears at first, because he had such a reputation for being tight-fisted, if not downright miserly. But on he went: 'You know, Jean, I was very frugal in my young days. I never squandered my pay packet in hotels, but always set something aside, every week, for thirty years. And I didn't just idle away the summers either, or spend all my time at the lakes fishing trout: no; summer or winter, I worked hard, cultivated my land like a good settler, and never spent a penny out of turn. As a result, you see, I have twelve thousand beautiful dollars in the bank, and my land in Saint-Donat is worth almost another three thousand. With that you could make those Finlays an offer. . .'

"You know the rest, Lucienne. My uncle died almost immediately after we got back from Acadia, and I was left alone in the world, the sole survivor of a family of five brothers carried away by consumption, like their parents before them ... I accepted the inheritance my Uncle Norbert had left me."

These words plunged Lucienne into a deep gloom, just as when Jean had first confided his plans to her during an evening at the Comeaus. That night, she had said nothing, but leaning closer to the window, had gazed out at the stars shining over the mountains. Hers was a simple, child-like faith, and instinctively, in times of stress, her thoughts turned to heaven. Once again, as she sat by Lake Pembina, her gaze turned to the mountains, to the nearest one on whose slopes an overgrown field and crumbling cottage bore witness to the tragic miscarriage of some settler's dreams. Turning from a scene too heavily laden with sorrow her eyes travelled to the more distant peaks lining Lake Clair. The hazy golden light which had vibrated about them all day had vanished, and already their slopes were darkening with the approach of night. Deeper colours were slowly gaining upon the golds and russets of autumn. The lake turned almost black, and cold breezes began to stir. From time to time the retort of a hunter's gun could be heard deep in the woods, a chain of echoes rebounding along the wild ravines like the painful repercussion of certain words in the human heart.

"Jean," exclaimed Lucienne suddenly, dejectedly, "I had hoped that you would eventually forget all these ideas. But I see now that it is hopeless."

"But how could I stay here? When I accepted the inheritance I also accepted Uncle's conditions. Now I am committed, in all honour and justice. No, it's far better that I should go . . . "

And Jean began to speak with enthusiasm about the magnificent opportunity, the challenge which was opening for him to realize and perfect his uncle's half-formulated plan. To him, he felt, had been entrusted a lofty mission which filled him with noble pride. At college he had deplored the mediocrity of his classmates' ambitions: almost every one resigned to a routine life in some ordinary profession, resigned to staying within well-travelled lines without even feeling the lure of the unknown, the unexplored. He would become despondent as he saw them behaving like the timid deer of his native mountains, reluctant to stray from their beaten track unless pursued by a pack of hounds. Born with a taste for high flying, Bérubé as a young student had waited impatiently to try his wings in some great cause. And this idealistic cause, he was convinced, had just been presented to him to test his will. Yes, he, Jean Bérubé, a boy brought up in the mountains, would be the one chosen to lead the Acadians back to their native land and reconquer it for God. To Lucienne he tried to explain the call he heard from that distant land, a call tormenting him day and night. "Come," the old land seemed to plead with him, "come, I need you, I miss the singing of my church bells . . . " And then Jean wondered: "Could it be simply that I took my reading every bit as seriously as Uncle Norbert? . . . Could it be that, having been sent back to the mountains after six years of study because of a delicate chest, I am nothing but a rootless person finding it difficult to live within boundaries set by my father and his father? . . . Could this feeling of mine be merely lust for travel and adventure? . . . Did I tell you, Lucienne, that I brought back with me a willow twig from the Park of Memories at Grand'Prée, and a spray of wild roses from Cape Blomidon? You would scarcely believe the ecstasy, and the powerful nostalgia which rise up within me when I contemplate those two faded bouquets . . . "

More exalted now, Jean continued: "No, you see, Lucienne, you and I and all the others, we are like pilgrims delayed for a while on their journey. Boston, Gaspé, Montréal, Sainte-Lucie,

Saint-Donat: these have been nothing more than temporary shelters for us ever since the Great Dispersal. Whatever the cost, we must all of us go back, to sleep at last within the earth that has been calling to us without respite in its long wait for our return." . . .

They were driving down the road to Grand'Prée, when Dr. Munster, who was sitting beside Jean, said suddenly in a worried voice: "I suppose I can confide in you, Mr. Bérubé: you are connected in a way with that house. I expect a harrowing scene this evening. The Finlays must have some dreadful curse hanging over them: when they are about to die, every one of them is filled with the most complete and utter terror . . . it's really frightening."

"That's strange," murmured Jean.

"Of course you know the rumour about them in this part of the country?"

"No."

The doctor, glad of an opportunity to gossip, launched into a brief summary of the Acadian expulsion and the subsequent arrival of new settlers. In particular he stressed the curt treatment these settlers had given the few Acadians who had sought refuge in the surrounding woods. Then he began to relate what happened one night on Robert Finlay's property. Instinctively, Jean slowed the car to listen.

"That Robert Finlay," pursued the doctor, "had always been a terribly hard man. He had been a great hunter of Indians in Connecticut and had even brought back an Algonquin scalp, which Mr. Hugh later discovered and promptly burnt. In any case, when Finlay saw the poor Acadians arriving to beg help, his immediate reply was to seize his gun and riddle them with bullets all four, one after the other, first the sons and then the father."

At that point the car swerved violently, narrowly missing the ditch. The doctor, terrified, clutched at Jean's arm.

"Sorry," said Jean, quickly steering the car back to the road.

"Tragic stories don't seem to agree with you," smiled the doctor.

"Some of them don't," muttered Jean, who was growing pale and could feel his hands begin to shake.

The doctor went on with his story.

"I wonder what happened in that final moment between the murderer and his victims? Did the old Acadian manage to utter some supreme curse before he died? Did the sight of those butchered men imprint its vengeful image for ever upon old

Finlay's brain? At any rate, throughout the course of his life and especially at the moment of death, Finlay was pursued like Macbeth by his victim's ghost. He died the death of a man foredoomed to hell."

"A just punishment!" Jean could not help exclaiming. The doctor did not appear to hear. "But now, here is what happened. Whether through some curious mechanism of hereditary memory, or, more likely to my mind, through suggestion as the story was transmitted from father to son, all the Finlays of Morse Cottage have experienced the same horrible vision on their dying day. And this has been confirmed by my own father and grandfather, both family doctors like myself. Death for the Finlays has been accompanied by the most unspeakable terror. 'The ghost! The ghost!' they shriek, like demented men, literally terrified out of their minds."

"How very, very strange . . . " said Jean, blurting out the first words he could think of to hide his agitation.

"But there is something even stranger," replied the doctor. "One day an old woman, probably a witch of some sort, who had never been seen before in the neighbourhood and apparently knew nothing of the whole story, appeared at Morse Cottage and very solemnly announced that the ghost would soon stop coming, for the true owner was about to return."

"And when was that?" asked Jean feverish with trepidation.

"Oh, about seven years ago, I would say. You'll probably think it's ridiculous to attach any importance to the words of an old crone, but you know in this part of the country people are pretty superstitious, especially when it comes to the past and the old Acadians. You can scarcely imagine how upset they were at the Cottage about this prediction. And do you know, only last week I was called out to attend that old woman, who had been found dying by the roadside about three miles from here. I arrived too late. She was already dead. But when I told Mr. Hugh about it, you should have seen his face . . . "

Just then, Jean, who was becoming increasingly perturbed, suddenly recalled the words he had heard one Sunday morning when coming out of church in Kentville: "They will come when I am dead. This was the promise of the Virgin of Grand'Prée."

They were arriving at Morse Cottage. Impelled by curiosity as well as by a feeling of sympathy, Jean Bérubé followed the doctor to the sick-room. Doctor Munster had warned him that the scene might be harrowing. What met the young man's eyes exceeded all his imaginings. There, sitting in his nightgown on his bed, with his beard and hair standing on end and his eyes unnaturally widened with horror, Mr. Hugh Finlay was beating the air with his arms in a futile attempt to ward off the dreadful nightmare. His flailing arms, his crazed eyes rolling in uncontrollable terror, his haggard face spread fear about him in the dim candle-lit room. At times the old man pulled the blankets over his head to blot out the hideous spectre. In a choking voice he stammered incoherent words and cries that turned into a desperate wail when through the sheets and blankets the vengeful apparition could still be seen standing there motionless and implacable. Then, staggering up from his bed, the old man turned his face to the wall, and wringing his hands, began to sob heavily, like a child. The doctor had not exaggerated: it was a terrifying and painful scene, awesome and heart-rending like one of Shakespeare's darkest passages. There was no respite: one wave of terror followed another, with the same shrieks, the same laments, the same gestures of utter despair. In the flickering candlelight every movement of the old man sent enormous shadows dancing like grotesque phantoms upon the walls. Crouched in a corner, Mrs. Finlay covered her head to shut out the sight. Near her, a younger woman cowered in her shawl, pale with fear. Jean Bérubé recognized Miss Bulrode. He noticed that at this critical moment, Allan was not here. Approaching the sick man in a moment of relative calm, Dr. Munster managed to give him an injection. Then he tried to quieten him with soothing words. But just as he was becoming calmer, the old man turned to the door, where Jean was standing, deathly pale as he surveyed the fearful scene. What visions then arose within the dying man's over-wrought mind? Immediately, his eyes dilating, he jolted to an almost upright position in the bed and screamed, this time very audibly:

"The ghost! The ghost! He is there, there . . . !"

And, paralyzed with fright, the poor old man, enveloped in his sheet as in a winding-cloth, burst into loud and racking sobs.

The doctor waved Jean Bérubé away. The young man did not have to be asked twice. As he was leaving the room, overwhelmed by the scene, a woman caught up with him, quivering, almost frantic.

"Your car is just outside, Mr. Bérubé? Drive me away from here, I never want to come back again!"

And before Jean, in his surprise, had time to object: "Immediately, I tell you, immediately, or I shall die in this hateful house."

"But who will drive the doctor home?"

"He can wait."

In a few moments the young woman was ready. Jean put Miss Margaret's two small suitcases beside him, on the front seat, and drove off. But hardly had they gone a few hundred feet than a shriek of terror came from the back seat.

"A face," said Miss Margaret, "appeared at the car window."

Jean got out, searched the darkness, but saw nothing . . . or perhaps a shadow fleeing in the night.

Two minutes later, Jean Bérubé was driving at forty miles an hour along the road to Truro. At times he thought he heard a muffled sob behind him. Her head buried in a large scarf, Miss Bulrode was trying to erase the horrible scene from her mind. An hour later, without having uttered a word, she was deposited on the threshold of her parents' house. Then Jean drove back at the same speed towards Grand'Prée. Dr. Munster was waiting for him at the door of Morse Cottage.

"Ah, there you are! Poor Mr. Hugh! I've at last managed to calm him down," he said. "He should sleep for two or three hours now. But I have another patient whose condition is worrying me in Wolfville. Will you drive me back?"

Then, glancing at his watch, he jokingly remarked: "It's three o'clock. With a bit of speed, you could still catch a few hours' sleep."

The night had grown still blacker. A few drops of rain had fallen, and a high wind was moaning through the trees like the rushing of ocean waves. Just as he was about to turn out of the Morse Cottage driveway, Jean Bérubé braked abruptly, stopped the car, and switched on the high beams of his headlights; then, slowly turning the steering wheel, he explored the sides of the road. The two broad stripes of moving light swept over the road and lawn, making countless drops of rain glitter for an instant like glow worms in the dark.

"What are you doing?" asked the doctor.

"I thought I saw something or someone lying near the road," explained Jean as he drove off again.

Ten minutes later he turned off the Wolfville highway into the driveway of Morse Cottage once again. As he was preparing to change gears to drive up the incline, a shadow suddenly loomed up beside him on the left side of the car. Jean started nervously, stalling the motor. He was trying to start it again when a fist clutching a pistol emerged from the darkness just on the other side of the window, and a round face pushed forward, its wild eyes searching for the driver's face. Jean Bérubé immediately reached for the door handle, planning to spring upon his assailant. But the other man had foreseen his reaction. His left hand was already tightly upon the handle. Then he waited, with his weapon poised, as if savouring the idea of prolonging his victim's agony. Jean was calculating whether he could reach the door on his right, open it and escape. But he did not dare, convinced that he would then be shot in the back. The two men observed each other for long and suspenseful seconds. Even in this moment of terror, Jean's courage and lucidity did not desert him. With a spontaneous act of faith he had recommended himself to the Virgin, and almost in spite of himself he could not help wondering at the dramatic twist of history which, years after the event, brought the sons of victims to confront the sons of murderers in attitudes so similar to those of their forefathers. He thought of that cruel manhunt that had taken place on this very spot so long ago, on a dark night like this one. Suddenly, a shot rang out. Fragments of glass and slivered wood flew into Jean's face. But the hand had been too unsteady: the bullet had missed its target. It had merely shattered the glass, skimming along the dashboard. Seeing the assailant preparing to shoot again, Jean drove his hand through the broken window pane in an attempt to seize his wrist. But at that very moment, another shadow rose up behind the first and seized his weapon: after that there was only one large black mass rolling and groaning on the grass. At last Jean Bérubé could jump from his car. He looked, he searched, and listened: there was no longer anything to be seen or heard. Far away came the muffled sound of running along the highway, but that soon faded into the howling wind and the jet black night.

# Vocal Groulx

## The Tradition of French Literature in Canada

L. Groulx, "Les traditions des lettres françaises au Canada," a speech delivered at the French Language Congress, Quebec, June 25, 1912. *Dix ans d'Action Française* (Montreal, Bibliothèque de L'Action française, 1926), pp. 7-21. Reprinted by permission of Mme J. Rémillard.

Ladies and Gentlemen:

One truth which even our greatest hair-splitters no longer challenge, for the simple reason that it has now been established beyond all controversy, is that Canadian literature must of necessity be ... Canadian!

It will be Canadian or it will not be at all!

Ladies and Gentlemen, a day was bound to arrive when people would wish to abandon their differences in the face of such a serious problem. They would then no longer expect the blossoming of a great work, "A messenger to carry all earth's cries/And pleas with it up to the skies ... " from any but an artist of true, free, genuinely Canadian genius. Such an artist would be like a cock's cry rousing the dawn: from his communion with the soil – the Divine soil – he would sing not songs housed in foreign books, but hymns "born of our native soil and rising from deep roots."

And so there was agreement on this first point: a not entirely heroic concession, since there remained so many other issues providing grounds for endless discussion. Should we lend an ear to the highly seductive, if somewhat haughty tones of nationalism, and opt for absolute autonomy in the creating of our independent art? Or, conscious as we were of being a young nation, would it be better to accept the tutelage of great art, and, before writing masterpieces of our own at least learn to read those of others?

Modesty and common sense made us opt for the latter alternative. Of course Brunetière helped us along a bit by persuading us that "it must be the height of insolence and barbarity to think that despite our brief life span everything that counts begins with us!" And how could we avoid the feeling that to break with the past was to break with our very life-blood?

In any case, the most serious and complex question immediately arose. It was all very well to set ourselves to the study of great art. But first we had to find, in the literature of France, those works whose pith and marrow we could convert into "our own blood and sustenance."

You will immediately see, Ladies and Gentlemen, that the problem is an important one, inasmuch as the entire future of Canadian literature rests upon it; upon it also rests the integrity of our French soul, in other words the question of our survival. And how can we postpone facing this problem when we see a tendency among our own people to choose as their masters the least French of all French writers? Fashion – and it is a tenacious fashion, refusing to fade as all others do – fashion dictates that the preferred writers are those who have only the poorest following in their own country, who have mastered their over-refined and subtle art but are imprisoned within their small, pompous coteries with little hope of any external, Pentecostal enlightenment.

A nation's literature must be at one with its people – a nation can benefit only from those influences which it is destined to undergo. Gentlemen, these are commonplaces which I am so solemnly asserting, and I assure you that I am fully aware of it. Since when have venerable commonplaces not formed part of the profoundest eternal Truth? Since when have we not known that tradition and progress cannot be divorced? (Others, though, have forgotten it, much to their grief.) We no longer need to learn, or indeed repeat, the sad truth: writers without strong roots, déracinés, can never be anything but an inferior species. For some reason, I am suddenly reminded of those two maple trees I found in exile, their familiar, nostalgic leaves now shading the grounds at Crec'h Bleiz, the Count of Cuverville's manor in Brittany. Uprooted from their own New France, the two plants had grown as best they could on Breton granite, alongside Celtic oaks. From their country of origin they had brought with them a proud stature and lofty, virile foliage. But when tapped one spring morning, they were found to contain none of the rich sap which flows within them in their native land. A fact, Gentlemen, which has more than merely symbolic value: at all costs, we must weld the present and the future to the past. Progress can only be achieved through perseverance, through the continuity of a single effort, through the intelligent assimilation of a nation's inheritance, just as a young tree can only thrive and grow strong upon the remains of those that have lived before.

From all this you will have gathered, Ladies and Gentlemen, that the literature which is to inspire and guide our master-pieces must be one that is most characteristically French, most expressive of human dignity, and hence best suited for its task of education and to the needs of our collective soul. Do we truly wish to pave the way for a Renaissance of French literature in Canada? Are we willing to become workers devoted to the exaltation of New France? We must then listen warily to the belligerent appeals of those who, like Du Bellay long ago, would have us "plunder remorselessly the sacred treasures of the Delphic temple." Nowadays there are indeed intellectual robbers deliberately plundering, but here is the rub: everything French comes to us from France, but not everything which comes from France is French.

What great risks we would be taking, for example, if in order to encourage the flowering of young talent we penetrated too deeply into that eighteenth century which Mr. Faguet so rightly characterized as "neither Christian nor French". Nor can I see any need to enshroud our French lucidity with Romantic mists; for Romanticism was nothing more than an abortive revolution in literature, a violent assault upon traditional common sense; indeed, the origins and philosophical bases of Romanticism must be sought not in Chateaubriand, not in Victor Hugo, not above all in France itself, but in a foreigner from Geneva, Jean-Jacques Rousseau. I need scarcely mention here that host of aesthetes whose contribution to French literature was entirely negative, and whose greatest claim to immortality, now that they lie in scented shrouds, is that they had at last the grace to die.

The conclusion is that we must study those writers who created, in France, that rare and noble thing, a classical century. There, Ladies and Gentlemen, we shall find models fit for us just as they have been for the past 200 years for anyone with the fearsome ambition to write French.

It might be rashly objected that the special quality of seven-teenth century literature was non-national and indeed quite pagan. What a waste of time and effort to arrive at such a superficial judgement! Even if it were true, would this criticism apply to more than a small minority of the works? At issue here, I suppose, would be the century's dramatic literature. But has not a wealth of latent Christianity been found in a single trag-edy of Racine's, more indeed than in the whole of Romantic literature? Would it not be wise, furthermore, to bear in mind that a nation's true characteristics are revealed not in the themes chosen but in the way of treating them? The Cid may be Spanish and Andromache Greek, yet nothing could be more truly French than Corneille's *Cid* and Racine's *Andromaque.*

No literature could be greater than that of the *Grand Siècle*, for none has embodied greater ideas in greater language. None could be more truly French, for there has never been so complete an expression of the very soul of France, the splendour of her history, the perfect integrity of her traditions and her incomparable ideal. None could be more human, for of all world literatures none has been able to contribute ideas of such universal value, none has so well seized human thought and endowed it with dimensions of eternity.

Ladies and Gentlemen, these truly are reasons that classical literature must become for us in Canada a heroic sustenance to build our strength, to fortify our soul. But would you press me for further reasons? Shall I say more? With French delegates before me and in the presence of one of the Forty Immortals, I tremble to utter what must appear to many a most horrifying blasphemy. And yet, Ladies and Gentlemen, I fear I must, the words will come out: the reason we turn to classical literature, to that beloved literature of Corneille, Racine, Molière, Boileau, Pascal, Bossuet, the reason is simply that no literature has ever been so . . . Canadian!

Gentlemen of France, I beg your pardon. Your noble literature is so naturally a part of our traditions that the question of ownership does become something of a problem. Witness the many points of consonance which have survived to link our French Canadian souls to the classical souls of the century that saw Champlain, Talon, Frontenac, and even Montcalm.

We are an offshoot of the old country and have grown upon alien shores. But like a seedling arising from the tiniest acorn, we have inherited from our mighty parent that need for a strong vitality coursing like sap within our veins and that pride to stand erect in the same clear light of the sun.

Coming as we did from that part of France where thrive the purest language and the most robust French temperament, abruptly severed from our mother country and left without communication for so long, we managed to retain the beautiful and clear impression, the moving image of seventeenth-century France we had taken away with us on the day of separation. We retained her faith, and with it the same instinctive bent for idealism. A parallel history, a natural evolution without irregularity have only served to strengthen native tendencies.

France has always been, by its very nature, a land of crusades. Occasionally the desire for conquest took her to the battlefields; but mingled with that instinct was almost always an equal desire to disseminate ideas or doctrines. We too have had a taste for crusades. During the hundred and fifty years of French domination, our forefathers were filled with chivalric ideals. Nowadays, in this feverishly materialistic America, it sometimes happens that our history is overlooked when people seek the names of the earliest explorers and conquerors. But when the time comes to erect statues in belated tribute to idealism, just look: from the distant mouths of the Mississippi to the haughty Capitol, from Detroit in Michigan to the prairies of the Far West, the heroes immortalized in bronze are French, our people.

After the separation, the time came for us, as it did almost simultaneously for our mother country, to rise toward new freedom; we had no catastrophe to tear us violently from our traditions. The establishment of constitutional freedom may have claimed a few victims, but it did not attack our soul. And if it was feared that British institutions might deprive us to some extent of our French idealism, we now have history to prove that such was not the case. We have remained, as always, incorrigible idealists. In 1792, we undertook our first parliamentary battle to safeguard our language, and it led to our first "resounding victory", a French victory. Did not Lord Dufferin, one of our Governors, praise us later for being true supporters of constitutional liberties? As you well know, it took a half-century of magnificent and unremitting effort, effort which goes on even today and which, despite our weakness and poverty, has always taken precedence over more practical matters. In the meantime, following the pattern of the France of old, oblivious to our own interests, we have thrown ourselves into countless great imperilled causes; places as far away as Rome have witnessed the flashing swords and epic deeds of our youthful officers.

Don't you see then, Ladies and Gentlemen, that we have defended ourselves much too well. We cannot change. A nation's history usually consists of efforts to assimilate other races, to chase intruders from its territories, to gain control over commerce, to push back its frontiers and expand its homeland. Ours can be summed up in a single ideal, a single struggle: that of survival. Survival! To that aim have we marshalled and co-ordinated all our energies. Strengthen our spiritual position by vigorous cultivation of the inner life; surround ourselves with strong defenses: such has been the constant motto of our history for the past hundred and fifty years. And we have been true to that motto: even the settlement of our land has not demanded more blood or more sweat. For the efforts of our settlers and labourers have been entirely subordinated to the supreme task of preserving and building our nation. When pioneers move into a new area, sowing new fields of wheat, they are merely adding a further buttress to that cathedral-like structure which houses in its innermost altar the heart and soul of New France.

Gentlemen, this noble faithfulness to the past, this jealously guarded predominance of spirit over matter are sufficient evidence of the continuing health and equilibrium of our ancient race. They attest to our French and classical character. They indicate to us, if I am not mistaken, the literary works of France which can provide us with protection for those traditions most conducive to great art. Should you require yet another reason for turning to classical French literature, you need only look at our best Canadian writers: those whose work was truly remarkable were also the most classical.

What matter if these old works of France are not, like more recent ones, laden with exotic language and purple passages? Is that not in fact a reason for preferring them, since by using "old words sufficient for our forefathers" they alone can remind us of those thoughts, those words most vital to the defense of our race?

There, indeed, lies the crux of the problem. To ensure the progress of Canadian literature, we must first guard the integrity of our French souls. But could we ever surround our souls with too much protection? Remember the expression which Maurice Barrès used to describe our survival – "simply miraculous". There are false prophets everywhere, haggling over our future existence; they must be ignored, if we wish to survive at all.

How very untimely it would thus be to allow enemies into our fortress. At all costs we must avoid risky experiments, which are never very beneficial to anyone, least of all to small nations; we must close our minds to foreign ways of thinking and woolly aesthetic theories which could undermine not only our moral and rational stature but also that clear and vigorous common sense so basic to the French temperament.

Nothing can ever replace the study of classical letters as a safeguard for our spiritual inheritance. It would be futile to search elsewhere for a closer or more complete expression of our ancestral spirit. Nothing in France's past has been so homogeneous and so purely national, especially since a wave of cosmopolitanism has swept over all literatures in the last two hundred years, blending and obliterating national characteristics. Nowadays, when a people cannot remain in complete isolation, when free-trade in ideas is practised around the world, a nation can only hope to survive by strenuous effort and active participation in universal competition. Surely the best system of defence, the strongest guarantee of survival is for a people to augment its intellectual capital, and thereby to carry into the fray the brightest banner of civilization. Let us not delude ourselves with grandiose but dangerous schemes. As French Canadians our only hope of resisting assimilation in

America is to be always in a position to confront the larger English Canadian civilization as an equal rival.

In order to attain such conquering intellectual vigour, to whom shall we turn for sustenance if not to the great masters of all time? For us their literature alone can offer a promise of life. France herself is indebted to them for her intellectual supremacy. For the issues with which the masters grappled forever constitute what Bossuet considered essential to the civilized world.

I have said enough to show the Delphic temple open to us: here we may indeed enter and plunder as we will. Let us boldly seize our portion of that superb inheritance. It will endow us with the rights to survival as a race and the hope of a noble, glorious literature.

It was Brunetière who said: "The literary success of a language does not depend upon the number of people speaking it, but upon the number, quality, and importance of the truths which have been bestowed upon it by its great writers."

Any nation, no matter how humble, has the right to a continuing existence in the New World if it can strike gold among the spiritual wealth upon which young nations must rely. Our distinguished guest from the French Academy, Mr. Etienne Lamy, proclaimed this in an article that was as widely read and discussed as any book. "The nineteenth century," he remarked, "saw a period of unitary governments and vast collections of states. But the work of liberation must be carried out in each State; and wherever a State still comprises groups of different origins, each one of these groups must be given the power to express freely its particular form of thought and action. When there ought to be collaboration among free spirits, any imposition of uniformity is to be regretted." ("Nationalities", Un siècle, p. 59 ).

To Mr. Lamy, we now say: enriched with a wealth of classical heritage, our Canadian France will have views on life, duty, truth and beauty, which will not otherwise be present in American culture. Would it be an excess of pride on her part, pride in her traditions and in the role Providence has marked out for her, if like Emile Faguet in other circumstances she were to cry out to all those who wish to crush her: "We are not learning to be French, we were born so, and we have every reason in the world for obstinately remaining so."

Ladies and Gentlemen, whatever the cost in terms of struggles or sacrifices, let us keep our French Canadian soul. So many generations of pioneers, soldiers and labourers have given it their heroic and loving devotion that our spirit has become a fountainhead of beauty, of energy. Let us keep it intact, with all the virtues of its faith and universal language, so that works of the future may profit from it. Then will our brothers of France pay us the tribute of recognizing the French sentinel their country forgot a hundred and fifty years ago – a sentinel still standing guard with weapons drawn upon the old cliff at Quebec, and sounding still the old alarm: in spite of everything, we shall be French!

# Duties of the University Community

L.Groulx, "Le devoir des universitaires," a sermon delivered at the Mass of the Holy Spirit, October 6, 1915. *Le Devoir*, October 7, 1915. Reprinted by permission of Mme J.Rémillard.

My Lord Bishops,
Professors,
Students:

You are here this morning to bear witness to one of the loftiest truths of our faith. In attending this Mass of the Holy Spirit you proclaim your deep commitment to a belief in the Third Person of the Divinity – eternal and uncreated Love, source of all good and of all forms of life. Source of all forms of life! From the simple vitality quickening a blade of grass to that most exalted manifestation of life throbbing within our temples – even to that supernatural life which fills our souls with the sweet certainty of divine presence!

You believe that the Holy Spirit inspires the life of our intellects in accordance with Catholic truth. You believe, therefore, that we are no longer alone facing the powers of darkness, of evil, and error; we are no longer alone, for our Master, in fulfilment of his promise, has sent unto us his Spirit of truth. Confronting those terrible powers there now arise the forces of truth and of knowledge. In the eternal struggle against evil we have gained God as our ally – a God who inhabits our minds and hearts, who dwells in amity within us, and who inspires our intelligence and our will.

### DUTIES OF PROFESSORS

Professors and students at Catholic universities: if you enter into communication with the Holy Spirit, as you are now doing, you obviously intend to devote yourselves to the fostering of truth in our country. It reflects great credit upon you that you have come here today to beseech the Spirit of Knowledge to grant you protection against error, as well as strength and guidance in order to discharge completely your duties to your faith.

I will not say the time has come; rather it is always the time for Catholic universities to examine earnestly their own motives and activities. Universities, within the jurisdiction of the Church, represent the foremost institution for the dissemination of intellectual and spiritual values; is it not therefore always time for them to question whether they are truly fulfilling their original purpose, whether the ability of their professors, the perfection of their methods of teaching, and above all their constant regard for truth embody the authoritative voice of Catholicism? Must they not also ask themselves whether their moral doctrines, and the integrity of the lives of their professors and students, are such as to constitute a visible example of the highest standards of morality for their countrymen; whether their graduating students carry with them the authentic stamp of their Catholicism; whether they are indeed a force for truth, a social force at the service of both Church and State.

## THE GREAT IMPORTANCE OF THESE DUTIES

It is urgent for us to consider these grave problems. We have witnessed the incredible influence of doctrines emanating from university communities. The terrifying chaos engulfing Europe, and to some extent the rest of the world, is a testimony to the terrible vengeance that can be wreaked by truth when it is betrayed. Would it not almost seem that we are entering upon those dark days foretold by Biblical prophets when our reeling planet shall stagger to its crumbling ruin among the stars? We feel the soil slipping away beneath our feet, we search in vain for some firm ground upon which to plant our hopes. And yet, I am mistaken; for in that chaos, in that black night into which we seem to be rushing, there remains a single ray piercing the dark; in the general disarray one doctrine remains unshaken, one has not betrayed its promise of eternal life. And we Catholics, steadfast now in our faith and hope as in the days of peace and triumph, we still proclaim the ancient phrase: "The universe may crumble, the cross remains!" *Stat crux dum volvetur orbis!*

## THE NATURE OF OUR DUTIES

Professors, is it your wish to carry out fully your duties as

Catholic teachers?

Do not then withdraw entirely into your professional studies. Above all worldly sciences, above all human truths, there is a truth – nay, there is Truth, which deserves your most valiant efforts and at very least a tithe of your time. Shall I tell you the reasons for such devotion? To cultivate this Truth is to ennoble the mind, because it furnishes the intellect with its most immaterial object; it is at the very source and conjunction of all branches of human learning; it is the beacon lit on high to illuminate all earthly sciences below. And since it forms the necessary base for any intellectual structure, since its inherent, divine quality attunes the soul to the supernatural, would it not be futile to strive for a normal, complete education, or for the skill and mentality appropriate to Catholic professors, without first acquiring this fundamental understanding of one's faith? As that great Catholic Louis Veuillot exclaimed: "Oh what superior knowledge it is to know Christ!" And Saint Paul too, even when in the company of intellectuals from Corinth, Rome, and Athens, considered that all the knowledge he needed was that of Jesus Christ on the cross.

Are these principles held in sufficient respect here in our country? What can be the source of that weakness which even our best minds must occasionally acknowledge? It seems they suffer from a lack of balance in their intellectual training. The base is missing. Instead of being in first place, religious truth has been relegated to last place, after all other fields of human learning. While men have been absorbed in mastering their professional discipline, time has worked upon the sand-like surface of their soul, erasing all faint traces of their early religious training. Hence we find, here in our province and indeed almost everywhere, minds that are strong and well filled, but like certain stars, possessed of a single luminous side; hence we have such incoherence of thought, such fluctuations of doctrine, such imprecision and uncertainties – all sorrowful indices of a neglect of priorities.

Gentlemen, beware of accepting such fatal mutilations; more than most, we must protect the education of our minds.

Our intellectual colonialism, if I may be permitted such an expression, presents special dangers. A nation which is still young, which lacks its own independent intellectual life, satisfies its thirst elsewhere – and God knows how great the risk is nowadays of drinking from troubled waters!

In the sphere of morality, the danger is equally great. We are citizens of a Catholic province, but of a province which because of that very faith is placed in an isolated position. We are in daily contact with men of other faiths or of no faith at all, men who do not recognize the supremacy of our Biblical, Christian morality over all forms of human endeavour; we mingle with them in all our activities; we witness and are deeply troubled by the daily compromising or indeed negation of truth. Have we not thereby contracted a fatal tendency to dissociate Christian morality from our activities in the sciences, in the arts, and above all in politics and business? Let us not exaggerate, you say: it is merely a tendency, merely a question of Protestant infiltration. Very well; but these tendencies, these infiltrations exist and constitute a real danger. Persecutions and false bigotry are not the only instruments of death for a nation's faith. Death can as often result from indifference, negligence, imprudence, or cowardice; it occurs when the intellectual aristocracy, whose duty it is to instruct and educate, lets fall the standard of truth and betrays its sacred mission.

Professors, remember your duties as you approach your classes. Remember, as you contemplate those young faces avid for truth, Pasteur's noble thought: "What can I do today to elevate the minds and hearts of my students?" In this country, you are, by virtue of your position, the militant representatives of Catholic thought. Remember, therefore, that you do not have the right to remain neutral – nor is it sufficient merely to respect the truth. In your role, to fail to serve truth actively is to work against it. Remember that your words, after the priest's, carry the most profound influence and that to you falls the prime responsibility of maintaining those unchanging principles which uphold the structure of society. Whether in literature, in the sciences, in business, or in politics, you are called to proclaim the rights of religion and morality. Yours is the task of restoring those principles which have been banned, of rescuing those truths which have been abandoned, of waging a crusade on behalf of all those sacred causes which have been defeated.

### DUTIES OF STUDENTS

And now a word for you who are students. You have a right to seek from your masters both truth and moral guidance, as they have the duty of implanting truth in your minds and virtue in your hearts. But in return, you also have the duty of lending them your active, respectful, and intelligent co-operation.

Need I tell you that you must regard your studies as a sacred intellectual duty? My young friends, I would say to you: believe in this duty; and I would say more: believe in it energetically. It is a tenacious faith that we need in a country where many do not believe – or if they do, in too superficial, too lethargic a fashion – where spiritual training is too often considered a superfluity, where bank notes take precedence over truth. You, as young Catholics, must believe and profess loudly that man is accountable to God, to the Church and to society for the resources of his intellect and for the use he makes of them.

But what Truth must be acquired? I say to you, as I said to your professors and for the same pressing reasons: religious truth first and foremost. After you have secured that, acquire your professional training. Whether you intend to devote yourselves to the law, medicine, teaching, journalism, engineering, industry, or agriculture, whatever you do, do it to perfection. Not only appear but actually be the most knowledgeable and the best trained in your field. This is necessary because a leader's value rests largely upon his professional merit, and because it ill befits a man to urge others to do their duty if he has not fulfilled his own. You, Sirs, would have no right to claim leadership if your studies, your professional skill and the dignity of your lives were not such as to stamp you visibly as leaders of men.

SOCIAL DUTIES

I would like now to address myself to those among you who do not consider your duties to be limited to your profession, but to extend far beyond, to your society, your nation, your faith. To you, young Catholics pursuing higher studies, and to you, young French-Canadian Catholics willing to take up arms in the cause of righteousness, I say: the future has the right to expect an organized movement representing French and Catholic thought. Lift your eyes from your textbooks occasionally and meditate upon the future and upon these most important duties.

On the social level, think of the humble people, the workers bending to the yoke of their daily labours. Confused by seditious charlatans preaching social revolution, our workers fear the choice they are told they must make: their faith, starvation and slavery or revolution, prosperity and freedom. Consider what need the Church will have of apostles to help the poor solve such dilemmas! It is among you, young, socially conscious Catholics that the Church will recruit its help.

On the level of philosophy and literature, it is equally clear that both nation and faith must be able to rely upon the work of intellectuals. Our ability to protect them both will depend entirely upon our success in creating works of such superiority as to assure the dominance of a French, Catholic way of thought. As public and private wealth steadily increase, as all classes gradually rise towards a higher standard of living, so should we turn more ardently to spiritual matters. Young men, is it your wish that the arts and letters of this province be devoted to the service of truth? Is it your desire to fashion a literature befitting the spiritual nature of this nation, a literature from which our people could derive the consciousness of their duties and the courage to shape their destiny? Is it your desire to formulate a truly French-Canadian spirit, one based on the old alliance of common sense and faith? If so, I say to you: in the aesthetic as in the social sphere impose upon yourselves the logic and the law of Christ! Give us works embodying the complete expression of your French, your Catholic souls. Sing to us of your noble hopes; show us the ideal realms of the divine so that we know them as our home; let beauty triumph and let eternal truth shine forth.

REASONS FOR THESE DUTIES

I ask you to accomplish these intellectual duties because you are believers. As believers you must be more aware than others of your obligation in justice and charity to render unto God the service and homage of your minds, and to devote your studies to Him, for they are the prayers of the intellect. Such homage is due to God more particularly in our present days. The time is past, if indeed it ever existed, when it was possible to believe privately, for oneself. The issue at stake in all countries now is who shall obtain dominion over the minds of the people. The honour of governing human thought, which should be the prerogative of Catholicism can only be claimed if Catholics are constantly faithful in discharging their duties toward the truth.

I would add that this obligation is imposed most urgently upon you, Gentlemen, for you are young French-Canadian Catholics. There are historical circumstances which increase the importance and gravity of certain problems. Do we have the right, we who are French Canadians and Catholics, to forget the fellowship of interest and honour which we have contracted with the Church? At no time has it been more appropriate to cry out: we are given as examples unto angels and men.

Alone in the midst of people of alien faiths, forced constantly to compare our social values with theirs, we daily form a living testimony upon which rests the honour of our faith. It can never be a matter of indifference to the Church whether we are or are not a highly educated nation, whether we can or cannot solve our social problems, whether our standards of public morality rise or fall. If, lacking truth or devotion, we are not able to maintain peace in our society, if our public and our private lives are neither better ordered nor more righteous than those in Protestant provinces, if our inertia prevents us from rising above inferior modes of thought, then we must face the harsh fact that our nation and our Church will be held to blame.

Gentlemen, you will, I feel sure, act in such a way as to justify your nation and your faith. You will not wish to go against that old logic of words which implies that students study. You will not wish to remain the only young people to be idle in our province. Then, when you go out among the others, those virile young workers in the factories or on the land, when you summon them to their duties in the name of your ideal, and when they in turn give you their work-roughened hands as a token of their willingness, you will be able to display with pride the marks of another sort of labour on your brows.

My young friends, in the name of all the noble, sacred causes for which I have spoken today, resolve firmly that there shall be a time in our nation's history when young men, strong in their faith and love of duty, scale the heights of the intellect; a time of belief in the beauty and seriousness of life, when hearts throb with enthusiasm and high ideals; when our own nation is revived with the breath of a new hope for the future; when the Church is loved and served like a mother. For the honour of our Saviour Jesus Christ, resolve that yours shall be such an epoch.

# L'Action française

L. Groulx, "Pour *L'Action française*," a speech delivered at the Monument National, Montreal, April 10, 1918. *Dix ans d'Action française* (Montreal, Bibliothèque de L'Action française, 1926), pp. 43-73. Reprinted by permission of Mme J. Rémillard.

Ladies and Gentlemen:

I have come to speak to you about a journal and this in itself is rather strange. Here in Canada there is only one event more commonplace than the birth of a journal ... and that is ... the death of a journal. *L'Action française* was born about sixteen months ago. In the normal course of events it should already be dead; and yet it lives on – in spite of its great age. It has managed to survive the high rate of infant mortality, overcome its teething problems, and every day now it grows larger in size.

Indeed, were it not for the journal's obvious concern for elegance, we could openly congratulate it for becoming so prematurely plump.

L'Action française, however, bears a name with rather belligerent overtones, a name that seems to be sounding a charge. I shall therefore begin by simply clarifying a few points about it.

## I

L'Action française is not a belligerent journal. Perhaps it is the very opposite. To be quite honest, however, we are not such pacifists that we ignore obvious dangers. We would not care to deny, for example, the existence of the sun [Le Soleil, Quebec City newspaper] and of Orangemen. When we are attacked we feel we must defend ourselves and our defense cannot be lax. Just recently – as I am sure you are all aware – our opponents ceased sniping at this or that one of our rights and began attacking them all. Our most extreme enemies – they are also the most forthright – have told us quite openly that ours is not to be the freedom of small nationalities. We are a nuisance which must disappear. Quite recently, of course, some of them have suddenly acknowledged our courage and even our good citizenship. Are we then simply being churlish? These belated and meagre amends for so many insults have not exactly inspired us to shout our love from the roof tops.

The most serious implication in all this is that peace does not exist in our country – it has gone forever. Behind this struggle to crush the French language lies such contempt for what is right and equitable, such pride in sheer power that no part of our political constitution is secure. A courageous archbishop recently denounced Manitoba as "a province of empty forms, mere bits of paper". How many Manitobas are there in this country? Incurable optimists may well try to pacify us by claiming that these attacks are merely the "whims of Orangemen or bigots"; we regret that we must counter by showing them how universal the oppression really is. What difference does it make to know that there are magnanimous men who deplore these outrages? Their customary silence makes them into secret accomplices. Just as the arrival of a single swallow does not bring Spring, so too one or two of these rare and silent men cannot represent the fundamental thinking of four million people.

In this situation, we of L'Action française are resolutely assuming our share of the burden of defense. Of the many steps which we considered urgent the first was the maintenance of an up-to-date war bulletin. The essence of strategy is to know one's opponents, to know where the blows are coming from, and what tactics are being used. Then too, some people are not even aware of the war waging in Canada, a war against us. While so many sceptics try to avoid facing the truth – the harsh realities of battle – readers of *L'Action française* will gradually find in the documentary part of the review masterful pieces of evidence, the complete dossier of aggression against us. At the same time, we have to reply to so many disloyal attacks against our past. A certain number of historians have promised us their support and those who spread calumny against the French Canadian race will henceforth find people ready to answer their charges. Just last month, Mr. Benjamin Sulte made short work of our supposed Breton origins and of their derogatory consequences. We intend to continue in this vein. Our aim is to furnish ammunition to all those modest but courageous men in their factories or offices, in cafés or on trains, whose duty it is to avenge the slightest insult to their race. We shall furnish arms to all those who believe that truth and justice have a right to defend themselves in this world and to those who consider that the best and most appropriate form of charity is often to provide truth for the ignorant.

Why not admit that we have set our sights even higher? Would it not be a magnificent result if the various campaigns of *L'Action française* succeeded in rousing our nation's awareness, stimulating its pride, and instilling into even the smallest of our groups such a strong desire to survive that no one could ignore it, either in Winnipeg or in Toronto? It is easy to delude oneself about one's real power, especially if one speaks English. Why not destroy once and for all the hope of all those who desire unity through assimilation, of all those fanatics rallying to the motto "one flag, one language, one nation"? Since we intend to remain ourselves and since we wish people to know this, why don't we, in all of French Canada, speak with one voice, without rancour or violence, but with the old determination of our ancestors: "No, your efforts are quite useless. We have not changed since 1760. We shall keep to all our vows. Our loyalty shall remain unshaken. Considering who you are and what we are, we refuse as proudly and firmly as we did a hundred and fifty years ago the honour of Anglo-Saxon assimilation: we are content with the glory of being French."

II

Let us, however, take care. There are dangers more threatening than the external ones. Nations do not die simply because others have decreed their death. Are we not witnessing at this very moment a time of revenge for nations which have long been subjugated? The more far-sighted among our would-be assimilators are not deceived about the extent of their power.

Goldwin Smith once confided with keen disappointment: "Canada by itself is not powerful enough to bring about the assimilation of the French element or even to prevent the permanent consolidation and growth of a French nation" (*The Canadian Question*).

Ladies and gentlemen, the true dangers are those we carry within ourselves, those which our organism no longer sloughs off. Decrees from outside cannot kill a race, but it can die as a result of a whole series of small acts of neglect or cowardice.

That is why we of *L'Action française* try to defend our language at every level. We wish to establish it wherever it has the right to exist in this country: in the speech from the Throne read by His Majesty's representative and in the official acts of Parliament, as well as on postage stamps, railway tickets, and street car transfers. If these concerns be labelled 'childish' or 'trifling' then we at *L'Action française* claim the honour of fighting for such worthy child's play and such glorious trifles. But who could seriously challenge the importance of this struggle? We sometimes complain of being misunderstood by foreigners; we deplore the fact that so many of our relatives from France have to rediscover us each year; we are distressed that so few people believe in our survival and that in certain places we are already considered a race threatened with extinction. What are we complaining about? How could strangers travelling in our province or in our cities not believe in our abdication and our disappearance when so many French Canadians hide their French origins behind English signs, when railroad companies spread the network of their English geography over the French countryside? What tourist, for example, could have guessed the existence of a French city at the mouth of the St. Maurice River when, not so long ago, all he could see at the station was the English name 'Three Rivers'? Can we really pretend to be a vigorous French race when we accept notices and advertisements from transport and other companies in English only with the sole exception of *Défense de fumer* and *Défense de cracher*, when we tolerate English as the sole language of business with clients, when we invariably ask for a telephone number in English or accept from our public utility companies letters written in English only, when we consult only English menus in our restaurants and cafés? Do you think many other nations, proud of their origins and determined to live, would tolerate such a situation for any length of time?

But these are such childish and trifling matters!

Can we forget that these encroachments come from a people who are unconcerned with abstract or written rights, but who attach sovereign importance to precedent and custom? Can we forget that we are a minority, that poor and weak people cannot afford to sacrifice the slightest portion of their patrimony, – the treason of a single person becoming a crime in these circumstances? "The defection of a single one of our people," said Edmond de Nevers, "every manifestation which does not reflect the old French spirit of pride, intransigence and magnificence encourages that chimerical hope so fondly cherished by English Canadians: our assimilation" (L'Avenir du peuple canadien-français, p. 366).

Childish and trivial matters! Meanwhile, the language of our people is changing rapidly; foreign sights and sounds abound. In commerce, industry, technology, the various trades, and in administration, English alone is spoken. The French Canadian has time only to learn another's tongue! At the same time our people are becoming so negligent, so apathetic towards this secret but continual invasion that soon they will be incapable of reacting at all. One of these days we shall find ourselves speaking the horrible jargon of Torontonians: from that day Quebec and Toronto will speak the same language and will understand each other!

Ladies and Gentlemen, those people who are struggling to salvage at least a few French sounds are saviours who deserve all our praise. "When a nation is slumbering or enslaved its tongue is coated with foreign words," writes Edgard Quinet, "but these words do not really implant themselves within the very tissue of the national language. They merely adhere to its surface. These impurities are like a disease: as long as they persist the language is incapable of expressing the true character of a nation."

Trivial matters! The men of the Orange Sentinel take a slightly different view of the matter: just recently they instigated an immense survey throughout the country and what do you suppose it was about? About bilingual notices in post offices outside the Province of Quebec! One should sometimes learn from one's enemies: the minute details of a campaign should be as important to the noble defenders of the French language as they are to its detractors. Why should we humiliate ourselves to the point of consciously conceding victory to Dr. Edwards and the venerable Mr. Hocken?

Trivialities! However, having ignored such trivial matters, can we not now see the symptoms of an advanced disease attacking the very fabric of our French nature? The assimilation of one race by another is accomplished through marriages or through deliberate, voluntary abdication of a language. Who would deny a tendency towards this abdication in our own nation? What patriotic indifference causes so many of our French Canadian families to teach their children English from the very beginning and to send them to English schools? All this is necessary, so they would have us believe, to ensure the child's future success in life. But how can they be so sure of this result? Unless something quite unpredictable happens, these children who are deprived of their national characteristics, and hence of their natural qualities, must surely be inferior to others of either race! Such denationalized children run a great risk of seeing their Anglo-Saxon rivals preferred, other circumstances being equal, in the very circles they have tried so hard to enter. Has not experience shown us, and by dazzling examples, that our compatriots who have risen to dominant positions in this country have done so only because they initially possessed the highest qualities of French culture? Is it really worth it, then, to opt for some problematical, material advantage by sacrificing the very thing which men of valiant heart prize above all things?

Moreover, how dangerous it is to take these risks with the education of children when serious ailments threaten our ethnic character!

I cannot remember which one of our writers – it may have been Edmond de Nevers – said: "the young French Canadian is perhaps the only child in America who has what could be called an ideal, and whose dream is not merely to become an Astor or a Vanderbilt!"

Alas! All that is changing; the dubious value of this American ideal may yet satisfy us. Who then shall denounce the agent which is distorting our Christian and French soul, attacking our youth, invading even our rural areas to corrupt us to the core? I refer to the cinema, the 'movies'! Never before in our entire history have our people so stuffed themselves with such foreign and worthless fare! The film has become the foremost, indeed the only book, the only novel, pamphlet or play. In the majority of our families people live by it and dream of it. What a distressing thought! Our youngsters – our nation's potential – while ignorant of the heroes and epic deeds of their own history are infatuated with notorious bandits and second-rate ham actors, with the gun-fights or court scenes of this vulgar, ridiculous art, with all the despicable heroes of American magazines and foreign melodramas. Is this not an extremely serious situation? We must lack the very rudiments of psychology to imagine that we can feed on these spectacles with impunity. Let us not delude ourselves: a disastrous standard of morality makes its way into our minds along with the shady stories of this coarse art; our system of values is toppled; our artistic instincts depraved; the very foundations of our old family traditions gradually undermined. We begin to feel and think like Americans and will soon be living and talking like them. Let us not assume that we can retain our language and our hereditary character if we accept ideas and customs totally opposed to both. Language is the expression of the soul. It requires a certain native distinction – at the very least a French soul – to speak French.

Ladies and Gentlemen, is it not high time that we recognized the danger and reformed the cinema? Should it remain as it is now, a ravaging blight, the worst kind of denationalizing agent, we will have to undertake a campaign against it like the one waged against alcohol.

In the meantime, we members of the League for the Rights of the French language constantly alert our compatriots to the danger of neglecting these 'childish' and 'trivial' matters. *L'Action française* is willing to act as a sentinel in the matter, nor would it ever seek to be relieved. Through Pierre Homier's column "Incidents From Daily Life", it keeps a watchful eye over all the various aspects and events of the great battle. It keeps a roll of honour to pay tribute to all the heroes, great or small, who impose respect for their language wherever they are; it castigates the apathetic or negligent and the sycophants of the superior race. In this way the ardour of battle is maintained and diffused; our compatriots learn the value of tenacity and the effectiveness of many small efforts put together.

You will perhaps object that this means a great deal of hardship and costly sacrifices. What matter if these hardships ensure salvation? Our duty is to accept them unequivocally, joyously, in the firm conviction that no one can defect without compromising the whole effort. If we are not prepared to do this, we might as well dry our crocodile tears, stop trying to conceal our cowardice and admit openly that we wish to capitulate, to betray our nation. Surely it would be less dishonourable to die freely than to succumb gradually to this slowest of dissolutions.

Conscience and honour immediately arise to warn us that capitulation would be a serious crime against justice and against our ancestors.

Capitulation would be nothing short of a cruel repudiation of our ancestors. Would we ever dare to say to all those generations of poor but proud peasants who endured so much hardship to keep us in the French family: "You were mistaken. Your heritage is not really worth defending. It is too costly to be profitable. We repudiate your labours and your struggles. We choose instead to break with your tradition, to be the generation that refuses to continue." Ladies and Gentlemen, either we are seriously confused about the meaning of honour or more urgent reasons than mere profit or vanity are required to justify a denial of one's ancestors.

We do not have the right to take this way out. We are the

representatives of former generations and our task is to weld the past to the future. The inheritance we now have was accumulated over three centuries: we do not have the right to toss it to the winds. We are not the final inheritors of this patrimony: our descendants have the right to expect it from us and our duty is to maintain it for them. "What would become of humanity if the living denied the principle of fellowship which links them with the dead? What would become of all the incentives to action, of the ambition that makes us what we are, if nothing were to remain of the work of those who have gone before, if the seedling planted and nurtured with such care should be cut at the outset of its growth, if the field so painfully sowed should never be harvested?" (*L'Avenir du peuple canadien-français*, E. de Nevers, pp. XL-XLI).

III

Although defense and combat are necessary, because there are both dangers and aggressions, *L'Action française* nevertheless does not intend to devote the best of its energies to these concerns. The type of battle which involves merely a few brilliant charges is not in our line. What we desire above all is to do constructive work, to consolidate all our efforts into concerted French action. A patriotism of organisation and directives rather than a patriotism of militants. To survive one must first live.

The most pressing need could well be the co-ordination of our efforts under a vigorous leadership. We lack neither resources nor energy, but we use them badly or not at all. Hands cannot get along without the brain; the brain cannot get along without the hands. All organs must co-operate with the life of the whole being. From the humblest labourer to the thinker of genius everyone must work side by side harmonizing his labours to the same directive. The efforts of the nation will then be like the victorious strategy described by Fustel de Coulanges: "Only through order, unity of direction, constant collective effort and the organization of the masses does strategy produce its greatest effects and win its battles."

We must therefore redress those errors which have been perpetuated for too many years. We owe it to ourselves to consider the economic organization of our province as an urgent priority in our programme of French action. Too long have we been oblivious of the fact that, even if a nation does not live by bread alone, it still needs a few slices to survive. The question is not whether we shall or shall not buy in Toronto, or on the west or east side of Montreal. The problem is of an entirely different order of magnitude. The important question is whether we can keep and exploit for ourselves our own gold, our savings, the resources of our land, and all our wealth, before they are exploited by foreign capital. And let us make one thing clear from the very beginning: to talk in this way is not to declare war upon anybody. Why should methods and principles advocated and adopted by all other nations become a provocation when adopted and advocated by us? Who can call it a crime that we shift for ourselves? Can we believe that to have good relations with others we must create our own yoke, our own economic slavery? Our wealth is our own. It must be right to keep it for ourselves.

What is involved here is more than simply obtaining justice for ourselves: national charity is at stake. So many elevated undertakings – charitable, intellectual, social and religious works – depend on the power of money; to stop the flow of their resources would be a sin. As sons of the French family, we reap benefits and profits: we do not have the right to refuse to give in return. We must surround our race with all possible signs of strength and legitimate pride. It is not beneficial for a young country like ours to feel its poverty too much. If the power of money is manifested too strongly on the other side, those of us who are weak and vainglorious, will adore foreign gods while the ordinary people will feel even more the crushing sense of our inferiority as a conquered nation.

*L'Action française* has tried to make our compatriots aware of our prime capital, human capital. A masterly lecture by Father Louis Lalande brought attention to the serious problem of our birth rate. The 'revenge of the cradle' should naturally lead to thinking about 'the protection of the cradle'. We have been eloquently told what this entails. Now we are beginning an inquest into our principal financial institutions, comparing them with similar English institutions in the province. French Canadians will gradually learn how rapidly their vital forces are ebbing away through their own indifference. Mr. Edouard Montpetit, who has agreed to participate in our enquiry into 'our national strengths', will soon tell us the extent of our wealth and how it should best be used. Mr. Henri Bourassa will discuss, within the framework of the same enquiry, the problem of colonization, always a current one. Finally, Ladies and Gentlemen, other initiatives will be undertaken at the appropriate time. We have resolved that this question of our economic reorganization shall remain on the agenda until it has received a satisfactory solution. Obstinacy must once again become a French virtue.

This economic effort is subordinated in our eyes to another campaign of incontestable urgency: I mean a truly national patriotic effort. However strange such a question may appear, we are forced to ask it at the present time: are we really preoccupied with patriotism? Whatever our profession or trade, how much time do we devote to patriotic duties? Whenever we make some grave decision, undertake some business deal or give our vote, how often do we ask ourselves: "Am I doing something for my people, for my nationality, for my language?" Is our national awareness sufficiently aroused, sufficiently widespread, so that the French cause in America can summon not only the devotion of a few élites but also the collaboration of all our people, indeed the collective soul of our nation? There is not a moment to be wasted, not a source of strength to be neglected; are we sufficiently aware that "every one of the descendants of the sixty-five thousand people conquered in 1760 must stand up and be counted?"

At *L'Action française* we are convinced that our indifference arises from ignorance of our history. We lack patriotic conviction because we do not really know our own country. We are ignorant of the pride and sense of brotherhood from which patriotism arises. To cure this ignorance we have undertaken the task of exhuming our history. *L'Action française* must surely be given credit for having done its share over the past two years in reminding the masses of our great anniversaries. Our journal celebrated the 257th anniversary of the founding of Montreal, the 50th anniversary of Confederation, and the anniversary of the Papal Zouaves. The public has been invited on more splendid occasions to commemorate, for example, the stand LaFontaine took for French in 1842, or to hear Father Louis Lalande S.J. recalling the reasons for our national pride. Then there is our *French Language Almanac*, a small handbook of popular and practical patriotism which we distributed throughout the country. First published in 1916 with 10,000 copies, it has now reached a printing of 25,000. Last month we inaugurated a publishing firm, the *Bibliothèque de L'Action française*; over 10,000 copies of *Our Pride* will be diffused through the French groups of North America. Next May, as a first step until circumstances allow more elaborate demonstrations, the Directors of *L'Action française* and the members of the League for the Rights of the French Language will retrace Dollard's route to Long-Sault. This will be the first of what we hope will become a series of annual pilgrimages for our people and our children. Because so many threats close in on us, because even the most courageous cannot help shuddering at our weakness and isolation, we shall set out to seek inspiration at Carillon. Together we shall relive the story of that brave handful of Frenchmen who, praying as they fought, penetrated deep into barbarian territory. And there the memory of those immortal victims, those men from our own nation who took an oath never to give ground or plead for mercy, will teach us of what stuff our nation is made and how our cause must be served.

IV

Ladies and Gentlemen, you may think I have outlined a great number of projects: yet *L'Action française* hopes to take part in all these movements and attain a few of its goals, its intention being to provide the country with an intellectual stimulus. I would say, if it did not sound so pompous, that our work is one of intellectual charity. Resolute action requires both knowledge and truth. "A civilization," Victor Bucaille has stated, "is a mixture of the intellectual activity and the economic development of a nation." The spiritual power and diffusion of a culture depend to a certain extent on the material development and financial energy of a country. On the other hand the material development can only attain its full growth with the support and guidance of the intellect. If, as so many people now say, our nation has been stagnating since 1867, it is because we lack a great intellectual élite. We have had far too few men of wide ranging, generalizing minds, men of leadership capable of calling upon the assembled energy of the people and of detecting and drawing out the forms of the future from a great mass of unformed dreams. In any work of construction there are the labourers, those who transport materials and do their bit without having to think of the whole. There is also the mastermind, the architect who watches the walls rising and, without waste of labour, unifies all the work to create the harmonious beauty of the whole. For the past fifty years, we French Canadians have not seen walls rising or being strengthened to protect our homeland. Our people bent over their tools and became absorbed in their little corner of the country; all too rarely did a great, guiding intelligence arise to give the knowledge and leadership needed to unify and co-ordinate the efforts of the masses. Too often the work was intermittent, isolated, unrelated to an overall plan, one group very often demolishing what others were building.

Our task is too great to allow us to continue in this haphazard way. We must awaken our people from the somnolence of their routine lives, cure them of their obsession with politics, the most barren and demoralizing of passions, and make them return to those proud and purifying labours which contribute to the national patrimony. To keep our own possessions, our own means of action, we must organize our economic activities and stimulate our pride, for through our ignorance of the past it has become so debilitated as to be almost non-existent. We must unite all the French groups of America and forge a coalition, a solid fraternity in the face of the ever-increasing peril.

There are serious social problems which we must resolve. The situation we shall have to confront as soon as the war is ended will be as formidable as it is difficult to anticipate. But one thing is quite clear: for this vast project of reorganization and regeneration a few superficial or divided spirits are not enough; we need unified planning; we need an élite that sees far and wide; we need to create the highest form of guidance and direction.

By means of its enquiry into 'our national strengths' which it began last January, *L'Action française* intends to prepare the way. It attempts to expose the various aspects of our problems. It thus hopes to reveal some general ideas and contribute to further knowledge.

To make its undertaking of intellectual charity as successful as possible, *L'Action française* also plans campaigns on literary or artistic levels, for such campaigns are urgently needed.

Brunetière said: "to propose one must oppose". Ladies and Gentlemen, a nation can only be itself by being distinct and different. It exists and has value only in so far as its national entity cannot be confused with any other and in so far as it asserts itself with full originality. But what is the best means of sharply delineating the particular genius of a race? Expressing it in works of the mind. A nation is captured and revealed to a greater extent in its forms of art than in the creations of its commerce or industry. Spiritual works: these are a nation's highest activities and they are most expressive of its soul and life. They are the golden seal to stamp the most accurate of national images.

These artistic creations are at the same time promises of survival. Intellectual achievements partake of the immortality of thought. As soon as a nation has produced artists and thinkers of genius, it can be said to have found a way of enduring. Through them a particular part of humanity – the very character of a nation – is poured into statues of bronze against which neither death nor foes shall prevail. Once it is created, the work of art no longer belongs to a nation; it is incorporated into the patrimony of mankind and mankind, in keeping it, will perpetuate the civilization from which it originated. At the same time these creative works nurture an entire nation and thereby establish forever certain traditions of beauty and certain intellectual habits which also help maintain continuity between the generations.

It is thus a supremely important task our artists and writers have of retaining a distinct French life and soul and of daily increasing its power. How we must strengthen our young race, that solitary isle buffeted by the waves of the encircling Protestant and [Anglo-] Saxon sea!

Above all, you writers or artists of French Canada, do not claim that it is chimerical to attain a distinct national genius when our race is still so small, so embryonic, almost amorphous. Doesn't the infinite variety with which God has endowed individual minds and races give them each some basis of originality? In the vast poem of the world no one stanza is exactly like another. The rhythm is everywhere different. No two spots on the globe are perfect duplicates. No two men look exactly alike. Each one carries his own spark of life and reflects one particular aspect of the Infinite Being. Three hundred years of isolation have given our people a distinct soul and character. Do we resemble anyone else on this continent? We differ from them in every way, in our faith, our language, our customs, and our history. If it should be objected that this difference merely shows our poverty and insignificance I would reply: look at our past. It will perhaps demonstrate what substance we are made of. "When I consider the history of our people," wrote Edmond de Nevers, "it seems to me that I hear the murmur of a mysterious germination deep in our French Canadian souls and I tell myself that there lies a latent world of poetry, art, intellectual achievement, moral nobility, straining towards the sun and only waiting to spring forth into life" (*L'Avenir du peuple canadien-français*, p. 63).

Lift your eyes now and look at our country, our homeland. You will see the characteristics bestowed upon it by the Creator, its features great and beautiful if somewhat austere. You will see its own unique history: the traces left upon it by the race which has inhabited it. In little plots of land, painfully cleared, as well as on the historic slopes of Long-Sault, on the Plains of Abraham, as well as in the dark interiors of the old homes near the cradles of our revenge, wherever our ancestors toiled with blood and sweat, you will find the homeland has acquired a kind of mystic aura! It will appear to you as a sacrament of heroism.

Would that our intellectual youth be kindled with enthusiasm as they contemplate their country in this way and so prepare a flowering of great achievements! "We shall be a nation only if we are a great nation." Our fathers penetrated with sword and book into the depths of savage wilderness; their axes made luminous clearings through the forests. Now we young French Canadians of the twentieth century must contribute our minds, our spirits, and our noble labours to let the triumphal light burst forth.

The hour has come for a decisive effort. We have attained the age of majority; we have sufficient numbers of workers; the tools have been made ready. Now is the time to use this power to establish our French individuality and conquer survival or otherwise, through criminal indifference, let the opportunity slip forever.

Do we not need the glory of such achievements to strengthen our pride? There are so many snobs among us who look down on their compatriots for the insignificance of their literary and artistic achievement. There are so many among us who turn through vanity and ambition towards the stronger side, towards an opulence which they mistake for elegance. Even if it were only to protect these weaklings, Ladies and Gentlemen, let us make it *chic* to be French Canadian.

It may be objected that we can surely serve the national cause without trapping ourselves in a narrow, nationalistic creed of art. I know that specious argument. I am also aware that it is quite possible to glorify our French character by displaying its versatility, by showing what flexible, diverse forms it can take; I know too that it is good to borrow from any rational aesthetic. Nevertheless, it remains true that certain dilettante forms are luxuries which are very costly for us – we are very poor to be playing the aristocrats! Here are even more disturbing considerations: if art is not the expression of the national soul, it will not be popular nor will it be able to establish and perpetuate our French individuality or renew our pride. If exotic forms should become so widespread as to be universal, if the most bizarre aesthetics should have their adherents, the inevitable result would be the undermining of our French originality; our minds would become deformed and our spiritual forces would turn against our own country. In art, as in all else, we can only be enriched with that which is in profound harmony with the requirements of our own nature.

Let our intellectuals ponder these truths. Their patriotic conscience will do the rest. Instead of the very questionable ambition of being mere 'accidents' in the art or literature of their country they will associate themselves entirely with the sentiments expressed in this valiant song from Mistral's *Mireille*: "I sing of a young girl from Provence ... through the Crau, through the corn, to the sea, I, a humble scholar of Homer shall follow her. She is not known outside this region. Though her forehead shines only with youth; though she wears neither a golden diadem nor a damask coat; yet I would elevate her like a queen and praise her in our despised tongue for we sing only for you, shepherds and inhabitants of the *mas*."

Ladies and gentlemen, these are some of our campaigns. To help them succeed we have founded our journal. You will not be unaware of the effectiveness of this means of publicity so appropriate for our busy, hectic generation. "The essay form," wrote Mr. Victor Giraud in his *Maîtres de l'heure*, "is the most appropriate one today for writers eager for action." The writings which have given rise to action in the past quarter of a century are not books, but articles, "extracts" as they were so aptly called in the past: Brunetière's article "After a Visit to the Vatican", for example, and eight years earlier the article Mr. E.-M. de Vogue published under the title "Affairs of Rome" (volume 1, pp. 217-18).

Has *L'Action française* let itself be carried away by too much ambition? It aspires to be a laboratory of ideas which men of action could find both instructive and stimulating. In inviting our most intelligent writers to contribute to it, it hopes to provide gradually some much needed directives.

It keeps a close and watchful eye over its format which must be French and consequently impeccable. We feel that this is necessary if we wish to argue our case in other lands, for we are convinced that in the past our intellectual exports have been far too slipshod. Are the journals or reviews we send overseas perfect enough, from a literary point of view, not to discredit unduly our young culture? You know that last year Marshall Joffre took away with him three years of *L'Almanach du peuple* bound in green leather. Would it be rash to set our sights still higher? How often have we been asked by French or Swiss friends interested in things Canadian: "Can you suggest a review or a newspaper I could obtain to keep me in touch with what is happening in your country?"

As early as 1908 there was a demand for the kind of journal which we are now attempting to provide. It has already been sent to France and Rome to counter the odious calumnies which have so greatly harmed our cause there. Thanks to subscriptions from generous and patriotic people – and these subscriptions are still open – we have been able to offer the journal free to some French bishops, members of the Academy, the Union of French Journalists and a few intelligent people who are friends of French Canada.

And that is our work, Ladies and Gentlemen. That is what our journal has become in just two years. Last year, *L'Action française* had thirty-two pages. This year without raising its price by a single penny it offers its readers fifty pages of very substantial reading. Only the encouragement of the public is needed to develop this project, to have it keep pace with the growth of our national ambitions. Until now our sole capital has been the charity of our subscribers and the devotion of our collaborators. If this undertaking has survived, it is because independent writers have considered the honour of serving a great cause sufficient remuneration for their labours. *L'Action française* now turns to you, Ladies and Gentlemen. If you believe that fostering a sincere and courageous effort, at this point in time, is worth the sacrifice of a dollar a year, *L'Action française* strongly and confidently solicits your subscriptions and your support.

We are among those who have unshakable faith in the survival of the French nation in this country and in the great nobility of the devotion which will perpetuate our race. We may have met with violent opposition; but nowhere have we been entirely defeated. Neither in Manitoba nor in Ontario has the teaching of French declined in recent years. Perhaps it has been reinforced. What strengthens our hope is that at no previous time in our history have we so concentrated all our energy and all our efforts. In 1760 we thought only of surviving. In 1840 we thought only of political action. In 1867 we thought only of the daily routine. This time we are making an effort to think of everything. We are prepared to use any weapon, political, social, economic, in our peaceful but decisive struggle.

Let us be fearless. The time of violence passes like all others. We merely need to organize and defend ourselves. Our nation is the repository of the highest culture and the highest truth – the only truth. Let us simply keep our flame alive. Some things are too necessary to be allowed to die; some too sacred for profane hands. One evening in March I noticed a flight of crows winging over the snowy landscape towards the setting sun. The black birds seemed to be holding the luminous disc at bay. Soon from the dark forest other croaking hordes rose to join in what seemed a terrible and pitiless harrying of the weak declining light. I closed my eyes for a moment, pondering the painful, brutal truth of this symbol. When I opened them again the light was still shining, still inaccessible in the depths of space and the sinister flock had vanished into the shadowy twilight.

Some things are too necessary to be allowed to die; too sacred to be destroyed by profane aggression.

# L'Action nationale

L. Groulx, "L'Action nationale," a radio broadcast, CKAC, Montreal, December 31, 1932. *Le Devoir*, January 3, 1933. Reprinted by permission of Mme J. Rémillard.

Ladies and Gentlemen:

I would like to begin by thanking the Saint-Jean Baptiste Society which has kindly allowed me to present *L'Action nationale* to the public.

*L'Action nationale* is the title of a monthly journal of 72 pages whose first number is to appear January 15th. Its managing editor and editor-in-chief will be the well-known journalist and man of letters Mr. Harry Bernard, editor of the *Courrier de Saint-Hyacinthe*. He will be assisted by an editorial committee consisting of Pierre Homier, abbé Groulx, Eugène L'Heureux, Anatole Vanier, abbé Olivier Maurault, abbé Albert Tessier, Arthur Laurendeau, Esdras Minville, René Chaloult, Hermas Bastien, Wilfrid Guérin, Léopold Richer.

The title and editorial committee of the new journal will, we believe, tell you something of its character and programme. If it appears to give priority to matters of "nationality," it will not neglect other, perhaps more profound implications of the concept. Catholics above all, the editors of the journal and its contributors do not intend to evade even the slightest dictate of their faith. They intend to work for their nation as Catholics; they are aware that any effort lacking in spiritual motivation would divorce the highest interests of the nation from an indispensable source of support. From this it should be quite clear that *L'Action nationale* intends to be guided in its policies by the superior principles of the faith and to devote its highest energies to the religious interests of our country.

Let me be equally frank in explaining what we mean by a so-called "national effort." In Canada, a political federation, the word "nation" clearly has two meanings: the Canadian state, and the French Canadian nationality. *L'Action nationale* fully intends to respect these two usages, subordinating one to the other according to political and judicial considerations. In the sense that one of the essential characteristics of a nation is the will of its people to live together as a nation, then there is indeed a Canadian nation, an association of provinces, nationalities and individuals, related and united by means of the Federal State and of their common territory or homeland. But there is also a French Canadian nation based, like the first, on the desire of its people to live together as a nation, but a desire in this case supplemented by natural and positive right, by a long and distinct history, and by ethnic and cultural similarities.

And here we could extend the word "national" to give it a third legitimate meaning. It would then refer to all the various groups of French origin in America, united by bonds of blood, culture, language and faith.

This, then, is the very wide perspective within which *L'Action nationale* proposes to work. You may be sure that it will devote generous space to the problems and interests of Canada as a whole. But since it is above all a French-Canadian journal, it is determined to give priority to the problems and interests of the French people of America and more particularly to the French Canadian nationality.

Need I say that we consider this to be nothing more than our right? There could hardly be any nationalism more legitimate, more legally justifiable than ours. A historical and social milieu imposes duties all the more immediate and pressing in that mankind finds his very being, develops his very personality therein. As one of the contracting parties to the agreement of 1867, the pact which made of the Canadian federation a bi-national and bilingual State, the French Canadian nationality fully accepts its duties, as well as any legitimate subordination to the Federal Government; it acknowledges that it must help the latter carry out its civilizing task; but in return it claims the right to retain its autonomy, and believes that the Federal State must give it positive assistance in maintaining and developing its culture.

As it is only natural to expect from a journal such as ours, we intend to treat these national matters or problems in detail, basing our discussions on principles of order. All the various elements in the life of a nation should support one another. A doctrine and a programme of action intending to provide guidance and inspiration must respect that principle and always support it integrally. You will no doubt have noticed, as well, the prominent place given to the younger generation on the editorial board. Recent events have shown that young people, until now considered to be quite dead, intend to bridge the generation gap. The editor of *L'Action nationale* belongs to these young people. Every interest of French America will be sturdily championed by this journal; but the mark of its youthful contributors will be evident in its greater concern with social, economic, and scientific questions and perhaps also in its prouder, more conscious sense of national dignity.

\* \* \*

These are our plans. Do they seem too ambitious? We are quick to admit it. Since it is without capital, *L'Action nationale* must rely on the contributions of its subscribers to set itself up and subsist materially. Editors, contributors, administrators, all will be and indeed are already obliged to supply their time and work free of charge. The editors have personally underwritten the cost of setting up the journal and advertising it. We are not unaware that times are hard. And everyone knows how completely and utterly indifferent a large segment of the population is to projects of this kind. We are neither a political club nor a political journal; and it is a well-known fact that journals of intellectual and national substance are not valued as highly as tickets to a hockey game. A great many members of the public – very often the most well-to-do – will therefore be unlikely to loosen their pursestrings for our benefit. In the end we shall have to rely upon an élite – always the same and unfortunately always small in number – an élite of people who care about the fate of our nation and who understand the honour and the benefits to be derived from a truly French life.

We hope nevertheless that everyone realizes the gravity of the present times. The serious plight of the world has prompted someone to say that we are at a turning point in history. Could that phrase not apply to our small nation as well? When we consider the situation French Canadians face in this country, their declining role at the federal level, their growing helplessness in the economic sector, the great and ever-present American domination of their material and moral lives, how easy it is to feel the bitter taste of defeat upon our lips.

At all costs we must regain the lost ground; finding the solution to these problems within the next few years will be essential to our survival. Even if our situation were not that of a tiny minority in this vast and powerful North American continent, there are nevertheless certain truths and ideals of which a nation must never lose sight, certain problems that must ever be solved, certain dangers that must ever be avoided. Today French Canadians are unhappily discovering the high cost of negligence.

Despite the adversity of the times, we intend to remain optimistic. For the restoration we are about to undertake along with many other good workers, we know that we can count on the friendly cooperation of the intellectual élite of French Canada. History has also taught us what deep and hidden reserves of energy our French-Canadian people can draw upon if only leaders can be found to inspire them and harden their resolve. Do we need to be taught what can be accomplished by an active minority through its determined spirit and tenacity?

And thus it is with confidence, after all, that the editors of *L'Action nationale* set about their task. Nearly all of them, already deeply involved in other activities, would gladly have avoided this new labour. Nor is it obvious why they rather than many others should be the ones to shoulder these responsibilities. But in this hour of crisis they are determined to place an instrument of good-will at the service of their compatriots and their country. They are convinced that they shall receive the response they so fully deserve.

Ladies and Gentlemen: if this project seems to you a worthy one, send your subscription, $2.00, to the following address: *L'Action nationale*, la Palestre Nationale, 840 Cherrier Ave., Montreal.

Thank you and a Happy New Year to what will soon become *L'Action nationale*'s large family.

# French Canadian Nationalism

L. Groulx, *Le nationalisme canadien-français*, a speech delivered and published in Ottawa, 1949. Reprinted by permission of Mme J. Rémillard.

I was asked to give you a definition of French Canadian Nationalism. Since this is a subject I have been discussing all my life, my first reaction was: where to begin?

Let me nevertheless offer a few old ideas, bearing in mind that ideas only become clichés through being so very old and so very true.

Speak to us, I was asked, about healthy French Canadian Nationalism – the emphasis being on "healthy." It made me wonder: is there any other kind? And have you by any chance been called upon recently to snuff out volcanic eruptions of national fervour? Nationalism in itself is not an artificial reaction. It is the natural, vital and hence legitimate reaction of any nation or people wishing to live according to its own inner spiritual laws, to the prime dictates of its own nature; it is the specific reaction of peoples or ethnic groups which are subjugated or in a minority and not, therefore, entirely masters of their own lives. Hence it is a reaction which can become aggressive when threatened with oppression. A simple desire to continue to exist, to remain what we are, what providence and history have made us, – not to remain inert or static of course, but to grow naturally, with the unhindered development needed by any living organism – such a formula could well describe French Canadian Nationalism.

I

The essence of our being can be expressed in two words, French and Catholic. French and Catholic we have been, not merely since our arrival in America, but for the past thousand years since and even before Tolbiac and the birth of the Frankish nation. Our rights go back far enough to inspire respect, and surely we are of quite respectable lineage as well. We are the direct descendants of the French people who left France around 1660-1680 when she was the leading nation in the world. Moreover, our faith teaches us that as Catholics we are, through our spiritual birth, of a stock that is more princely than any on earth. We are of a divine race, we are the sons of God.

How did we come to merit such noble birth? Consider the cumulative privileges of our religious origins. We were the sons and subjects of a European state which had retained Catholicism as its official religion and had maintained a harmonious relationship with the Church. In America, we were the sons of New France, a colony whose religious homogeneity was even greater than that of the mother country, and whose political authorities collaborated even more closely with the Church, leaving her almost complete freedom to fashion our little nation according to her divine laws. And what for us could be the logical, one could almost say the inescapable, result of this accumulation of privileges? – social, judicial, cultural structures essentially superior in quality. Any historian or sociologist will vouch for this if he is willing to scrutinize our type of family, our type of education and hospitalization, our parochial institutions, our civic laws, even our system of land-holding, that seigneurial regime so different from that of the old country, more heedful than the latter of human dignity, admirably structured to better the condition of the peasant.

From a purely objective viewpoint, such appears our first cultural treasure, the initial foundation stone of our nationalism.

Here is the second. From our French birth we inherited the cultural traditions of a nation which, at the time of its colonial expansion, had attained the highest pinnacle of its culture, a culture which has ever since been recognized as one of the classic cultures of the entire world. We still retain the tradition and the discipline of an order that is founded on reason; a somewhat severe order no doubt but one which continues to protect us against the rash or fatal adventures of the modern spirit and more particularly against the excessive temptation of foreign cultures. From our French birth we still retain – or at least we long retained – the sense of dignity and pride that the French nation possessed during its 'great century'; a pride which serves largely to explain the spirit of independence our small colonial nation had, even before 1760, and has maintained continuously ever since, despite some frivolous wavering in its policies.

Here then, in its entirety, you have the ideological and emotional substance of French Canadian Nationalism. Of all the colonial nations that are branches of modern Europe, there may be some which are richer materially; but how many could boast of greater spiritual wealth?

## II

What has become of this wealth, these privileges of birth? What have we done with them? Did our small nation seize upon them with that jealous passion, that tenacious faithfulness which any nation will instinctively attach to what it considers the basic, essential part of its own soul? Was there any law prohibiting our nationalism? In our history, 1760 intervened. For any people, and above all for a tiny people, the experience of conquest must be considered one of the worst catastrophes, whatever the attitude of the conqueror to the conquered. All unbiased historians are in agreement on this point. Even if, as is sometimes maintained, the conquest saved us from a greater disaster, the fact of replacing one disaster by another remains catastrophic. An ethnic group cannot be cut off in a single blow from its natural roots without suffering some serious consequences. Not with impunity can a country's political, moral, social, and cultural climate be suddenly changed.

Would you care to gauge the vigour, almost the violence of our ancestors' determination to remain French and Catholic in spite of 1760? Consider in the first place the Quebec Act wrenched from the conquerors a mere ten years after the Treaty of Surrender. The Quebec Act, which has been rightly called one of the most astonishing constitutional texts in the history of the British Empire, was certainly a willing or unwilling tribute paid by the masters of the Empire to the daring moral vigour of a minuscule nation – for after all we are talking of a hundred thousand people at the most, or something like twenty thousand families! "The birth certificate of French Canadian Nationalism," one English Canadian historian has described the Act, somewhat inaccurately, since in order to make such a mark upon history nationalism must surely have been born some time before! Consider in the second place the year 1791, when the Province was divided into two parts, Upper and Lower Canada. This further stage of constitutional evolution still maintained the small French state of 1774, another willing or unwilling acknowledgement of the vigour of its nationalism. Remember too the long political struggle the small state underwent after 1791 to obtain self-government; here the French found themselves setting precedents for the British. Remember the uprising of 1837-38, a movement which, in spite of a few exaggerated ideas and actions, was profoundly motivated by the same touching desire for emancipation and even for independence. Then after the strong measures taken in 1841, remember the abrupt, astonishing political reversal of 1842, made possible and indeed inevitable by the same burst of French energy. Then, the later definitive reversal in 1848, a result of the same causes. Finally, remember 1867 when the province of Quebec reappeared in the new Confederation, when the small state of 1774 and 1791, which had been thought destroyed in 1841, rose once more, this time with full political and cultural autonomy, and now, if it so wished, master of its own fate for ever.

The achievements I have described were primarily political

ones. There were others, as you know, tending along similar lines towards the same goals: the protection of our French laws, and the protection of our religious freedom. The latter implied, in spite of the ambition of the new rulers, independence for our religious leaders and our parochial system. Nowhere, however, was a more astonishing vitality manifested than in the cultural domain, that domain closest to the heart of the nation. I am thinking in particular of the almost incredible step taken by a group of our people in 1770, ten years after the conquest, when they daringly offered to set up a Royal George College in Quebec to be, despite its English name, a great centre of French culture for North America, and for the entire British Empire. This handful of isolated Frenchmen were thus the first to work for the establishment of higher education in Canada. In 1790, barely twenty years later, they returned to the project. In that year, Simon Sanguinet of Montreal bequeathed 15,000 *louis* towards a project for university education. Still in 1790, the Seminary of Saint-Sulpice offered to pay the costs of a similar undertaking, and in particular to devote to it the revenue from two of its seigneurial domains. Consider also the long parliamentary struggle against the Royal Institute, for freedom of education, a struggle which started in 1814 and continued without respite for 15 years. Our historians have often written in praise of the popular movements which arose in 1822 and 1828: in 1822 against the first project of union for the two Canadas, and in 1828 to protect the rights of the House against the whims of Lord Dalhousie: movements which took the form of vast petitions supported by 40,000 and 87,000 signatures. What is perhaps not so well known, however, is that the first of these national petitions to the Government in London was organized by French Canadians as early as 1821 to obtain freedom of education. The only thing which halted this attempt when it was already well under way was the intervention of Monseigneur Plessis for reasons which are not now under debate. And after all that, remember the law of 1829 establishing elementary schooling. The French Province of Lower Canada, so strongly criticized both here and in England for the ignorance of its inhabitants, nevertheless managed to have such a law passed four years before France passed Guizot's law establishing primary schooling in 1833, and ten years before England itself decided to take similar measures.

At this point in history I shall stop. You know as well as I what has happened since that time. If we now take all these occurrences and replace them in their proper historical perspective – a perspective in which such continuity of effort or the very idea of the effort no longer appears very easy or indeed very natural – can we help being profoundly moved?

We come face to face here with one of those constant factors of history, one of those laws which, while themselves invisible, nevertheless reveal the secret, profound intuitions of a people, intuitions which come from the distant past: at critical times they determine the decisions which must be taken, the roads which must be followed in all honesty to fulfil a nation's destiny, to accomplish its mission; intuitions of collective possessions to be preserved, possessions of sufficiently high quality to command persistent and obstinate devotion; intuitions not perhaps entirely divorced from the mysterious aims and inspirations of God's providence.

We come face to face, moreover, with our ancestors' slow building up of that sociological reality we call the national milieu: a group of institutions, an atmosphere or moral climate eminently suited to the development of the human personality; a milieu whose preservation and flowering is based upon natural law and, for us French Canadians, thanks to the struggles and victories of our forefathers, upon positive constitutional law. French Canadian Nationalism – *honi soit qui mal y pense* – is far more than a mere whim, a nation's vainglorious ambition. It is a right! Not a right graciously given, but a right victoriously conquered.

### III

What duties are dictated to us by this right? Would there be any reason for abandoning our national background, our Catholic and French nature? Any reason to allow them to be damaged or sabotaged?

Some dreamers occasionally conjure up the vision of a shrinking world, and the evolution of the human species towards an international, cosmopolitan type of man. "We are living in a large garden which is daily growing smaller", Pierre Lecomte de Nouy has written. We may observe this phenomenon but that does not give us the right to blind ourselves to another which is manifesting itself with equal vigour. This second phenomenon is that, as the world becomes more international, there is a progressive hardening of national realities. Is there any need to explain this when everyone is witnessing the breaking up of empires, and observing the bitter determination with which small nations shake off the last remnants of the yoke and take their future into their own hands? Against the crushing weight of the new universe, all nations, large or small, seem to prefer to buttress themselves, hastily creating for themselves within their national framework a last, secure haven of liberty.

Others, contemplating what they call the decline of the Latin countries of Europe, and in particular what they are pleased to call the lamentable and apparently irremediable state of France, wonder what could be the purpose of deviating so thoughtlessly from the broad highway of the future and binding the fate of a young nation to an archaic, outmoded culture? Without going into such immense problems, we can well ask how many countries among those which underwent the two great wars can boast of not having been vitally affected? Disturbing as the state of France may seem to us – for she bore the brunt of those two wars – who would dare maintain that French culture no longer ranks first among European cultures? And in what respect could others claim to be superior? The culture and civilization of the Anglo-Saxon nations, which are in the forefront of today's world scene, are praised to the skies. In this case I would ask the question I have already asked elsewhere. Are these cultures presently at the beginning of a climb to further heights, or are they at the beginning of a decline? Numerous observers have noticed the first faint cracks in their sumptuous façade. The learned Louis de Launay has commented that England seems torn by some mysterious trouble: "At present it seems to be floating at the mercy of the winds, as if its old island were badly anchored on its marine base." And of the United States he has added, "America is a prey to wandering, nomadic bands of anarchic workers, revolutionaries, outlaws and IWW (Industrial Workers of the World) – all of whom could well bring into the country the social ills from which it had thought to be free, once the prosperity resulting from the war has evaporated." Has Louis de Launay not seen through the dazzling and formidable phenomena of American expansion to the symptoms of decadence concealed within? "Within this rapid expansion of Yankee imperialism, within this growing folly for mere size can be discerned, as in the gigantic proportions of the prehistoric reptile, the seeds of degeneration." Gentlemen, if we really must choose, is it worth abandoning the ship which may be ancient and outmoded, but in which we willingly took refuge in times of war, simply to throw ourselves upon other doomed vessels, their shattered hulls hidden below the water line? Furthermore, if I needed to strengthen our position by adducing an actual, concrete fact, I would say that our mother Province, the Province of Quebec, has remained constantly faithful to French culture; surrounded by an Anglo-Saxon world, she has even managed to retain her educational disciplines. Quebec has its troubles and its disturbing problems, but are they more disturbing than those of other provinces? And in what way is this Province, which is so often described as backward – backward because of its faithfulness to its cultural traditions – in what way is it so inferior to its rivals?

Too many others, alas, echoing some of the weaker minds among our own people, see our desire to unite and preserve all French-speaking territories as an unhealthy form of isolationism – a rather muddled way of thinking, I admit, but one which so conveniently replaces wit and commonsense in our present world. By this argument, French Canadians would be isolating themselves simply by remaining true to the most pressing, the deepest requirements of their inner nature! That may well be isolating oneself, but everyone does it, even those who denounce our faithfulness simply because it happens to be different from theirs. It quite often happens that I am asked for an interview by our Anglo-Saxon friends, and when they approach the question of Quebec nationalism, I simply tell them, "Yes, we are nationalists, but less so than you." This reply always baffles them. Then I go on, "You reproach us because we buy our own things from our own people, and because we insure and bank with our own people. But – and I am not criticizing you – when do you English Canadians ever buy from anyone but your own people, or bank with a French Canadian bank, or insure yourselves with one of our firms? The only difference between you and us is that you do spontaneously, through racial instinct, without having to be told, what the French Canadian only does when he is reminded because he belongs to the least nationalistic people in the world." And I go still further: "In politics it often happens that our representatives hesitate when a choice has to be made between their party and their nationality; and occasionally, much to the dismay of our historians and many others, they sacrifice the interests of nationality to their party. Once again I have no wish to criticize, but has it ever happened that you had to sacrifice your English interests to those of a political party? We love France, but we would never sacrifice the vital concerns of our country for her. But during the last half century and more, when have you English Canadians ever refused any appeal whatsoever from Great Britain on the grounds that, as you say, 'blood is thicker than water'?"

No, it is definitely not right to say that nationalism and isolationism are synonymous only for French Canadians. And do we really need to refute the childish claims made by those false prophets who are always wailing that to become more nationalistic means to turn inward upon ourselves and live stupidly narrow lives within closed frontiers? An individual does not isolate himself by developing all the resources of his personality to become more fully human, more filled with life and better able to communicate it; an Englishman, or an American, is not turning inward when he tries to fulfil and develop as best he can the basic characteristics of his type of race; why, then, should the French Canadian's personality become shrivelled simply because he remains faithful to the laws of his origins and of his nature, especially when he has the eminent privilege of belonging to the most universal of cultures and to the Catholic faith which embraces all the horizons of the universe?

Let us determine to be French Canadians, fearlessly, resolutely, without half measures. We cannot, on the one hand, maintain that our French culture has a contribution to make to the spiritual and cultural enrichment of our country and, on the other hand, offer this country a mere pale shadow or caricature of that culture.

Let us meditate upon the recent statement made by the Apostolic Delegate to the Committee on Survival, surely the most explicit and encouraging words ever to come from a representative of the Pope in Canada. "Your mission is a two-fold one. First you have the mission of preserving your religious and national heritage. Secondly, you have the mission of disseminating that heritage. I would add that it is your right to preserve your heritage and your duty to disseminate it." A right and a mission. We cannot expect a right to be respected by others unless we first respect it ourselves. As for that duty – that mission – shall we be able to carry it out if we are mere half-French and half-Catholic Canadians?

Wherever possible, let us preserve our national background in its entirety, especially in Quebec where we are fortunate enough to possess an environment made exactly to suit us and which is, as you know, as good as that of any other province in Canada. Wherever a national background does not, and cannot, coincide with a province, let us preserve it in our families, in our schools, our parishes, and even, if possible, in the diocese. Let us live our culture to the full. We can take account of the various differing requirements of our surroundings, – what I would call our political or geographical context, – without yielding to the blandishments of integral bilingualism, if such a thing does indeed exist. In our present atmosphere we must shun the sort of bilingualism that would mean being unable to speak our mother tongue better than the other, and that might introduce confusion as to which language should receive our strongest emotional attachment. Hermaphroditism is too flagrant a deviation from the laws of nature to make it viable as a general rule in culture or linguistics.

Let us proceed with confidence. To begin with, you who are here today and who possess some influence throughout the entire country, do not minimize the role you can play or the effectiveness of your efforts. Is history not made of such efforts? It may happen of course that a single man affects the historical evolution of an entire nation and indeed of all mankind. Our own era has provided us with shattering proof of this possibility. Thinkers, philosophers, statesmen, these leaders do indeed carry awesome responsibilities. But on the more mundane level history is shaped for better or worse by a series of decisions made by individuals, by heads of families, leaders of small societies, educational leaders, religious leaders, all of them responding to a common call, acting together, and thus determining the collective life of the country for a century to come.

Let us seek encouragement, also, in the greatness of our venture. It is an awesome consideration for a small nation to know that it is the bearer of eternal values and truths. If there is one fact which has been made brilliantly clear by the tragic events of our own era it is surely the unique and eminent value of Christ's doctrine in bringing back peace and brotherhood to our poor world and preventing it if possible from destroying itself through its own folly and hatred. In these times, what countries could be more fortunate than those which possess the true faith? After the elimination of both France and Catholic Spain from the North American continent, it was surely not for nothing that God willed this exceptional thing at the tip of our continent: a small people united by the true faith, living in its own state, and, if it so desires, radiating the living splendour of a Christian civilization.

We need not have undue fears of being engulfed by a flood of artificial immigration. Nations who do not have children cannot continue forever to export their herds of human beings. Our strongest and most pressing danger from the outside arises from the fact of our being a minority group, a minority in nine provinces, a minority in the whole of Canada. That is the terrible situation in which we have been placed by Confederation. It gave us the immense advantage of reconstituting Quebec into an autonomous state. On the other hand it transformed us into a minority throughout the country and at the federal level. Before 1867 we had never been a political minority, not even under the Union which had given equal parliamentary representation to Upper and Lower Canada. We have now been condemned to the role of a political minority for 82 years. Have our representatives in Ottawa during that time succeeded in finding the exact synthesis, the fair balance between what is due to the Federal government and what is due to the country, the Province, the nationality, the party – as would have been done by the English, the Irish, or the Jews? Who would dare claim that they have? There is the dark blot on our record.

It is made darker by the fact that here the external danger is compounded by an internal danger: our national conscience is far too weak. For the past few days you have been discussing national education. Let us beware of the lazy complacency which would make us pin our hopes for survival and for our future on the good-will of others or on some vague euphoric feeling in the country as a whole. Let us be quite clear about this point. We shall not be more French simply because the *Winnipeg Free Press* or the *Toronto Star* suddenly start showering us with good wishes; or because French is treated as generously as possible at the federal level and we are at last given an equitable share in the civil service; or because *bonne entente* between the two nations, instead of being simply a mirage for naive people and a rhetorical theme for after-dinner speeches, suddenly becomes a loyal and durable reality. No, none of these reforms or reversals of opinion, however desirable in themselves, will make us become more truly French Canadian. We shall become French Canadians by ourselves, by our own determination, by our own efforts, by turning inward to become more fully conscious in a lively, vigorous way of our national and spiritual values, of the mission they confer upon us, of the magnificent destiny they have power to give us. To become fully conscious of our French and Catholic nature, that is the issue. Experience will teach us what we have too long neglected or disdained: the wonderful treasure amassed by our ancestors, the leavening to swell the heart of a young nation.

The other evening a few hundred of us went on a pilgrimage to Midland, the land of the martyrs, the very heart of Huron country. We went by bus to St. Ignace, the site of the old Huron village where the Jesuits Brébeuf and Lalemant were hideously martyred. The beauty of a fine evening, the silence of that small plateau still hemmed round by forest and encircled by a melancholy river almost hidden at the bottom of the ravine, the skeletal outline of a restored Indian hut, the stakes driven into the ground to mark the site where houses stood in the old village, the memory of Brébeuf's enshrined skull which we had honoured in the afternoon as it returned to Huronia after three hundred years: all this no doubt favoured an evocation of that historical scene. After listening to a brief summary of the saint's life we walked towards archaeological reconstruction number 26, which is thought to be the exact spot where this hero of the faith underwent torture; and suddenly a wave of emotion swept over the little group of pilgrims. Many of them spontaneously fell to their knees, some to kiss the soil where there now grow ferns, brambles, and wild cotton, and then to arise with tears glistening in their eyes. A collective shudder of emotion had passed through these men and women. And yet these pilgrims to Huronia had simply become conscious of the merest fraction – a glorious one perhaps – but still a fraction of our incomparable past.

# Historical Groulx

## The Teaching of History in Our Colleges

L. Groulx, "L'enseignement de l'histoire dans nos collèges," letter to the editor of Le Devoir, October 27, 1913. Reprinted by permission of Mme J. Rémillard.

Mr. Henri Bourassa,
Editor of Le Devoir, Montreal.

Dear Sir,

When I resumed my course on the British regime in Canadian history the other day, I found in my papers a note referring me to one of your recent articles. It reminded me to mention to my students the present requirements of the public as well as the profound convictions they must seek in the history of their country. It also made me think that it might be an appropriate time to inform the media of the efforts now being made in our colleges to give our children an education in patriotism by teaching them their national history.

In Le Devoir of September 3rd, referring to Lord Haldane's speech to the Bar, you made to my mind some rather severe comments about the patriotic education presently given in our various schools and colleges: "We must admit that the teaching of this history (the history of England and Canada) in such a way as to ensure that our Canadian youth have a knowledge of the rights and obligations of the Canadian people, – such teaching is deplorably defective, or rather non-existent, in our secondary schools and colleges, French as well as English."

Sir, I do not know what historical studies are like in the High Schools and Collegiates of Ontario; nor could I really assess the value of the courses in constitutional law taught in our universities. But do you not think that your statement might be somewhat unfair to the teachers in the secondary schools of the Province of Quebec?

As proof of your assertion, you mention the disconcerting ignorance shown by most of our legislators and magistrates in matters of constitutional law. Certainly this ignorance cannot be denied, for there are so many examples of it as to put it quite beyond doubt. And it can be explained, at least partly, by the almost total inadequacy of the teaching of our history thirty, twenty, or even ten years ago. If I may be allowed to give my own case as an example, I have to admit that when I left college around 1900, the only knowledge I carried away with me was the result of my own private reading of Canadian history. I would add that, along with all my contemporaries, I was more than a little indifferent to that history, which was taught from primary school textbooks – and bad ones at that – and which we all treated with slightly less respect than the annals of the Babylonians or the Ninivites.

But, if I can trust my memory and my own observations, I would say that this regrettable situation came to an end at least ten years ago. Many circumstances combined to change it. The hard-fought battles over educational questions which we have engaged in for the past twenty years; the growing public awareness which resulted from these struggles; the foundation of the French Language Society; the foundation of the Catholic Association of French-Canadian Youth, with its study programme of national questions; and yes – I do not hesitate to recognize it – the foundation, too, of the Nationalist League; and especially the "nationalizing," if I may use that expression, of topics for French composition set in the final exam at the *Rhétorique* level and hence of topics set for composition throughout the year; all these causes and many others brought us to a fuller and more methodical study of our history. It would not be an exaggeration to say that the teaching of Canadian history has been completely reformed and renewed, I would even say created, in our colleges within the past decade. Here at Valleyfield we now devote two course hours a week to it, at both the *Belles lettres* and *Rhétorique* levels.* I am assured that a similar programme exists in the majority of colleges and seminaries in Quebec. I am well aware that we still lack an official textbook for use throughout our secondary school system. But in many schools – in Valleyfield, for example – students are given their history Professor's manuscript text, and this is geared to their needs and intelligence. Will you allow me to give a more precise, more personal testimony? I am quite familiar with the text used in Valleyfield, because I wrote it myself eight years ago, for the *Rhétorique* class I was then teaching. I am certainly not blind to its flaws. But I know that it contains within its nine hundred pages the pith and marrow of our best historians:

*The fifth and sixth years of the now defunct eight-year classical college programme in Quebec.

Ferland, Garneau, Chapais, Salone, Gérin-Lajoie, Decelles, etc. In the section which deals with the British regime, for example, I know that every political regime from 1764 to 1867 is discussed at some length, sometimes even with the texts of the statutes illustrating the gradual evolution of our political liberties. All the constitutional struggles of Bédard, Papineau, LaFontaine and Cartier are related in lengthy chapters. This textbook also contains conclusive chapters which explain the judicial position of the French language since 1760, and the role French Canadians played in the gradual conquest of constitutional liberties. In the chapter on Confederation, the students of course learn the history of the Quebec Conference, the division of federal and provincial powers, the clauses concerning the French language, marriage, and the educational rights of minorities. But they also learn the advantages of Confederation from the commercial, military, religious, and national points of view. There is another section on the disadvantages of the federal system, and a conclusion which establishes the *Anglo-French* – instead of *Anglo-Saxon* – nature of the Canadian Confederation. In another chapter, which deals with Article 93 relative to minorities, the whole question of education in all the provinces is discussed in minute detail. The book concludes with notes on the limits to our autonomy, on the prospect of independence or of annexation to the United States, and on the future of French-Canadians. Finally, I would add that in the study groups of our Catholic Association of French Canadian Youth – these exist in almost every college – national questions are constantly on the agenda and all the most serious problems of the time are prudently but openly discussed.

Given, therefore, what I perhaps naively believe to be real progress, I wonder whether, considering the intellectual receptivity of secondary school students, we can really demand much more of our history teachers, apart of course from the continual perfecting of teaching methods. Since they are not after all Professors of constitutional law, since they are not involved in higher education, could and should their teaching be of a more substantial, more profound nature?

Sir, I would ask you to believe that I put this question sincerely, and without complacency. It is increasingly rare to find in our colleges the kind of person which a Senator denounced so harshly at the last French Language Congress, the kind of person who believes rigidly in the absolute perfection of the system. I have instead found teachers with a real desire to be worthy of their task and to comply with the legitimate requirements of the intelligent public. We have nothing but contempt for the surly attacks of those masked enemies whose aims are entirely different from the ones they show; but on the other hand we welcome and gratefully acknowledge the advice of sincere and disinterested men who are of a calibre to grasp the importance of these questions.

Believe me, your devoted

L.A. Groulx, priest.

# The Role and Traditions of the French Canadian Family

L. Groulx, "La famille canadienne-française, ses traditions, son rôle," a speech delivered at the fourth annual Semaine Sociale, August 31, 1923. *Semaines Sociales du Canada 1923* (Montreal, Bibliothèque de L'Action française, 1924), pp. 334-358. Reprinted by permission of Mme J. Rémillard.

"One of the most wonderful phenomena the Catholic Church has produced within the past two centuries," wrote the biographer of Mgr. Taché, "is the French Canadian family." Since men of faith value moral beauty above aesthetic beauty the same historian did not hesitate to add the following rather solemn comment: "It is a phenomenon we admire more than the most magnificent Gothic cathedrals of France."

What influences, what moral, historical or other conditions combined to produce this wonderful masterpiece? I propose to investigate these causes with you this evening. But first I believe I can state two related principles: the French Canadian family has flourished and been able to perform all its duties, firstly because it so admirably fulfills the natural purpose of the family and secondly because Catholicism has been the supreme law governing its life.

The family we are studying this evening is the rural family created by the old regime and perpetuated to this day. I need hardly explain that I do not intend to pay much attention to exceptional cases: they do not enter into an historical synthesis. If, as a result, the picture seems to be all sun and no shadow, it is not because the shadows do not exist or because I am unaware of them; it is simply that history, unlike painting, determines the place of shadows not by artistic principles but by the laws of truth.

One of the founders of our nation, the first Bishop of New France, resolved that the sources of life in this country should be sanctified. Conscious of his role as the spiritual father of an entire people, he strove to inculcate deep religious feelings into the seminal families of this country. Courageously carrying on the work begun by the Jesuits, this great apostle set before the eyes of our ancestors the ideal example to be followed: the miraculous family created by God the Father for his Son; the sublime family of Nazareth. In his ecclesiastical letter of 1665, François de Laval established a Confraternity of the Holy Family. It was intended primarily for married women, but – note the spirit of the times – young girls were also welcomed. Here, from a chapter of their rule book, are the virtues recommended to the members:

Towards *God*: dread of offending Him, promptness in all things connected with His worship, complete submission to His will even in the most distressing circumstances, and deep respect for all holy things.

Towards their *husband*: sincere and cordial love, so that great care is given to anything which concerns him spiritually or physically; constant desire to win him to God by prayer, good example and other appropriate means; respect, obedience, sweetness and patience in bearing his faults and bad temper.

Towards their *children*: continual concern and desire to bring them up in the fear of God, to teach them their prayers and ensure that they say them every day, to inspire them with a great horror of sin, and let nothing pass which might be offensive to God; gentleness in reprimanding them, patience in bearing their little weaknesses, always regarding them as living embodiments of the child Jesus; the enjoining of cleanliness in their habits and the avoidance of luxury since it can only serve to foster vanity in both parents and children.

Towards the *household*: great care and vigilance that nothing be wasted or spoiled; cleanliness without ostentation.

Towards *oneself*: the ambition of relinquishing all things displeasing to God and incompatible with the spirit of the Holy Family; the constant questioning of one's behaviour as follows: How would the Holy Virgin act in this situation? Would she speak in this way? Act in this way? Dress in this way?

With his usual mixture of practical commonsense and high Christian idealism, the first Bishop of New France then proposed this lofty goal to the members of the group: "Work towards the conversion of infidels in this country through the example of an irreproachable life."

This, Ladies and Gentlemen, was the first constitution set up for the French Canadian family. Because of François de Laval's initiative, our young nation has been praised – in a momentous document, one of Pope Leo XIII's encyclicals – for originating this devotion to the Holy Family.

The first couples of New France could thus contemplate the best example of domestic life known to history as they learned their essential duties: to procreate children and bring them up well.

In order to fulfill its potential for the future, the home must above all be founded on a true matrimonial bond and on the love of a married couple. Care for children and desire to perpetuate the species can never exist in cases where the encounter between man and woman has come about through the ephemeral motivation of mere passion.

I need hardly mention that the French Canadian family has always been established by the sacrament of a Catholic marriage, never by any other means. Even in the very early days of the colony with the arrival of shiploads of *filles du roi*, it is an historical fact that the first missionaries and the first Bishop would not allow any couple to leave without having first received the blessing of the Church. *Marriages of Canada*, those parodies which were performed in Paris theatres around 1734, were nothing but sheer invention, the pastimes of a leisured society desperate for smutty entertainment. One need only look at the collection of pastoral letters written by the first bishops of Quebec to see what infinite precautions were taken to protect the sanctity of marriage. The most rigorous measures were taken against any deviation, however accidental. To maintain the dignity and honour of the matrimonial bond, parish priests were not allowed to administer nuptial rites to dissolute soldiers and their victims. In any case New France was a country over which the discipline of both Church and Christian mores ruled supreme. The sanctity of the conjugal bond was considered a principle above question, a natural law. Not only was immorality not tolerated: it condemned itself by hiding from public view. When need arose, the arm of the law assisted the Church and public opinion. A moral wrong is also a civil wrong. The courts, which did not trifle about the matter, deported without further ado, not only lower class offenders, when they were men of scandalous or bigamous lives, but also, to name but a few, a certain Mr. de la Frédière, a daughter of the King's Attorney in Quebec, and a Mr. Gallifet, Governor of Trois-Rivières – all of whom learnt as they sailed into exile that even the nobility could not trespass with impunity against public mores.

Protected by these energetic measures which helped to maintain public morality, the honour of our origins and of French Canadian homes remained unblemished. Our earliest ancestors were often poor, but rarely were they debased. When, having fetched his barrel of lard and his barrel of flour from the Intendant's shop, the peasant of New France led his bride to his pioneer's hut, he could well have inscribed over his doorway: "our wealth is not in gold and silver but in honour."

The government records in Quebec show one single illegitimate birth among 674 children baptised before the year 1660, and only one more before 1690! In a survey of all births in the colony, carried out by abbé Tanguay, there were found to be only 1,366 illegitimate children from a total of 165,194, a proportion of 8.03 per thousand children!

With such evidence before us, Ladies and Gentlemen, we may indeed speak highly of the great moral rectitude of our forefathers. If other people affect to scorn these statistics, it is undoubtedly because they could never hope to match them!

There is something more here than simply a sense of honour and respect for women. With social mores so well regulated by faith, people who were choosing a spouse were more likely to take into account the moral qualities which are the basis of sound and durable love. In an environment where fortune was not the first priority, young men seeking rich heiresses were thought simply to be lacking in judgement. 'Happiness is more precious than wealth' our forefathers would say, so regularly that it became an axiom; and when they commented that a young man had chosen his bride for her money, they were virtually predicting a swift, disastrous end to the honeymoon.

In any case the prevailing testimentary custom left most girls with more or less equal fortunes. Rarely was the family wealth bequeathed to a girl and so, if one was more attractive than the others, it was not because of the kind of possessions which count in marriage contracts, but because of her greater virtue or beauty.

"A wealthy settler," relates Mr. de Gaspé, "would buy his daughter a calico dress for her wedding, as well as shoes and a pair of cotton stockings. Often these clothes would eventually be handed down to the bride's grandchildren." Mr. de Gaspé is perhaps exaggerating a bit, but what is certain is that the early settlers' way of dressing was far from extravagant. Weld, an Irish traveller who passed through the country at the end of the eighteenth century, described the costume of a village girl as follows: "It consists of a sleeveless bodice, blue or scarlet, and a petticoat of a different colour." He adds, and we believe him, "Her straw hat makes her look extremely interesting!" "In over a hundred closely scrutinized descriptions of marriage contracts, inventories, or wills," writes Mr. Edmond Roy, "we found only one silk hat, one pair of leather gloves, one black velvet waistcoat and one shawl ... as for furs, we found only coats of lynx and bob-cat. Jewelry was rare. Apart from the gold ring and silver band which every good housewife wore on her finger, we found only one necklace of mother of pearl. On the other hand everyone owned a silver crucifix." In brief, the French Canadian fiancée would very often have only one possession to give her prospective bridegroom: that venerable and spacious piece of furniture so solemnly described in the old notaries' acts as 'the great bed of the household'.

Well, you ask, what about the bride's dowry? Her only dowry was in her heart, given totally to the bridegroom of her choice, in her arms, those heroic arms which never ceased working until death, in her valour and proud faith, stronger than any obstacle, in her sense of honour, brighter than her sweet Canadian eyes, more glittering and purer than the gold of her engagement ring.

The wife may have brought her husband more honour than riches, but this did not mean that he could take advantage of her because of his greater fortune. In this respect Catholic virtue gradually transformed the old laws to redress the excessive inequality between man and woman. Whatever the wealth of the prospective bridegroom, he could never be richer than his wife once the marriage was concluded. Community of property between husband and wife was the common law in the Canadian family. As far as our ancestors were concerned, conjugal love would have been flawed had there been any division in either possessions or interests. How interesting nowadays to read those old marriage contracts with their archaic expressions:

The intended spouses mutually agree to take each other through form and contract of marriage as husband and wife and lawful spouses, and to have the said marriage celebrated and solemnized with the least possible delay in the presence of the Holy Catholic, Apostolic and Roman Church. They avow their desire to share all their goods, movables and chattels according to the customs of Paris in use in this country. The promised bridegroom endows his intended bride with the sum of money of 300 to 500 livres in 20-sol pieces. The *praesipinum* or first claim on inheritance of either spouse on the decease of the other is commonly a fixed sum of 150 livres which may be taken in ready cash or in movables. Linens, wearing apparel, armour and accoutrements, rings and jewelry belonging to the spouses, a buffet or a hope-chest and the great bed of the household also form part of the *praesipinum*.

Finally in recognition of the true bond of devotion between the intended spouses, they mutually agree to leave each other all their goods in the event of there being no surviving children born or to be born of the future marriage.

Thus was it intended that the community of property between husband and wife should be prolonged even after death. What wonderful, noble documents, these agreements which were made in a spirit of Christian brotherhood, which eliminated so many opportunities for conflict, stimulated joint labour, and added confidence to love! From the fact that husband and wife were associates with equal rights also sprang the excellent habit our fathers had of consulting our mothers in all their undertakings and of never concluding any serious business without agreeing about it together.

This was the basis upon which families were established in the old days. It seems to me that one would look in vain to find a matrimonial alliance in which the beneficial effects of Catholicism were more apparent, the unity of hearts more perfect, and the family consequently better able to achieve its foremost, natural goal.

Hence the French Canadian family was magnificently productive of life. On this point history and statistics are so eloquent as to need no further elaboration from me. The rule in self-respecting households, as I have often said and even repeated, was to reach the mark of the first dozen children and without undue pride occasionally continue beyond the second. I would simply point out that the French Canadian nation doubled its numbers every thirty years and sometimes in shorter periods. (By the way, let me add that our brother Acadians surpassed us in this respect and gave what may be the best example of human fertility by doubling their numbers every sixteen years.) I would also point out that in spite of their excessive concentration in towns, and in spite of an absolutely inexcusable rate of infant mortality, the 65,000 Frenchmen of 1760 had produced within two centuries a nation of almost four million people.

It would take far too long to list all the tributes that have been paid to our French Canadian fertility. Let me simply recall some of the more notable.

"Indian families," wrote Mgr. de Laval, "do not have as many offspring as our French settlers, who in most parts of the country have up to eight, ten, twelve or even sometimes as many as fifteen or sixteen children." De la Gallisonnière was struck with enthusiasm at the sight of this unrivaled production of men, and considered it a weapon against detractors of New France: "It is a source of riches far more important for a great king than sugar or indigo or even, if you will, than all the gold in the Indies." Montcalm's diary similarly reveals his awe at meeting a veteran of Carignan surrounded by 220 descendants who now populated four parishes on their own.

These statistics reveal their full significance only when

coupled with certain facts. In the past, fertility in this Province was not a matter of ups and downs. Neither bitter poverty nor harsh times could turn our ancestors from their duty. The day had not yet arrived when income or easy living would determine the number of births in any family. Is it not common knowledge that nine-tenths of the settlers who lived through that period of harrowing misery between 1608 and 1648 have thousands of descendants living today? Here is what Mère de l'Incarnation wrote about the fertility of that period: "It is prodigious to see the increase in population of this country ... Besides these marriages (of settlers sent by the King), those who have been established here for some time have so many children that the country is teeming in a most marvellous way." In 1671, when the colony was still in its heroic infancy, Talon wrote to the King giving a figure of 600 to 700 births for the year, at a time when New France had hardly more than a thousand families. During its long martyrdom in exile, the Acadian nation marked its route with as many cradles as tombs, never ceasing to produce new lives to oppose the men wishing its death. Furthermore we know that less than fourteen years after the dark hour of Conquest our ancestors had grown in number from 65,000 to 100,000, a fact which prompted Carleton to remark that the English could implant themselves in this country only at the dire risk of being swamped.

This fertility which was maintained throughout our history was characteristic of all classes. Because everyone was bound by the same law, and because the task was not a duty to be submitted to but a duty to accomplish, the large family was not the exclusive privilege of any social class. Seigneurs and bourgeois did not leave the burden of enlarging the population to the lower classes. In 1719, when French Canadian merchants protested against competition from foreigners arriving from abroad, one of their arguments for requesting the protection of the Marine Council was that most of them had to support very large families. As for the nobility, we know that every one of the leading ladies of New France deserved the phrase with which the solemn Mr. de Tracy once complimented Madame de Linctôt: "A pretty woman who amply fulfills her duty of bearing children." How often the Intendants and governors, pleading with the King on behalf of the colony's noble families, attempted to impress His Majesty by mentioning the large number of children these families had! Denonville wrote to the Minister in 1686: "I must inform *Monseigneur* of the extreme poverty in which several of our large noble families are living, reduced to beggary: the family of Saint-Ours is such a one. Then there is the gentleman, Mr. de Dauphiné, who has the responsibility of a wife and ten children ... the Sieur de Linctôt and his wife, who have ten children and two more belonging to one of their daughters, complain that they lack bread." The following year Denonville wrote again about Tilly: "There is this good man Tilly, one of our councillors and a gentleman. He has fifteen children and we must supply him with wheat for them to survive." And finally was it not Mr. de Muy who once undertook to count the grandsons of Pierre Boucher and stopped after he reached the 150th?

Surely, Ladies and Gentlemen, there was once in this country a small people who did not worry about their material resources when it came to filling their cradles. The truth is that our valiant ancestors drew their support from other sources.

To start with they married when the heart was young and both blood and courage strong. From 1669 marriages became obligatory in New France: it was henceforth forbidden to remain a bachelor or a spinster. His Majesty had indeed decreed, "That there be established some pecuniary penalty ... for fathers who do not marry their sons by the age of twenty, their daughters by sixteen." At the same time, to stimulate the obedience of the settlers, the King endowed large families generously. An edict recorded by the council in 1676, and very progressive for that period, granted to all parents who had ten or more children who were born of lawful wedlock and were neither priests nor members of any religious community, an annual income of three hundred *livres* plus a sum of twenty *livres* to the children on their wedding day. If ever there was a superfluous law, however, it was surely the decree enforcing obligatory marriage! His Majesty had to pay many pensions, but there is no evidence that he had to impose many fines, in a country where one became an old bachelor at the age of twenty-five and an old maid at twenty-two. Some nations are enamoured of celibacy, almost unto death: the family must not be broken up until each child has become "a man of property"; the building of new nests is postponed until the nest serves only to comfort aging and rheumatic limbs. Quite the contrary in this country! Candidates for matrimony appeared at the Church door in the full vigour of their virility, their virgin strength promising the race continued health and vitality. In the majority of cases, we must admit, they were richer in aspirations than in pieces of gold. What matter? At the outset of their married life they would be more frugal. They courageously did without those luxuries in dress, furniture or food which so many others afford by 'economizing on births'. They believed that there was plenty of room for courage and hard work; that four sturdy arms working together would still create the happiest life, no matter what hardships were encountered. Then, too, children were the prime wealth. At the arrival of the twelfth or the twentieth there was as much rejoicing as for the first, and they would exclaim, in the popular phrase, that they were 'enriched' with a boy or a girl – if not two at once! The christening of a child, no matter how many siblings had preceded him, was always an excuse for a joyful reunion of relatives and friends. And if new born children necessitated more bread in the pan, more space at table, more thread or wool for the spinning wheel, well, there was always Providence on high which was known to be more solicitous of full than of empty nests. The mind is rather staggered by these dizzy heights of faith, but Mr. Etienne Lamy reminds us that "these beliefs (those of our ancestors) are after all those of the Church – the most notable thing about these Catholics is that they were consistent."

## II

Magnificently constituted to create life, the French Canadian family was equally well equipped to develop and discipline this life, so naturally do principles of order, once accepted, develop along harmonious lines, and so true is it that the laws of Catholicism are indeed the very laws of life.

True education, unless we are mistaken, presupposes a certain law and a certain authority: the basic law for any human being is the orderly development of his faculties; the authority executes the law and causes it to bear fruit.

The French Canadian family was never without such law and authority. It was at opposite poles from the modern family invaded by democratic ideas, a family in which parents share the government of the household with all the children, and authority vested in everyone is finally vested in no one. Our families have a head and that is the natural head, the father, who embodies, as Frederic le Play said, "the only authority instituted by God and incorporated into eternal law."

When the head of the family in those days was worthy of his role, what moral influence he had! In the eyes of his household he appeared not only with the dignity of a father – since he was, here on earth, the author of the life he governed – but also with all the prestige of an austere worker, a labourer who reserved the hardest tasks for himself, who provided the family's bread and, in addition to all his other merits, was always present in his own home. Since he never made his family do anything he would not have done himself, his word was law in his household. If he did not have first say, he certainly had the last. "A father's word was the word of a King," said Mgr. Plessis. When the weaker, more gentle mother could not obtain obedience, he had merely to frown and duty would be enforced. It was well known that the frown could lead to sterner measures. Nor was this an idle threat in an age when Bossuet frequently administered corporal punishment to the Royal *Dauphin* himself!

Obedience to the father had no age limits. Little more than half a century ago the custom was still maintained, in accordance with old French laws, that children of twenty-five or over who wished to marry could not do so against their father's wishes without having first addressed to him, through a notary, three respectful "appeals" at appropriate intervals. These appeals were indeed "respectful," whatever Napoleon may have thought when he replaced the word by "respectful acts" in his code. Just note for instance the supplicating tone adopted by Jean-Claude Louet, the son, when in January of 1733 he pleaded with his father Claude Louet, a lawyer in the summary court at Quebec: "My very dearest Father: I am most deeply grieved to find myself deprived of the delight I was wont to take in your sweet company. With sharpest pain I see that the tender affection with which you oft rejoiced my heart is now extinguished."

To this first appeal the father did not respond. The son returned to the charge and, as is natural in a crossed lover, the tone of the second letter was even more pathetic: "My dearest Father: words cannot describe the depth of my affliction when I find your heart inflexible and set like flint against my supplications and appeals. Can it be possible that your tenderness for your child, always so great, should be so altered as to place him under a cloud of perpetual disgrace?"

And, as the father was still unmoved by this second respectful appeal, and this truly affecting style, Jean-Claude's tone became distinctly tearful: "Dearest and most revered Father: in deepest misery and woe I make appeal to that paternal tenderness whose sweetest tokens I have oft received. Can it be possible, my dearest Father, that you would deprive me of its grace in the very moment of my greatest need? No, I am certain you love the salvation of souls too ardently to condemn me in the course which I pursue . . . "

If you seek the secret of such great, almost fearful authority, you must look to its well-nigh supernatural nature. We must remember that the head of the family in olden days fulfilled an almost priestly role in his household. Did he not perform sacred rites? He was the one who had the power of benediction. He blessed the first handful of seed before it was sown; at table he blessed the bread before it was broken; and most important of all on the morning of the New Year he solemnly lifted his hand above the heads of his children to bless them, like a patriarch. A grandiose and moving ceremony, in which we see perhaps better than in any other tradition the spirit of our ancestors. Their faith and the prestige of the father were so great that no member of the family would have missed the New Year benediction, so strongly did they feel that it was sanctioned by God and that they were bound to this act of faith and homage towards their father, the Lord of his household. Married children living away from home would cover great distances in the bitter cold of the early morning to arrive before Mass on the first of January and throw themselves at the feet of the head of the family. On January 1st, 1842, the Honourable Augustin-Norbert Morin, who was then a Judge in Kamouraska, was on his way to Quebec with the intention of arriving at his parents' home for this New Year ritual. Delayed by bad roads, he was forced to stop at the Church in his native parish, Saint Michel de Bellechasse. The New Year High Mass was about to begin; the people were thronging around the Church. As soon as he had descended from his carriage, Mr. Morin began to look for his old father in the crowd; and then in front of the entire parish His Honour removed his hat, knelt in the snow and, like any good son, asked for the paternal benediction.

Given such authority, supported by the supernatural, the education of children in French Canadian families was bound to produce good results, as anything will that is in harmony with truth.

As much as possible this education aimed at developing the whole person. I will not dwell on physical education. In the early days, when people lived mostly outdoors, the climate and way of life took care of that. And climate and way of life did not do too badly, if we are to judge by this colourful description by Marie de l'Incarnation: "It is wonderful to see the great number of very beautiful and robust children, without bodily deformity except those caused by accidents. A poor man will have eight children who go about without hats or shoes in winter, with the thinnest shirt upon their back living off eels and bread, and yet there they are tall and plump." From a diary written by Mr. Aubert I extract the following lines:

The French of Canada have sturdy, well made bodies. They are agile, vigorous, perfectly fit, aggressive and capable of bearing all kinds of fatigue, which has meant that during the last war, French suppliers had to give them a quarter more bread than they gave the French men from Europe. All these physical advantages possessed by French Canadians come from the fact that they are born in a country with pure healthy air, that they are nourished with good and abundant food and that from childhood they have the opportunity of fishing, hunting and canoeing.

Commenting on the physical vigour of our ancestors and on their bodily perfection, La Hontan, Hocquart, and Bougainville make similar observations; Father Charlevoix even writes: "We have no provinces within our kingdom where people have such robust health, such advantageous size and such well proportioned bodies."

These, Ladies and Gentlemen, are the effects of our fresh invigorating Canadian air but helped, we may well suppose, by the purity of the young nation's blood and by the vigorous education of children. For example, children were brought up to respect sobriety. The older Canadian may often – perhaps too often – have enjoyed his glass of "Jamaican" with his friends and relatives; but in public drinking places it was against regulations to allow young men to have a drink before they had attained their maturity or had some beard on their chin. The same custom was applied when tea was later introduced and it remained a drink for adults and for spinsters who had attained the age of reason!

Physical education was completed by a working apprenticeship to which children were soon put, too soon perhaps, if not for their muscular development at least for their intellectual development. Life was hard for everyone in those days: children could not hope to escape the general rule. But in most cases they were not eager to escape, so thoroughly had they been inculcated with the idea that work is a natural duty for any valiant person. Surely no one could have felt greater pride than the fourteen- or fifteen-year-old country boy leading his first team of horses or oxen, ploughing his straight furrow and hearing himself praised in the evening in front of all the girls for being so strong and working like a man!

Work was for a long time the universal profession in New France. Were the daughters of Mr. Saint-Ours not seen working in the fields, handling the sickle and even the plough? The wife and daughters of Mr. de Tilly worked in the fields every day, according to Denonville. Yet Mr. de Tilly was a gentleman and a member of the Sovereign Council. Kalm tells us that the daughters of the highest placed families, even of the governors, would go down into the kitchen and cellars suitably attired and make sure that everything was in order. No, in those days it was not felt demeaning for a young lady to wear an apron, nor was it considered noble to remain idle!

This behaviour was very natural for children, since their parents worked at all the various trades, the family trying to be as self-sufficient as possible. Not only was the father a farmer, clearing and working his land, but he was also a mason, a carpenter, joiner, blacksmith, cobbler, saddler, and, during the long winter months, a weaver of cloth and a chair mender.

As for the mother, well, some of our extravagant, modern ladies might well find her rather old fashioned! Ladies, will you allow me to make a few impertinent remarks? As far as I am aware those mothers never wore the kind of elaborate costumes with which some of you so cunningly contrive to disfigure yourself and succeed so admirably; I am afraid they read their prayer books or their 'Guide to Household Management' rather than the fashion catalogues; their hands were roughened and red; but at least these simple women had not lost the arts of sewing and spinning and of moulding the characters of their children with as much skill as they moulded their delicious bread. We remove our hats and stand with swelling hearts to pay tribute to that early French Canadian mother, the best woman, the best wife in the world: a valiant woman who toiled hard all day and, late at night, was still working in the soft halo of the midnight lamp, only going to rest when the oil ran out; a woman of sound commonsense, adjusting her expenses to her income, setting aside small stores of money for emergencies or for the education of one of the sons; a woman of energy and foresight stimulating her husband's courage and preventing him from going astray; a woman of faith, capable of smiling even in the midst of the greatest sorrow, capable of singing with tears in her eyes to sustain the courage of those around her and to praise God.

The mother did not merely look after the house: she was also responsible for the garden and the hens; she found time to work in the fields, harrowing, mowing, bringing in the corn along with the men; in the evening she would sew, darn or knit and during the winter, the best time for domestic industries, she would spin or weave. The general rule and custom was that everything in the way of clothing should be made at home, so much so that old inventories have even revealed the existence of 'button moulds'. It is not surprising therefore that children soon learned these multiple trades which, however diverse, were all necessary for survival since, in these families, each member's clothing and his bread depended upon the combined efforts of the entire group.

Amidst all this activity, you may ask, what happened to the child's intellectual education? It may indeed have suffered from this way of life, but it suffered far more from the historical conditions, which it is not necessary for me to describe here. Perhaps our ancestors, with their sound commonsense, their great integrity and sense of justice, were subconsciously convinced that 'the complex of knowledge and emotion which constitutes the principal treasure of any nation arises from its practical life rather than from any scientific or literary teaching its masters might give their young pupils'. And to put it more briefly, perhaps they consoled themselves by reflecting that, in Le Play's phrase: "The great mass of men learn more from their upbringing than from school."

For our forefathers, education meant, above all, moral education. They wanted religion to govern the child's life from the moment of his birth; and the Church was ever present to teach them her wise customs. In the earliest days, when visits from missionaries were very infrequent, the custom arose of keeping newborn children at home for a long time before they were christened. But as soon as the supply of priests became more plentiful, Mgr. de Laval quickly reimposed a stern discipline on the community; indeed he went as far as to threaten negligent parents with excommunication. Soon the habit became firmly entrenched; the first time the infant was taken out was to the baptismal fonts. The church bells were even more rapid than the grapevine in announcing the birth of the newest parishioner.

As the child grew, the same faith grew with him, surrounding him. More than any other instruction, religious teaching permeated his soul. The law governing both his conscience and the religious life of the family was that of the 'eternal commandments', completed by the Gospels. And, therefore, one of the first words the child learned to say was 'Jesus', by which he might mean any one of those first objects he learned to recognize: the crucifix, or those old pictures of Saint Anne teaching the child Mary to read, or of Our Lady of the Seven Sorrows displaying her heart pierced with the dagger of grief – all these religious objects were indiscriminately called 'Jesus' by the toddler. He was taught that evil deeds and disobedience were infringements of the Divine Law, painful to God. The child's first lessons of catechism and his first prayers were also learned at home. As soon as he could utter a few words he learned to make the sign of the cross, or, as it was commonly called, the 'name of the Father'; he already knew that it was wrong to go to bed without saying his prayers or rise without offering his heart to God. From generation to generation these touching prayers were handed down in an oral tradition which very regrettably was never recorded in the prayer books.

Legend was often used to supplement doctrine, so that lovely images and concepts of faith were impressed on the minds of the very youngest children. In those days Christmas gifts were not brought by a repulsively obese, decrepit old man, almost as fearsome as Michelangelo's Moses. Which one of our fathers did not cherish a much happier memory, that of falling asleep as a young child on the 31st of December with a mind full of delicious visions of the radiant child Jesus in His manger? During the night, in the middle of those wonderful dreams, the child Jesus would descend and deposit gifts in the shoes that had been placed on the hearth, or better still in the long woollen socks which had so feverishly been suspended at the foot of the

113

bed and which suddenly began to rustle so mysteriously in the middle of the night!

Even the songs, those simple ballads which mothers sang as they rocked their cradles, had their share of spiritual message or imagery for the children. Mothers would sing them hymns, or Christmas carols, or even songs from the liturgy, imitating M. le Curé's solemn tones. One of the most popular lullabies concerned "a hen so black giving Baby its egg in a sack; a hen of pure white laying hers within sight; a hen of mottle grey in Church on Sunday," and the last verse was always about "three hens more laying eggs at Heaven's door."

Among the virtues to which children were trained there is one I would especially like to mention here, because none other so well illustrates the great delicacy of our ancestors' nature, and that is their modesty. I shall not dwell on this point because the most significant tribute to tht education we received on this score must surely be the very difficulty I have in mentioning it even in praise. Our forefathers practised an austere chastity which did occasionally become a rather excessive reserve. Young girls very often came to marriage with all their unsophisticated innocence. For a long time, and even today, children were taught that Indians had the monopoly of the very mysterious delivery of children and, to save the façade of this pious myth, it happened that these awesome messengers invariably chose the very moment after the other children had been suddenly whisked away from home to appear with their burden.

In houses which were often rather cramped human hives, the children's rooms or beds were always arranged to preserve a prudent division of the sexes. Our bishops, those early protectors of our families, had not hesitated to give precise and detailed instructions on these matters. There is a historical fact which, while tragic in the extreme, gives us a final insight into the scrupulous, almost fierce precautions our ancestors took to preserve decency: at the time of the great Deportation, History tells us that Acadian mothers aggravated the dismembering of families which had already been cunningly calculated by Lawrence, by refusing to let their adolescent boys board the same ships as their nubile daughters.

The best description I could give of those households of olden days and their religious traditions would be to quote a most venerable witness, Mgr. de Saint-Valier, who had become thoroughly acquainted with our rural areas by visiting them repeatedly, often going from door to door: "Each household is a well regulated little community in which everyone gathers for prayers morning and night, in which the rosary is recited together, and before every meal there is a communal examination of everyone's conscience, during which the father and mother make up for the scarcity of priests as far as the conduct of their servants is concerned."

And this is the kind of Catholicism whose sincerity and depth we occasionally allow ourselves to question! Ladies and Gentlemen, if to be Catholic is to accept with complete loyalty the words of Christ and the teaching of His Church, if to be Catholic is to conform to the morality of the Gospels and perform the duties they prescribe, however austere, then I for one immediately think of that small nation of French people who covered the continent with their crosses to profess their faith in Christ, the Son of God; I contemplate those forefathers who, lacking the knowledge of scientists, yet knew their catechism better than today's scientists and whose humble and simple faith was illuminated by supernatural insight; I think of this small nation, humiliated by defeat, attacked in its religious faith by threats and blandishments and nevertheless producing only five apostates during the thirty years following the conquest, according to its Bishop; I see in my mind's eye those old Christians who had their defects and their miseries, certainly, but who were willing to confess their sins to those severe parish priests of the day and who gathered their children and servants about them on Easter morning to take communion. I think of those fathers and mothers, devout believers who would so often pray before engaging in any action, who regarded sin or disorderliness among their children as the greatest of sorrows and wept more bitterly over the evil conduct of their sons or daughters than they would have over their coffins; I think of those poor souls who despite the cruel wounds and hardships of life never uttered a word in bitterness, far less in blasphemy; and then, more bent and broken by sorrow and bereavement than by the passing years, let themselves be taken by death as by a divine hand and, with the smile of the just, gave their children a final blessing ... Ladies and Gentlemen, when I think of all these touching examples of nobility, when I contemplate the greatness and purity of that faith, I could wish only one thing for our modern Catholicism: to occasionally equal the faith of those by-gone days!

### III

This brief sketch of our historical family would be incomplete if I did not add that its constitution was greatly strengthened by a social factor: the judicial and economic framework within which it developed. This was not the principal factor, but the spiritual qualities were so reinforced thereby that the French Canadian family became, by virtue of its customs and of its old legal system, that superior type of domestic society which sociologists call a 'seminal family.' By 'seminal family' they mean, as you know, a family which was perpetuated through an uninterrupted succession of heirs of the same lineage and the same trade or profession, each generation handing down not only their hereditary endowments but also their customs, methods of work and above all the sacred accumulation of ancestral traditions. Frédéric Le Play commented that it was such families, even more than the political constitution, that had ensured the greatness of England; and he added: "The small land-holder cultivating an inherited piece of land himself, under the 'seminal family regime,' was for a long time the system which best insured the well-being of a race both in England and on the continent."

To begin with, the concept of a seminal family assumes that the home and land were also the workshop. Life and work were in the open air, far from centres of corruption: that is to say in those hygienic and moral conditions most likely to maintain the vigour of the race.

The family domain, since it was inherited as a bequest from one's ancestors, was not, like the home of a nomad – I mean a rented home or furnished apartment – a matter of indifference, an ephemeral possession, an inanimate shelter. It was a living thing incorporated into the very character and history of the family; it was like some relative of one's fathers and forefathers who, through long proximity, had acquired some of their features; it was a precious reliquary, gathering and preserving the results of all their labours. Thus it had acquired a kind of immortal personality of its own, linking the various generations and helping them all to remain alike.

Furthermore, in such a type of family the old people stayed within the household, providing it with the kind of continuity which has a cohesive effect upon the family. Contrary to what happens in an unstable family where the trade or profession is not hereditary, where all the children leave, one after another, and allow the household to die with the parents and be reborn with each new generation, in a 'seminal family', one of the children always remained with the old couple after his marriage and took the title of heir and associate. Note, by the way, that the choice of the heir was not left to the hazard of primogeniture; the parents chose him themselves, very often on the basis of his greater ability to administer their hereditary possessions and to co-operate with the past. Until their death, the elderly couple cohabited with the heir and thus ensured the transmission of the family traditions in the most effective and wisest way, by a judicious mingling of the old and the new. With regard to the administration of the patrimony, or the education of the children, the heir profited from the accumulated experience of his ancestors without being bound by it, since he became his own master and recovered his own initiative with the decline and eventual death of the older generation. Le Play saw in this association of father and son such a guarantee of continuity and progress that he wrote: "For peasant families, the cohabitation and association between the parents' and the heir's household has always been an urgent need as well as an indispensable means of prosperity."

The truth of Le Play's observations can easily be confirmed by other arguments. Remember that one of the prime characteristics of the seminal family was that property was kept within the family through inheritance. Since the patrimony was indivisible and had to be transmitted integrally, there was only one way in which the heir could give his brothers and sisters their share of the inheritance: that was to procure sufficient income from the paternal property to establish them. This was precisely the intention of the father's will. Can you think of a system more likely to impose thrift on the young landlord or more likely to multiply the results of his efforts? If it is true that 'thrift is always the means of achieving ownership of land', it is no doubt equally true that possession of land is the best stimulus to thrift. In a period when most children were destined to be farmers and when all those sons of farmers felt irrevocably bound to the soil, fathers had to put all their savings into the purchase of more land; and sons in their turn would do the same in the best interests of their co-heirs and their own children. Thus the family's land was gradually used to acquire more land and consequently to multiply the number of seminal families; and so the law which created the system was the best guarantee of its prosperity.

Finally, need I mention how strongly such a hereditary system maintained solidarity and family feeling? Another characteristic of the French Canadian family was thus its admirable cohesion. I recognize that in this the climate certainly played a part, closeting families together for six months of the year and making it necessary for all members of the family to live in continuous intimacy and dependence upon one another. This also meant, however, that these families were full of good cheer, the contagious joy which derives from a great number of people living together. As the French Canadian family always had so many members, it was rare to find a moment altogether deprived of gaiety. It was surely not our nation which furnished the models for those well known paintings or prints depicting the classic household: two greying spouses sitting near the dying embers of their fire and, to cheer their solitude, the rather morose tenderness of a single, melancholy child. As I have said elsewhere: "What magnificent feasts they

117

had, all of them seated around an immense table – for when only the family was present they still numbered twenty-four or twenty-six." They learned to do without outside entertainment; the joys of family living were enough for them. But as Mistral says in *Mireille*: "When Christmas evening gathered all the generations under its starry canopy, the grandfather presiding over the table which had been blessed made all else pale into insignificance as he raised his wrinkled hand in sign of benediction."

Cohesion was also a result of the part played by the mother hive with regard to its new swarms. How could children fail to remain closely attached to the central household when their own work had helped to maintain it, and when it had now become their best source of help and support? Then too, the cohabitation of the old parents and their heir provided the original home with a magnetic attraction which did not entirely fade with the death of the parents. This attraction to the parental household was indeed so strong that under the French regime a law was required to force young couples to leave it and ask the Seigneur to give them new lands. In any case the predominance of two or three names in each parish shows how near their original home the offshoots would settle. In Rameaux's *France aux Colonies*, for instance, a historian describes a community on the slopes of Saint-Michel where five original families expanded into thirty new households all in close proximity to one another.

Throughout the fantastic scattering of population, which was caused under the French regime by the enormous expansion of the colony, when very nearly every family provided men for the new settlements, soldiers for distant forts and garrisons, officers and leaders for new strategic outposts, or boatmen for trade, the home still retained its mysterious and powerful hold over the young nomads of the new generation. At the slightest call from their family, for a death or a marriage, like migrating birds the children who had dispersed to the very limits of the colony, from Niagara, Detroit or Vincennes would come flocking home.

I have just described very imperfectly, alas, the life and constitution of the French Canadian family of former times. It will be clear to everyone, I think, what a great role this family played in our history.

In the face of endless wars and epidemics, in the face of a hostile opposition seeking to strangle them, in the face of dispersion, the most disastrous of calamities, our fathers valiantly kept populating and expanding the nation. If we their descendants had organized life at our end as well as those humble people did at theirs, our strength would still be such as to make us masters of this country. Our ancestors not only gave us numbers, they also transmitted pure blood and moral virtues to ensure the continuing transmission of life. Having opened the gates of that royal river they sent it forward with such impetus that it rushes still between its banks.

From the religion practised in those early homes and daily exemplified by acts of heroism, from the education imparted in this noble atmosphere, we have derived our power of quiet endurance, our will to live, which is stronger than conscious desire, our public and private virtues so envied by our very enemies.

From such an abundant harvest of children the Church was able to take a generous tithe of men for its priesthood as well as for the legions of men and women who have made services of charity and education so widely and easily available in our Province, and who have earned our young nation a world-wide reputation for apostolic work. Thus the eldest daughter of France indeed became an heiress worthy of the eldest daughter of the Church.

Ladies and Gentlemen, let us retain these few essential facts: if the French Canadian family has been the jewel of our history, if it has been able to accomplish such great things, this has been because it possessed the essential properties of a true family; and if it was a true family in the noblest sense of the word this was because God granted it the honour of being so.

Whatever decline we may be undergoing today let us not allow ourselves to be trapped into barren weariness or bitter scepticism. The old families are not all dead, the old homes have not all crumbled away, the sacred stones are not completely scattered. In his *Cité Antique*, Fustel de Coulanges wrote, "In very ancient times tombs were placed inside the family property, within the inhabited grounds, not far from the doorway. This, explained one of the elders, was so that sons entering or leaving their home could meet their fathers and offer up prayers to them. In this way the ancestor remained in the midst of his own family; invisible yet ever present, he continued to form part of the family and to remain its father. Although himself in a state of divine and immortal happiness, he nevertheless continued to be interested in what was happening to the mortals he had left behind. He knew their needs and sustained their weakness. A man always had with him the guidance and support of his fathers."

Ladies and Gentlemen, the God of our homes is the invisible God represented by the ancestral crucifix. Our tombs lie further away in the sanctified soil of the churchyard. But our imperishable glory – and tomorrow, if we so wish, our victorious strength – arises from the fact that there is not a single home in our nation where there does not survive the moral presence of some ancestor at whose feet it would be proper to kneel as before a saint, with tears in our eyes and a prayer on our lips; and also from the thought that there is no threshold in our French Province behind which does not appear, beside the crucifix, the sublime image of an elderly couple smiling the smile of the elect, the very personification of our history and lineage; she with hands joined in eternal prayer, her white hair surrounded now by a halo of divine glory as it once was by the soft light of the midnight lamp; he with hands radiating the glory of his labours, hands held high to grant immortal blessing to even the remotest of generations.

# The British Regime in Canada

L. Groulx, "Le Régime britannique au Canada," *Histoire du Canada français depuis la découverte*, 4th edition (Montreal, Les Editions Fides, 1962), Vol. II, pp. 7-12. Reprinted by permission.

A GENERAL VIEW

One great venture had ended; another was about to begin. Another two centuries of history of which we must now attempt a general view. It would be wrong to imagine some artificial, complete break suddenly intervening between yesterday and today, between the French and the British regime. The same group of human beings continued their life on the same land, in the same geographical environment. A single factor was entirely new: the English conquest which was to alter the pattern of life in French Canada. The circumstances which led to this calamity in our colonial history are well known. The period during which European nations were busy seizing possession of the New World was soon followed by a period of rivalry between these colonizing nations. Canada paid the price of such a rivalry. So too did Louisiana, the tiny Antilles Islands and some embryonic Spanish colonies in the southwestern part of North America; but it is perhaps worth noting that Canada was the only one of the more important European colonies on the American continent to undergo the supreme ordeal. What repercussions would the conquest have on future history? I mean not simply French Canada's own isolated history, but the whole historical complex whose effects it had to endure, or whose course it could itself influence: the history of North America and of England. With France all but removed from the continent, the Anglo-American colonies were still not entirely liberated from the old French nightmare. Having become an imperial power, England was soon obliged to face new problems. Through the annexation of Scotland (the Covenant of 1707), through the even closer annexation of Ireland, it had already lost part of its ethnic and religious unity. Its recent acquisitions during the Seven Years War had particularly increased the heterogenous quality of its dependent territories. What reactions this was inevitably to produce on its internal life and, even more, on its colonial policy!

Obviously the heaviest repercussions were bound to fall on French Canada. "The conquest of 1760," wrote an English-Canadian historian, A.R.M. Lower, "was a type of slavery." Strong words. Even if conquest merely entailed the transfer of government from one mother country to another, with the ensuing change of political, cultural, and economic ties, this would still create a dangerous turmoil in the life of a colonial people. The conquest of 1760 did all that, but did it not do far more? French Canadians were suddenly faced with a future full of uncertainty and as frightening, we may be sure, as the strange, unknown lands of America must have seemed to their forefathers, the first pioneers. Their first anxiety was what France would decide when peace was concluded. Would France wish to keep the Canadian colony which it had often found so burdensome? Would England retain its conquest and, if so, what place and what treatment would it receive within the British fold? Such a tiny people, those 65,000 conquered beings. Nonetheless a formidable people because of its geographical position, the extent of its territory, and its ethnic and social character so different from the rest of the Empire.

Serious questions which called for serious answers. To understand the situation more clearly, let us try to anticipate the future from that point. A mere handful of settlers, ten to twelve thousand families, are suddenly abandoned in a corner of America. What can be expected of such a minuscule group? If it were to yield and be swallowed by the stronger nation, who could possibly blame it? It could well disappear without fuss and even without shame. How many ventures as magnificent as this French one have known a similar end! But we have mentioned the vigorous character of these pioneer people, their impatience of any yoke, their passion for freedom. The time is now just after the conquest of 1760. Colonial history is rapidly entering its last phase: the arrival of young nations to adulthood. In America new currents are beginning to appear, disturbing to the mother country. Perhaps French Canada will determine to survive, will energetically refuse assimilation. And in that case? Well then, history takes a great leap and acquires an austere greatness, a tragic beauty.

But let us continue. Would we be relying too heavily on *a priori* reasoning if we concluded that the political factor had played a dominant role in this life of resistance, of continual reclamation of lost ground? Let me make myself quite clear. I would not claim that the political element played the most important role in the history which was just unfolding. The conquered people did not for a moment stop living their ordinary life, their economic, social, cultural, moral, and religious life. A people cannot live at all unless it lives a complete, full life. But how can a human group resist absorption and survive unless it first seizes control of the government of its own life and, consequently, attaches a certain importance to political activity? Let us not forget the milieu in which this conquered people would live, a milieu comprised of Anglo-American colonies brought nearer by conquest and in which political weapons were already wielded with great vigour. But also a milieu dependent on the mother country where the entire life of the nation revolved around parliamentary institutions. Under these circumstances and in this climate of opinion, is it so surprising that the conquered people should have seized the most effective weapon at hand for their own defence? They did not, of course, seek political freedom as an end in itself but what could be more natural than to consider it the necessary condition for all other freedoms, the indispensable means of resolving the whole problem of their existence?

Are we indulging here in elaborate, hypothetical speculation, in fanciful reconstructions? The facts are there. The central, most evident pattern in the history of Canada since the conquest has been that of a continual and progressive political evolution. At times a hesitant evolution, searching for the right path, and at other times a vigorous evolution, but never deviating from the overall movement towards greater political power. Into this evolution the vanquished threw their energies. And the evolution would not cease until, from a Crown colony, Quebec became a self-governing province, within an independent Canada. Not the least interesting part of this new history was that the French-Canadian, brought up under the rule of kings and allowed only a minimal participation in his own government, should have suddenly been forced to regard political action as a priority, if only from a tactical point of view.

In this perspective, then, it becomes easy to divide the British regime into its natural parts. Two distinct periods are immediately visible: the movement towards self-government (1760-1848) from self-government to independence (1848-1931). Each of these periods contains sub-divisions or various stages which we shall now define. The movement towards self-government can be divided into three stages:

1) Provisional Regime (1760-1764): an anomalous period, a transitional stage. A time of occupation by some detachments of the conquering army; a time of waiting while the fate of Canada is decided in Europe; a time of restoration during which Canadian troops, returned to their homes, rebuild the country and heal the scars of war.

2) Regime of the Crown colony (1764-1791). Following the Treaty of Paris (February 10, 1763), the first announcement of England's policy regarding its conquest: a policy of assimilation promulgated by the Royal Proclamation of 1763. As early as 1764, with the inauguration of the new regime, a first and decisive stand is taken by French Canada: it absolutely refuses to accept the religious and cultural alienation proposed by the conqueror. The following twenty-seven years of history can be sub-divided into two parts. Ten long years of struggle to recover lost ground, in this country as well as in England, and then success at last with the Quebec Act in 1774: an astonishing piece of legislation enacted by the Parliament of London, repealing the Royal Proclamation of October 7, 1763 and, in the process, seriously infringing some of the fundamental laws of the Kingdom. In summary, French Canadians obtained the preservation of their French civil laws in 1774, thereby ensuring retention of their system of property and their social hierarchy. New guarantees were given to protect their religious liberty; freed from anti-Papal oaths of allegiance, the 'new' subjects thus gained access to public positions; civil or political inequality between them and the 'old' subjects was theoretically at an end. In brief, the Quebec Act recognized the right of a French and Catholic people to exist within the British Empire, a most important right at a period when the influx of British immigrants and American Loyalists was about to create problems of cohabitation between the races.

There remained one freedom to secure: political freedom which would put an end to the authoritarian regime of the Crown colony. That was to be the target for the next seventeen years. In the end, a great many factors combined to sweep away the outmoded regime. To begin with the Quebec Act was very imperfectly carried out. Then there was a coinciding of historical events of startling vigour, creating cross currents of powerful ideas: the American Revolution, the French Revolution and the effect of these influences was compounded and reinforced in America by a clumsy attempt at repression of colonial liberties.

3) Parliamentary Regime (1791-1848). The first action of this regime was to partition Canada into Lower and Upper Canada (today the provinces of Quebec and Ontario), one French, the other British. This regime, said to have been copied from that of the mother country, was greeted with much enthusiasm. In reality it was a deceptive compromise: the old Crown Colony regime hidden behind a parliamentary façade. Parliament had no real influence over the executive; supreme power was perpetuated in the hands of autocratic governors who were not politically responsible to the colonies but only to the Imperial Government. As a parliamentary form, this might still suit the oligarchic England of the eighteenth century, but it was quite incompatible with the democratic spirit of the new continent. The results were easy to predict: continual, increasingly violent unrest in all the British provinces of North America. The agitation was greatest in Lower Canada, since this French province felt a greater threat to its freedom and its life. In 1837 and 1838 there were bloody uprisings in both Canadas. This was followed in 1841 by attempts to stifle the unrest through vague promises of self-government, through the enforced union of the two Canadas, and through renewed efforts to Anglicize French Canada. These policies were self-defeating. Bringing together the reformers, or liberals, of the two most heavily populated provinces meant simply doubling the strength of the anti-colonial forces. In 1842, and then more definitely in 1848, through historical processes and through the tenacity of a French Canadian, Louis-Hippolyte LaFontaine, a skilful strategist as well as a statesman, the Province of Canada at last gained self-government and so, simultaneously, did French Canada. One fact had been made abundantly clear: there could be no viable or stable government without the co-operation of the French Canadians. An appeal was thus made to them as a national group, "as a race, and as a people". In 1849 French became an official language of the state on an equal basis with English. In any case, the unitary state established in 1841 had had to change into what was, to all intents and purposes, a federal state which returned to each of the two provinces a part of their political autonomy.

From self-government to independence (1849-1931). Here again we can discern two stages: the first from 1848 to Confederation (1867), the second from Confederation to the Statute of Westminster (1931). In 1848 Canada had gained autonomy with respect to the mother country, but the degree of internal independence – that is the autonomy of Lower and Upper Canada with relation to one another – was soon found to be quite insufficient. In spite of their evolution towards federalism, the institutions of 1841 remained unitary in their structure:

a single parliament legislated for the two provinces. This created a congenitally uneasy situation which led to misunderstandings and quarrels on both sides and, eventually, to the dissolution of the union. Only one solution seemed appropriate and acceptable to Lower Canada: a federation of all the provinces of British North America. And so, in 1867 as in 1791, Lower Canada, now Quebec, recovered its political entity and its individuality. For Quebec the battle for political autonomy now seemed quite definitely won. What remained was simply to perfect the province's internal autonomy by ensuring its economic, social, and cultural independence, and then to defend its political and national autonomy against the encroachments of the central power. And since the foundation of this greater Canada was accompanied by a scattering of the French nationality from coast to coast, Quebec was also called upon to protect the natural and constitutional rights of minority groups of its religion and culture against the oppression of English-speaking provinces. Finally, and more particularly in the early twentieth century, it had to defend its own autonomy, and that of Canada as a whole, against an offensive resurgence of British Imperialism. French Canada's essentially Canadian spirit and concerns ensured that it remained at the forefront of the struggle to lead the country to independence.

In looking at this kind of history, which seems at first to be too exclusively political, we must be careful not to neglect all the other elements which the political situation shapes, and by which it is in turn shaped. However, nothing is more obvious than the effect that each new stage of political evolution had on all the other forms of the nation's life and, reciprocally, the effect a more robust and conscious life had in stimulating the conquest of new liberties. This vital impetus is the very soul of history, from which it derives its organic structure.

It is easy to see, furthermore, what similarities were maintained between the two regimes, the old and the new. The French regime seemed doomed by its tragic fate: there was always an enormous discrepancy between men and their task; the nation was forced to build its country and its life alone, or almost alone, while burdened with the crushing weight of its empire. Thus, its history was one of extreme tension. After 1760 the historical setting was the same. The constant factors remained, and there was still the old necessity of thinking and living perilously. There was the same gigantic disproportion between men and their task. Life had to be led in an even greater isolation on the continent from which France had been expelled; a tiny island of Latin culture had to be maintained in the vast Anglo-Saxon sea of North America; French and Catholic had to survive in a British Empire that had become the dominant temporal and Protestant power in the world.

A destiny of great effort and great risks but eminently worth it!

Need I say that I hope to write this part of history, as I did the first, with complete objectivity, at least to the extent that any historian of goodwill can presume to do so. I shall neither exaggerate nor minimize the inevitable conflicts which occurred between conqueror and conquered, between two cultures and two civilizations. This declaration of intent is not superfluous in these days when history is so often pressed into the service of propaganda alien to both its object and its discipline.

History may well favour national unity but it is not part of its function to work actively for that goal. Its place is above and beyond such preoccupations. In any case a solid and durable peace could never be established on a basis of historical lies. If two peoples are to inhabit the same country, they need to know what happened between them, if only to understand each other better and to learn what it is they have to forgive one another.

# The Explosion

L. Groulx, "L'Explosion," *Histoire du Canada français depuis la découverte*, 4th edition (Montreal, Les Editions Fides, 1962), Vol. II, pp. 162-169. Reprinted by permission.

THE PRECISE NATURE OF THE EXPLOSION

'Armed Insurrection': how often have we seen this expression used as a chapter heading in books! And how curious that this historical fact must be exaggerated, even in the terms used to describe it. Long preparation, concerted plans, clashes on a battlefield, armed attempts to topple a regime ... all these elements of the classic insurrection. But here we must forget them, especially if we confine our attention to 1837. We do not conceal the fact that there was a long, disturbing intellectual ferment; that, following the Russell Resolutions, our political leaders indulged in a kind of verbal insurrection without being too concerned about the inflammatory effect their speeches might have on the populace or about the possible reaction from the authorities. Nor is it possible to overlook the uprising of 1838 or Robert Nelson's 'Declaration of Independence', which signalled the start of an offensive. This second uprising seemed better organized. The exiled 'patriots', exasperated with rancour and misery, had prepared for it; they relied on the support of the *Frères Chasseurs* (The Hunting Fraternity), a secret society with an extensive network on both sides of the border. The general state of mind in Lower Canada seemed readier than it had been the previous year. Even the moderates had been pushed closer to revolt by Colborne's harsh measures of repression. Then too, Lord Durham's first blunders, his rash assertions concerning the fate of French Canadians, had alarmed even the pacifists. The Bishop of Quebec, Mgr. Turgeon, wrote to Lord Gosford in England, "As long as people thought of Lord Durham as a friend to whom they could confidently bring their real or imaginary complaints, everything went well; but when they suddenly perceived, or thought they perceived, that the administration was not listening, that was enough to plunge us once more into turmoil." The exiled patriots' appeal found a response in the northern section of the province, from Lavaltrie to Trois-Rivières, and in the southern countries around Verchères, Laprairie, and Beauharnois. For their supply of arms, the leaders seem to have relied on sympathizers outside the country; they also counted on the active co-operation of the rebels of Upper Canada. That at least was their hope. Strongly impressed and relying, as he said, on "the most competent judges of the situation," Lord Durham wrote that the revolution of 1838 "would probably have been successful even without the help of the United States had the French Canadians been better prepared and better led." But can one really consider this second uprising as anything more than a mere episode, a dismal venture which, in less than eight days, had completely collapsed?

In spite of their rash language, the political leaders never really wanted a genuine, well-planned insurrection. At Saint-Charles, as we have mentioned, Papineau definitely advised against this form of rebellion, as he would advise against the parade of the Sons of Liberty planned for November 6, 1837 in Montreal. On May 17th, 1838, he wrote to J. A. Roebuck: "Before the aggression committed by the Government against the people of Canada – papers confiscated from my home and from my friends will prove it – I had invariably advised against recourse to arms on the grounds that this gave us no chance of success whatsoever." Dr. O'Callaghan, a journalist at the *Vindicator*, and certainly the most audacious of all Papineau's followers, wrote: "On my deathbed I would continue to declare in the sight of God that, when I left Montreal for Richelieu with

Papineau, I was no more planning a movement of resistance than I am now planning to become Bishop of Quebec." Furthermore, and this surely gives the best insight into the basic strategy of the leaders of Lower Canada, in none of the documents of that period can we find a single plan of campaign duly worked out. In Upper Canada, Mackenzie's procedure was quite different. He had thought of attempting a surprise attack on Toronto, seizing control of the arms depot, capturing the Governor and his Executive, and then proclaiming the Republic. There was nothing comparable to this in Lower Canada. Except for the skirmish in which Bonaventure Viger and Dr. Kimber ambushed a cavalry detachment on the road to Longueuil and freed two prisoners, and except for 1838, at no time or place did the 'patriots' ever take or plan to take the offensive. Quite the contrary. Retrenched behind the imperfect protection of their improvised camps, they waited awkwardly for their enemies, when they could have engaged in guerilla warfare and harrassed them along the roads. In 1837 camps were organized along the Richelieu, at Saint-Denis, Saint-Charles, and later at Saint-Eustache in the north. There was not the slightest concerted action between these camps and practically no communication between them, except perhaps the vague plan people at Saint-Eustache formed of descending upon Montreal while the Royal forces were fighting south of the St. Lawrence. After their victory at Saint-Denis, the 'patriots' did not even venture to pursue Gore's company in its demoralizing flight. The reason was that these poor men – bands of men, rather than troops – lacked the most urgent supply: arms. In not one of their battles did more than a third of their combatants have access to a rifle. "When they met," Bouchette was later to comment, "there were three or four pitchforks and as many scythes and iron bars for every hunting rifle, and this very often of poor quality." This was the result of another, and far worse lack, the lack of leaders. Officers with some experience could not be entirely wanting in a country which still had an organized militia. Some, like Papineau, had even served in the war of 1812. And yet the most general lament during these troubled times was: 'Leaders, where are our leaders?' There was no one to impose a minimum of order and discipline in these camps; we can hardly imagine the resulting chaos. The few men who remained at the head of these bands of 'patriots' were very poor leaders, when they did not flee in the heat of battle, like Storrow Brown and Amury Girod. The bitter truth is that the men at Saint-Denis, Saint-Charles and Saint-Eustache were fighting for leaders who had already taken flight, preferring voluntary exile to combat and especially to arrest. Is anything more needed to show the complete lack of organization and, consequently, the absence of premeditation?

Was the explosion, then, simply a spontaneous accident? Long political struggle and the passion generated by it had gradually created a propitious atmosphere. At the last moment, an unfortunate combination of provocation and mistakes unleashed this pent-up energy. In Montreal, on November 6th, 1837, there was a brawl between the Sons of Liberty and the Doric Club. Windows were broken in Papineau's house; the presses of the *Vindicator* were smashed. Agitation spread through the countryside. Troops, it was rumoured, had joined the Doric crowd to fire on young 'patriots'. On November 9th, John Colborne moved his headquarters from Sorel to Montreal, thus causing movements of troops which added to the general unrest. Colborne then pressed Gosford to have the principal agitators arrested. On November 16th the Governor, losing control of himself and his advisers, issued twenty-six warrants for crimes of high treason: Papineau was among the accused. This was tantamount to lighting the fuse. Three days before-hand Papineau, duly warned, had left Montreal with Callaghan to go to Richelieu. At that point, a large section of the populace had lost all confidence in either the police or the process of law. The arrests of the leaders, it was thought, would mean their assassination. The Superior at Saint-Sulpice, Father Quiblier, warned Mr. Papineau accordingly. To give oneself up was to be massacred, claimed one of the accused, William Henry Scott, who was the Member of Parliament for Deux-Montagnes. A few men then appealed to the public and decided to protect the leaders who, not entirely without cause, felt they were engaging in legitimate defence. The explosion occurred. Such was its immediate cause, and its true character. We must believe Bouchette when he claims that the uprising of 1837 was nothing more than "resisting arrest." It was simple resistance to a police operation, completely unconnected or very indirectly connected with the political struggles of the 'patriots'. One of the more moderate men of the period, Jean-Joseph Girouard, wrote from prison to his friend A.N. Morin on April 1st, 1838: "What would people say in England if it were proved that there had never been any revolt as reported in all the newspapers, in the Imperial Parliament, and in the public acts – that the people were merely defending themselves and that the alternative of attack was never open to them?" If further confirmation were needed, it would be amply provided by the sequel of events. There were battles at Saint-Denis, Saint-Charles and Saint-Eustache – not very glorious days for the royal artillery, facing miserably armed and badly led mobs. "To be sure," commented Sydenham on the skirmishes at Richelieu, "it was a pitiful revolt, crushed with the utmost ease by a single regiment." Less than a month in 1837 and eight days at the most in 1838 were needed to crush the uprisings. The leaders were in prison or in exile; the so-called 'revolutionary' press, the *Vindicator*, the *Minerve*, and the *Libéral* were reduced to silence. A grim terror spread over the province.

EXTENT AND DEPTH OF THE UPRISING

Does this rapid failure allow us to conclude that these uprisings were purely superficial disturbances? A preliminary observation gives us pause: we are dealing with a rural phenomenon. The revolts of 1837 and 1838 did not break out in cities, where heavier concentration of people provided more fertile ground for the seeds of revolution. They broke out in rural areas, and there they remained. When he chose to flee towards the Richelieu, Papineau decided to a certain extent the site of the first explosion. But this does not explain the events which took place at Saint-Eustache, nor the events of 1838, when the new recourse to arms was again disavowed by the leader of the 'patriots'. No doubt some responsibility lay with agitators whose movements can be followed in the path traced by the outbreaks. On the whole, the Quebec region remained calm. A split had occurred in Papineau's party around 1834, a split between the Montreal and the Quebec factions and this had led to greater indifference in the Quebec regions. On the other hand, it is not surprising that the fertile valley of the Richelieu and the Deux-Montagnes region should have been more strongly affected. Over the past twenty years, Saint-Denis, Saint-Charles and Saint-Eustache had all been favourite sites for patriotic gatherings and violent electoral clashes. Indeed, it is hard to imagine the exasperation of people in these regions, especially along the Richelieu. The disaster at Saint-Charles sent a wave of shock over the whole province. The gleam of excitement which had been sparked by the victory at Saint-Denis went out like a tiny candle snuffed by a cold gust of wind. And yet when Wetherall was on his way to Montreal on November 28th, 1837, he came upon 1,000 to 1,500 French Canadian "volunteers" lying in wait for him near Saint-Mathias. There was a further confrontation with 300 men solidly entrenched at Point-Olivier and they did not yield until English troops were deployed against them.

It would be wrong, however, to minimize the extent of the uprising. There are many facts to show that the agitation was both profound and extensive. These people of Lower Canada, so often accused of being politically backward, heard the call to freedom and political emancipation earlier and more clearly than people in other provinces. They were more successful than the reformers of Upper Canada in resisting the intimidation and corrupting tactics of the governing establishment. In spite of the pressure applied by Craig, Richmond, and Dalhousie, they remained unshaken in their loyalty to their representatives. During the elections of 1834, following the 92 Resolutions, Lord Aylmer issued a sort of challenge to Papineau's party. The people of this province, the Governor claimed, had too much commonsense to believe in ills which none of them felt. During the electoral battle, most of the 'anti-resolutionists', as they were called, withdrew or were beaten. The result was 483,639 votes for the resolutionists, and 28,278 for the anti-resolutionists. During 1837 and 1838 the agitation seems to have been acute, especially in the Montreal region. Nor did any region remain completely indifferent. For its campaign of repression, the Government of Lower Canada recruited 3,000 volunteers and, in particular, a company of artillery. Of these 3,000 men, according to the historian Robert Christie, not one was French Canadian; not one had even volunteered. The letter mentioned earlier from the Bishop of Quebec to Lord Gosford, dated December 3rd, 1838, contains these most revealing lines: "I am aware that many men who used to declare themselves strongly in favour of authority now remain ominously silent." The clergy, the Bishop confessed, felt helpless when confronted with the state of public opinion: "It pains me to admit that nowadays, for reasons of prudence, and to avoid greater calamities, we must confine ourselves to giving private advice."

All this is quite impressive. Robert Shore Milnes, as we have already recalled, saw in these tough-minded peasants of Lower Canada "the most independent people" he had ever known. In 1837, the atmosphere was heavy with anxiety and violence. On August 9th, 1839, Lord Durham wrote to Lord Glenelg: "As the English move in, they (the French Canadians) discover that both the representative system and their nationality are threatened ... " The fact that there were so many peasants ready to shoulder their rifles, pitchforks or scythes at the first alarm, and face death on a battlefield, surely reveals the depth and gravity of the emotions sweeping the country.

NEITHER A RACIAL NOR A CLASS STRUGGLE

Must we then agree with Lord Durham's assertion that the whole episode could be reduced to an impassioned struggle between the two races? Almost as soon as he arrived in Canada, the High Commissioner wrote to the Minister: "The first point to which I would like to draw your attention, since all others are in some way connected to it, is the violent animosity which exists between the French Canadians and the English, not as parties but as two different races locked in a national struggle." There is no doubt that many of the regime's tactics, if not the regime itself, appeared to fan the flames of ethnic resentment. Recall, for example, the debates in the Assembly in 1792 and 1793 on the choice of a Speaker, on fiscal laws, and on the adoption of direct or indirect taxation, the latter affecting English trade, the former, the property owners and farmers, that is, 80% of the population. These debates had the unfortunate effect of dividing the Assembly into two clearly defined racial camps. No one has shown more clearly than Pierre Bédard in 1807 that such a regime, instituted or distorted, would almost inevitably lead to clashes. Nothing, claimed the editor of *le Canadien*, could be more subversive than to make the King's representative responsible for all ministerial advice and acts, thereby making the Governor and Ministers into a sort of opposition party to the majority in the Assembly – subversive not only because of the partisan role thus assigned to the leader of the Government, but because of the impetus it gave to ethnic rivalry. "For, since the entire Ministry is composed of Englishmen," argued Bédard, "all the Englishmen in the Assembly vote with it from sheer prejudice, and the Assembly is thus split into English on one side and French Canadians on the other."

Here was clear indication of the terrible path political struggles were likely to follow. But who did more to envenom the situation than the oligarchical caste, giving the "Official Party" – the two Councils and the Governor's circle of advisers – the appearance of a unified group identified with the rest of the English population in the province, and elevated to the rank of "Loyal Party," pillar of Crown and Empire, while the French majority in the Assembly was denounced, ever since Craig's time, as the party of sedition.

This kind of political division was no doubt fostered by Family Compacts in each province. Very few people, however, had any illusions about this vaunted Britishness. Frederic Elliott, secretary to the Gosford-Grey-Gipps Commission, was quite blunt: " . . . If ever the turbulence in Lower Canada threatens the tie with the mother country, the English would be the first to break it." The Commission was of the same opinion. While Lord Gosford could still write to Lord Glenelg, on May 25th, 1837: "In my opinion nothing is more erroneous than to suppose the French Canadians lacking in loyalty," the Commissioners warned that the English population of Lower Canada "would not hesitate to renounce its allegiance and seek help of the United States, if the Crown did not acquiesce in its desires." Lord Durham was no less categorical: "The English party," he wrote, "used these noisy protestations of attachment to England . . . simply to make us share their hatred for the French Canadian majority." He also added: "Although they show less animosity . . . more prudence, and far more presumption . . . the

English are no more loyal than the French . . . Neither party has the slightest confidence in the Imperial Government." Durham also demonstrated that the English party was prepared to allow the annexation of Lower Canada to the United States, rather than to submit to a Government with a French majority; and that it even wished to see a war break out between England and the United States to serve its own purposes.

A historian could no doubt overlook this Machiavellian Britishness. If ever there was a practice calculated to transform political struggles into racial struggles, it was surely the rash custom of creating two distinct parties along ethnic lines and stirring them up against each other by the most inflammatory appeals. But was the oligarchy successful in these designs? Certainly, it would be unfair to confuse the Official Party with the entire English population. Gosford saw that there were extremists among them as there were moderates; his administration, he said, could count upon the support of the majority of moderate men and men of liberal ideas in the province. Charles Buller, in his *Notes on Lord Durham's Mission to Canada in 1838* also distinguished between the "Official Party" and the English population. Of the highest officials in the province, he said that "with the exception of Mr. Daly, all had been involved in the old, pernicious system of this corrupt and cliquish government, and all had made themselves hateful to one or other group and, occasionally, to both." And he added: "The official group which still seemed to have as its head the senior judge of the province, Mr. Sewell, was a class unto itself. This body did not have the confidence of either the French or the English, and had no influence on public opinion."

Was the oligarchy more successful with the French Canadians? Did it force them to unite in harsh opposition to the minority? Describing what may have passed through the minds of the ordinary people is not an easy task. In the days preceding the explosion, how did these people react to the occasionally vitriolic and all too common attacks against them in the English press? And a few months later, what feelings were aroused in them by the implacable measures of repression and revenge, to which the authorities had apparently been pushed? It is easier to see clearly into the minds of the leaders. No sign here of any racism or desire for racial struggle. The leaders always refused to equate the great mass of the English population with the caste of "officials," the "dozen individuals" whom they called the "anti-French Canadian junta." "There are not *two* parties," protested Papineau one day, "there is one despicable cabal against the whole country, which is as unanimous as it could conceivably be in its hatred of that cabal." Need we refer once more to the 92 Resolutions, and especially the third, fourth and

133

fifth? In all sincerity, these men of 1834 could well speak of the "liberality and fraternity" they had shown British immigrants. As much as was within their power, they had tried to facilitate the newcomers' "participation in the political advantages and industrial resources" of the province. Similarly, they could boast of having worked for "the general prosperity of this country by ensuring the peace and contentment of every class of inhabitant without distinction of origin or creed." This spirit of generosity did not abandon them in 1836. When claiming its right to administer public lands, the Assembly declared that this was for the advantage of "all classes of His Majesty's subjects." That year it was again Papineau who, well aware of what went on in every English colony, exclaimed: "It is sometimes pretended that our claims result from our different origins and from our Catholicism, when it is quite obvious that true liberals are men of every creed and every origin."

And so to conclude. Seen in perspective, the outstanding features of these events of 1837 and 1838 are the following: nothing, especially the first year, resembling a civil war, long fomented and well organized; no rebellion in the legal sense of the word; an improvised movement almost spontaneous in its violent outbursts; a rather extensive and profound rural phenomenon; a popular movement which cannot be simply labelled a racial struggle, or even a class struggle, without narrowing its scope or distorting history. Its dominant characteristic was that of an episode in a political struggle for political ends.

# French Canadians and Confederation

L. Groulx, "Les Canadiens français et l'établissement de la Confédération," an article from *L'Action française*, 1927, reproduced in *Notre Maître, le passé*, 2e série (Montreal, Granger, 1936), pp. 233-254. Reprinted by permission of Mme J. Rémillard.

No province played a more decisive role in the establishment of Confederation than Lower Canada. The province was important, firstly, because of the size of its population. The census of 1861 gave a figure of 1,111,566 inhabitants. This was more than the combined population of the three Maritime provinces and more than a third of the entire population of the proposed state. No federation would have been possible without the consent of these million people.

This sizeable group possessed, in addition, considerable political power. It already played a predominant role in the Parliament of the United Canadas where it was the more stable group whose cohesion had defeated the Anglicizing policies of the Union. More than any other factor, Lower Canada was instrumental in determining the colonial emancipation which occurred first under Bagot and then under Elgin. In contrast to the parliamentary representation of Upper Canada, which was nothing if not variable, constantly reshuffling according to the whims of its ephemeral leaders, the party led by LaFontaine, Morin, and later Taché, treated the various parties and factions in an off-hand manner, combining with one or the other in turn, never ceasing to be itself, faithful to its principles and aspirations. A small, liberal-democratic faction was organized along one wing and then faded without weakening the main body. More important, the French Canadian group in 1864 had at its head a true leader of men. Lacking the personal magnetism of a Papineau, lacking the strength of character of a LaFontaine or a Morin, George-Etienne Cartier nevertheless had an ascendancy over his party and his compatriots unrivalled by any of his predecessors. To a greater extent than any of them, he possessed all the qualities of leadership. His was an imperious, wilful, highly strung, almost despotic personality; small wonder, then, that he managed to impose his rule on a people accustomed to monarchic traditions! Not that his nation was always willing to accept everything he wanted; but it never accepted anything he did not want. On this point all his contemporaries and all historians are in agreement: only one man, George-Etienne Cartier, could have made his province agree to all the serious political transformations of 1867; and only he, by uttering a single word, could have frozen them into indomitable opposition.

Lower Canada had another asset which gave it a good bargaining position, and that was its geographical situation. Historians have tended to neglect this major factor, no doubt because it was so obvious. For the architects of 1864, Lower Canada had to be either the central arch in their great structure or else a yawning gap in the very middle. Not only did its harbour of Montreal and its long navigable stretch of the St. Lawrence constitute an indispensable trade route and water way, the foremost marine artery; but more important, it was the land bridge between the central province and the Atlantic provinces. Already there were complaints that it was arbitrary and extravagant to create a political link between provinces separated by great, uninhabited areas at the lower reaches of the river. What masterpiece of artifice would have been needed to cement an alliance across a gap of three hundred miles? In other words, how could such an immense void possibly have been bridged? Such are the major factors in politics and history. Without Lower Canada, a federation of the Maritime provinces might have been established; but never a Canadian Confederation. Upper Canada had only three choices: it could live in isolation at its end of the country; it could enter into a bipartite federation with Lower Canada; or, it could maintain the regime of 1840, that unnatural coupling which was daily becoming more intolerable.

\* \* \*

Confederation thus depended above all upon Lower Canada; but this province was also the one which was likely to incur the most serious risks. Certainly it had grievances against the regime of 1841, although no more so than Upper Canada. "Are we meeting today in a spirit of amity to seek solutions for constitutional ills and injustices which have been a source of grievance to the conquered?" asked George Brown in 1865. "No," he continued, "it is the conquerors who are aggrieved." In any case, one fact can never be too strongly emphasized: the federal system, adopted for want of a better, is not the perfect political solution, which would be the acquisition of full powers within a completely independent state. Because of this fact there are many principles and worries surrounding the establishment of a federation. Small nations join in a federation to make their political and national situation more stable, not more precarious. They want greater security, not greater risks. In the speech he gave in Halifax, John A. Macdonald clearly underlined this essential aspect of any political federation:

> In any discussion of colonial union we must consider both what is desirable and what is practical; we must consult the prejudices and the aspirations of each party . . . I hope that we shall be able to produce a constitution which will set up a strong, central government, able to defend itself against whatever threatens it, but which will also preserve the individuality of each province and protect its particular aspirations. If we are unable to accomplish this, we shall fail to attain the goals we now have in view.

What particular assets and aspirations would Lower Canada have to place in the hands of the federal state? Upper Canada only had political or material interests to worry about. At most, it simply needed to protect its school system which it considered quite unalterable. Similar concerns were apparent in the Maritime provinces but, weaker than Upper Canada, they were more concerned about their political and social particularities.

Only in French Canada, however, were there truly transcending reasons for anxiety. French Canada was in a unique situation. Given the duels that had been fought between two civilizations in this province ever since 1760, it could only fear new and graver developments. After eighty years of relative isolation, during which it had only needed to defend itself against a tiny English minority within its own closed boundaries, in 1840 the field of battle was suddenly enlarged; French Canada was forced to fuse its life with a British province and an entirely British population. In 1864 the field of battle again widened dramatically to include half a continent. Lower Canada now had to gamble for its destiny against four provinces instead of only one. And the risks of the game were not only its political and economic interests, its special social conditions, but also its religious and moral interests: its entire national being and all its faith. As a son of the Church, Lower Canada could not forget that it was responsible for the souls of its people and that it was therefore obliged to create proper safeguards not only for itself but for all the Catholic minorities of the proposed state. For a nation endowed with Christian faith, these are the most serious of responsibilities.

French Canada thus had the duty of working out a dual political contract with its future associates; first, a contract which would completely protect its provincial autonomy and carefully delineate federal and provincial jurisdictions; and secondly, a contract of national and religious character which would settle the rights of the French Canadian nationality as well as the conditions of religious minorities in the English-speaking provinces. French Canada was alone, or almost alone, in determining the very nature of the political contract. Upper Canada, we know, would have preferred a unitary state or, as it was then called, a legislative union. Opposition in the Maritime provinces to such a form of government was neither universal nor irrevocable. If the alliance of 1867 turned out to be a federal rather than a unitary pact it was because French Canada demanded it so.

Would simple legislative guarantees, however, have been enough to reassure a nation which had so often been disillusioned in the past about the most sacred of contracts? How could we be free from anxiety when, in the midst of the talks, the two nationalities confronted each other with attitudes that were so completely opposed, if not downright hostile? On the one side was a willingness to create special privileges for the weak, a desire for justice so strong it became generosity, and a desire for conciliation so strong it became foolishness; on the other side was a headstrong determination to make the weak feel the superiority of the strong and to pin the French and Catholic minorities down beneath a weight of petty and rigid clauses. Far from being able to rise to the magnanimity required of founders of states, far from being able to see in the diversity of nationalities and their creative energies a means of stimulating and strengthening the national character, a whole section of the Anglo-Saxon population – the most dominant and powerful section – was determined to keep a lion's share when signing the Confederation Agreement and to admit associates only in the role of serfs. What a harsh light was thrown on this disturbing state of mind by the education debates of 1866! Antoine-Aimé Dorion was merely expressing the collective anxiety of his compatriots when, during the course of the Parliamentary debates of 1865, he exclaimed:

> I know that the Protestant population of Lower Canada fears that, even with the proposed restriction of Provincial powers, their rights may not be protected. Then how can Lower Canada expect happier results from a central government which will be given such wide powers over the fate of this part of the country? Experience shows that majorities are always aggressive and this particular case will be no exception.

Echoes of apprehension must have been aroused in the country when this warning note was sounded by Henri-E. Taschereau, the Conservative member for Beauce, one of the few men of his party to break with the leaders:

> I am not confident that our descendants will thank us for having made them a part of the immense empire of English provinces in North America. On the contrary, we will soon realize that this Confederation is the ruin of our nationality in Lower Canada. The day this constitution is approved will sound the death knell for our nationality just when it was about to take root in the soil of British North America.

The struggle which followed was of a violence unparalleled in the history of Lower Canada. To the bitterness of party quarrels were added the fundamental passions which are invariably aroused in people when they feel strongly threatened. For the first time, with the very life of their nationality at stake, French Canadians found themselves divided into two camps. Tragic situation for a little nation whose historical greatness lay in the high value it had always placed on its character and its survival! To be or not to be a Federalist at that time was a question of betraying or not betraying the nation. The resistance against Confederation organized by the younger generation immediately after the Charlottetown Conference was renewed and strengthened after the Quebec Conference. Public opinion was shaken first by Antoine-Aimé Dorion's vigorous manifesto, then by the cry of alarm set up by the *Union nationale*, a group which included young Conservatives who had broken with their party, such as L.-O. David. Anti-federalists were thus recruited from other sources than the liberal-democratic faction which had already been discredited because of its American leanings and its religious ideas. "We are not unaware," the Bishop of Saint-Hyacinthe wrote, "that there are men of loyalty and goodwill who fear Confederation because some of its details seem to imply the ruin of all Catholic and French influence." At their general assembly in Trois-Rivières in the autumn of 1864, the bishops of Lower Canada allowed Mr. Clerk, the editor of the Catholic paper *True Witness*, to discuss the principles of Confederation, "providing that he showed respect for Ministers."

The agitation of the populace became so great that the Canadian government took fright. Having previously allowed its newspapers to promise some sort of plebiscite on the question of Confederation, it now judged more prudent to abandon this scheme. Better still, it skilfully contrived to avoid the verdict of popular opinion altogether, convinced as it was that the slightest incident or tactical error could compromise all its plans. Macdonald wrote to Leonard Tilley on October 8th, 1866:

> Had we recalled Parliament during the year before your election, it would have been most inconvenient for you and would probably have resulted in your defeat. We would have been pressed by the Opposition to declare whether or not we supported the Quebec resolutions. Had we replied in the affirmative, you would have been defeated since you were not in a position to go before the electorate carrying the burden of these resolutions. Had we replied in the negative, declared the question to be open and the resolutions (Quebec's) subject to modification, Lower Canada would have risen to a man – and then goodbye Confederation.

What magical power was exerted to appease such anxieties and such anger in order to secure the support of Lower Canada for the 'Fathers' of Confederation?

This was the achievement of the political leaders and, above all, of George-Etienne Cartier, whose sway over public opinion is well known. The personality and prestige of the leaders, however, were less influential than the repeated assurances with which they saturated all their speeches. They were extremely careful to give assurances on every important point of anxiety. Amongst these important points were the very foundations of nationality: language and faith. The first terms to be hammered out at the Quebec Conference were too condensed and too vague. Gradually, after long debates motivated by a desire for justice and foresight, more ample and more precise formulas were found. The official language rights were protected by Article 133, which seemed to foresee all eventualities and protect all rights; the education rights of minorities were protected by the highly detailed Article 93.

These guarantees could only be effective, however, if French Canada had an autonomous political framework, avoiding the unitary state so destructive of any particularism. On this point again, Cartier and his colleagues multiplied precautions, demanding firm assurances on the genuinely federal nature of Confederation. The provinces were to be not mere shadows, but true political entities, endowed with wide powers. In Quebec, during the Conference, and later in London, the vote taken on each one of the Articles of the constitution was not the personal vote of the delegates: voting was by province; and, to indicate its ethnic and political duality, Canada had two votes: one for Upper and one for Lower Canada. The preamble to the new charter unequivocally asserted the retention of provincialism: "Considering that the *provinces* of Canada, Nova Scotia and New Brunswick have expressed the desire to contract a federal union ... considering furthermore that such a union would have the effect of developing the prosperity of the *provinces*..." Although in this preamble Quebec was fused with Ontario under the title of 'Canada', it recovered its distinct political entity in Article 5: "Canada will be divided into four Provinces to be called Ontario, Quebec, Nova Scotia and New Brunswick." It would be wrong to tar Cartier with the brush of 'new-nationalism', as it was called in those days, an expression meaning an 'unhyphenated Canadianism' resulting from a fusion rather than a federation of nationalities. From the very beginning the French Canadian statesman, with his realistic turn of mind, had quite rightly disentangled the true from the false, and the possible from the chimerical, in this dream of a 'new nationality'. A Canadian nationality might emerge in the political sense of the word, not in the ethnic sense. "People have objected to our project because of the term 'new nationality' attached to it," observed Cartier; "if we unite we shall form a *political* nationality independent of the national origin and religion of individuals." To make his meaning quite clear, he immediately added:

Some people have expressed their regret that our country should have this diversity of nationalities, and their hope that the diversity would eventually disappear. The fusion of races into a single nationality is a utopian dream, a sheer impossibility.

The French Canadian nationality, master in its own home within the autonomous framework of its province, would also have, according to Cartier, sufficient safeguards at the federal level. Cartier also clearly indicated the only decisive tactic his people could adopt on this more dangerous battlefield (the abandonment of this strategy has perhaps been the partial cause of our defeats):

> When a leader from Lower Canada has sixty-five elected representatives to support him and can count on a majority of both French and English Canadians of Lower Canada, do you not think he could succeed in bringing down the Government if his colleagues objected to its policies? That is our guarantee. At present, if I meet with unreasonable opposition, I have the remedy at hand: simply withdraw and thus provoke the fall of the Government. The situation will be the same in the Federal Government.

True, the speeches of Cartier and his colleagues show little foresight. Some of the declarations made by the Conservative leader or by Langevin and Cauchon would make us smile today if they had not cost us so much. Should we doubt the sincerity of these men? Their illusion and their fault – both remain great – consisted in putting too much faith in the goodwill of their political associates, thus placing the future in jeopardy. When one remembers the stormy history of the last quarter of the century, their optimism surely seems inconceivable.

Their excuse, if they can be excused, was that they never promised anything which had not been authorized by verbal assurances from the leaders of the majority. What could be clearer, for example, than this declaration by John A. Macdonald, who was better qualified than anyone else to express the sentiment of his people at the time of the signing of the federal pact: "The delegates from all provinces have agreed that the use of the French language shall be one of the founding principles of Confederation . . . " And how could one not put faith in these declarations when Lord Carnarvon himself confirmed them in the Imperial Parliament:

> Lower Canada is rightly proud of its customs and ancestral traditions. It is attached to its particular institutions and will enter into union only with the clear understanding that these will be preserved . . . On these conditions only and with these sentiments, Lower Canada now consents to enter into this Confederation.

And further:

The object of Article 93 has been to place all minorities of whatever religion in a position of perfect equality, whether these minorities be *in esse* or *in posse*.

\* \* \*

The speeches of political leaders weighed heavily with French Canadian opinion. But would they have overcome all resistance if they had not been confirmed by more authoritative voices? No one could deny that the fate of the emerging Confederation lay in the hands of the ecclesiastical hierarchy of Lower Canada. The speed with which Cartier sought the approval of the Bishops and the fury of the liberal-democrats at the pastoral letters of 1867 are evidence enough of how seriously the opinion of the Bishops was taken. To stifle the project before it had even got under way, the prelates would not even have had to put their moral influence behind the opposition; their silence would have been enough.

The attitude of the Bishops we must admit, was far more discreet than that of the political leaders. Moreover, prelates in Lower Canada were not as enthusiastic as their colleagues in the Maritime provinces. Basically they were quite worried.

"We understand the hesitations and even the fears of a certain number of our compatriots," commented Mgr. Cooke of Trois-Rivières, "and it is not without strong apprehension that we have recognized the fearful necessity of adopting measures so serious both in themselves and in their consequences." These fears were felt most strongly in Montreal, in the circles surrounding Mgr. Bourget, that great figure of the Canadian hierarchy. When Cartier boasted in Parliament that he had the support of the episcopal authorities, Mr. Truteau, the vicar-general of Montreal, hastened to make the following reservation:

Mr. Cartier is reported to have said in Parliament that the highest authorities of the Church in every diocese of Lower Canada were in favour of Confederation. I do not know what other Bishops may think of the matter; but as for the Bishop of Montreal, I am sure that I can say that he did not wish to give an opinion on the question yet. Before leaving for Rome, he said that he would rather wait before committing himself. As for myself, I feel that the country is in an exceptional position. I am convinced that Mr. Cartier's intentions are excellent, and that he would never wish to do anything prejudicial to the Church. But I must admit that every day I pray God that, if Confederation does happen, the results are not harmful to Lower Canada and that we never have the grief of seeing our happy country persecuted by the Protestant party as is unfortunately the case in Switzerland, where the Protestant districts persecute the Catholic districts.

In Montreal one article of the new constitution in particular led to great anxiety: the legislation on marriage and divorce, which it was proposed to place within the jurisdiction of the Federal Government. Mr. Truteau would have liked to see all Catholic members opposing this unhappy scheme. Why not leave "the right of legislating on divorce to each particular Legislature"? "The Legislature of Lower Canada," continued Mr. Truteau, "which would, of course, be composed primarily of Catholics, would not force upon us the hideous spectacle to be seen wherever divorce is authorized." All the Bishops of Canada were also alarmed about the future educational rights of Catholic minorities. When the Langevin bill, proposed during the session of 1866, seemed to leave out of account the minority of Upper Canada, the religious hierarchy did not feel it had the right to remain silent. In a collective appeal to the Governor-General, Lord Monck, they stated "that, as a matter of justice, the rights and privileges granted to the Protestant minority in Lower Canada should be equally granted to the Catholic minority in Upper Canada." A few days later, to show their support for the popular feeling which had been aroused over this question, the Bishops, on the suggestion of the Bishop of Montreal, decided to make their petition public.

In fact, it was only after the federal constitution had been approved by the Imperial Parliament, and published in the *Official Gazette* of Canada – that is on the eve of the elections of 1867 – that the Bishops of Lower Canada decided to reveal their feelings about the new political state. This 'interference' on the part of the religious authorities was furiously decried by the liberal-democrats. Was this tactic very clever? The most skilful way of reducing the effect of the episcopal letters, from their point of view, might simply have been to show the deliberate understatements in these letters, the extremely faint praise the Bishops gave the project of the 'Fathers' of Confederation. In vain would one search the letters for an explicit judgement on the objective value of the constitution. To recommend the charter of 1867 to their faithful, the Bishops could only find extrinsic reasons such as the necessity of this political form for the material development of the country; the great urgency of the need to find a solution to the threat of annexation to the United States; the presumed wisdom of this project since it was the work of 'the most eminent statesmen of each province'; and, above all, after the approval of the Imperial Parliament and the sanction of Her Majesty, the duty of obedience to the established government. They were careful not to say anything about guarantees for the protection of ethnic and religious rights. If they saw any guarantees it was indirectly, in the extent to which the new political state would preserve

143

Canada from annexation to the United States and put an end to the intolerable regime of the United Canadas. They had very few illusions as they faced the future: the only means of achieving survival seemed to them a moral and political union of French Canadians. One of them, the Bishop of Saint-Hyacinthe, foreseeing the inevitable struggles to come, could find no better way of recommending the acceptance of these struggles than to say that they were beneficial:

> No doubt our position within Confederation which is exceptional because of our faith and customs is rather uncertain and fraught with difficulties. Dearest brethren, we say to you with conviction: it is better for us that it should be so, since for nations as well as for individuals struggles which are met with courage and energy are sure means of increasing our strength and imposing respect for our people.

The attitude of the venerable Bishop of Montreal reveals greater caution. To Cartier, who had sent him a copy of the *North America Bill*, Mgr. Bourget replied by merely acknowledging receipt. When the time came to give guidance to his flock on their conduct in this matter, the Bishop fulfilled his duties by sending out two documents: one, a circular letter to all his clergy dated May 25th, 1867, the other a pastoral letter on July 25th of the same year. In these, we notice a significant detail: unlike similar letters from Trois-Rivières, Saint-Hyacinthe, or Rimouski, which were entitled, for example, 'Pastoral Letter' or 'Episcopal Letter on the Occasion of the New Constitution . . . ' or 'Concerning the Inauguration of a Federal Government . . . ' or 'On the Proclamation of Confederation', his were called: 'A Circular Letter on the Proper Conduct to be Maintained During the Coming Elections' and 'Pastoral Letter calling for Public Prayers on the Occasion of the Coming Elections'. Contrary to other episcopal documents, the circular letter and the pastoral letter from the Bishop of Montreal did not have the slightest appearance of pleading for the new regime. Occasionally, in connection with a discussion of the principles of social morality, there is a simple reminder of the obedience due to 'all legitimately constituted governments'; in his pastoral letter, to support this reminder, the Bishop recalls the history of the Church in Canada on this matter.

This was a deliberate and calculated reserve from which nothing could make the Bishop of Montreal deviate. Despite the attempts of the sensation-mongering liberal-democratic press to make capital of this attitude compared to that of all the other Bishops, and despite the pleas from his colleagues who wanted him to take a more explicit stand, Mgr. Bourget was not to be budged. When Mgr. Larocque wrote to him: "Confronted with such a harmful state of affairs, could Your Grace not make his views known openly and publicly, if only to prevent the weak from being misled by works of malice and bad faith?" the venerable prelate refused categorically: "In all sincerity, I must declare that I think I have said everything in my circular letter and my pastoral letter . . . that I thought I could and should say on Confederation for the guidance and instruction of the clergy and the people."

In summary, the Bishops of Lower Canada asked the faithful to accept the federal regime for reasons of circumstance and of Catholic morality. They could not in all sincerity recommend Confederation with secure confidence. At most, Mgr. Cooke of Trois-Rivières felt he could guarantee that the Fathers of Confederation were acting in good faith: "We know of nothing which would authorize us to think that Confederation is an act of *treason*." The fact remains that they unanimously reminded the faithful of their serious duty of obedience to constituted authority. This teaching, combined with the authority of the political leaders, crushed opposition to the project. Approved in the Parliament of 1865 by a narrow majority of 27 French Canadian members to 22, Confederation, having become a *fait accompli*, was able to obtain the vote of 53 out of 65 [sic] constituencies in the elections of 1867.

\* \* \*

When they recall the prominent role they played in the establishment of Confederation, next July 1st, will French Canadians wonder how their goodwill was rewarded? Will our political associates today remember that we gave our assent to the pact of 1867 because we believed in the security and good faith of our political and religious leaders who, in turn, relied on the good faith of Anglo-Canadians? Surely anyone would admit that, had they foreseen even one tenth of the things that did happen – the persecutions over the school question and the many broken promises – the Bishops of Lower Canada would never have written their pastoral letters in favour of Confederation. We do not deny the delusions, the naive lack of foresight to which our leaders were prone at the time. Still, we do recall that the reason they did not take stronger precautions was that they did not think them necessary when dealing with fellow-citizens!

We must concede, as well, that after a half century of existence the Canadian Confederation remains an anaemic giant carrying within itself numerous seeds of its dissolution. There is a principle of biology which states that an organism begins to deteriorate and decay as soon as the causes which have formed it cease to operate. If the Canadian Confederation is to be more than an artificial state, a mere façade along the American border, it is time to stop repressing the forces and principles which gave rise to this great political body, and which were to have breathed life into it. Whether in the past or the future, every attack on the security of French Canadians in this country diminishes their interest in maintaining Confederation. Our nationality did not enter to die, nor to let itself be gradually undermined; but to lead a life of integrity within Confederation. Now is not the time to rarify or even to narrow the federal spirit. Quite the contrary, it becomes more important than ever to strengthen and disseminate it throughout the whole of Canada, as the contact between the two nationalities increases. The French Canadian nationality is no longer cloistered in the eastern part of the country: overcoming all barriers set against it, it has exported men into every western province and as far as the shores of the Pacific. The present reaction against injustice and administrative pettiness should warn Ottawa that while support for Confederation may once have been cheaply bought, today's generations will never admit that they have sold their right to live and, more, their right to live honourably.

# History as a Guardian of Living Traditions

L. Groulx, "L'histoire, gardienne des traditions vivantes," a speech delivered at the Second French Language Congress, Quebec, June 29, 1937. Directives (Saint-Hyacinthe, Editions Alerte, 1959), pp. 189-223. Reprinted by permission of Mme J. Rémillard.

Your Eminence, [Cardinal Villeneuve] Your Excellency, [Lord Tweedsmuir] Your Worship, [Mayor E. Gregoire] Ladies and Gentlemen: I come before you very late with a subject that is very old. Luckily, nothing at a Conference could be more novel than to discuss the set subject!

History as a guardian of living traditions ... a wonderful title on the whole, and one which I intend to take as an homage to my craft, the great discipline of history, and to historians, those meddlesome craftsmen who, not content with disturbing the dead, must also disturb the living. 'History', the most dangerous product ever engendered by the chemistry of the intellect: a "narcotic, an artificial paradise to intoxicate whole nations, breed false memories, maintain old wounds ... " So say the decadents in their fit of pique and paradox, taking great notice of history for fear that it should later take no notice of them. History would indeed be a silly and futile discipline if all it could do was conjure up lifeless, unreal reflections of a nation. The past is nothing if it is not the truth, if one cannot expect from it, as from a grain in the earth, the potential for life, the germ of a vital thrust towards the future. But this is precisely the question: is all history simply a lie? Is the past really dead, a charnel house of impotent and deceptive shades? Must we refuse to allow it any extension into the present, any influence on life? Only those who have a most childish conception of the dynamic sequence of historical periods could possibly think this way. Without any paradox, I would say boldly that history is the most living of things and that there is nothing so present as the past. Nor even is there any need to write or relate history in order to release its driving force. We carry its potential in our minds, in our eyes, in our veins. The doctrines our fathers preached, the monuments their genius erected, the human features they stamped upon their homeland, in short, the sum of hereditary elements they transmitted – all these act upon us, upon our senses, our intelligence, our emotions; they condition, often without our knowledge, most of our reflexes and our actions. We carry in our very bones the mind and marrow of our forebears. No, a nation cannot separate itself from its past any more than a river can separate itself from its source, or sap from the soil whence it arises. No generation is self-sufficient. It can and does happen that a generation forgets its history, or turns its back upon it; such an act is a betrayal of History. And if we are here today in quest of faith, our hearts heavy with anxiety, is it not because a preceding generation may have lacked faith and forgotten to be anxious?

History, a reconstitution and condensation of the past, thus carries within it an awesome dynamic quality. As long as nothing distorts its teaching or renders it inadequate, then history can act as more even than a rudder or compass in the life of a nation. History not only indicates the goal, it advances, surges towards it through some irresistible inner force. History preserves something essential to any nation: a living tradition. Here again – a weighty word, an august reality about which we must not be confused. For some, tradition is synonymous with minor customs: family customs, parochial or national customs, such as our own New Year's custom of paternal benediction and the distribution of gifts by the child Jesus. Traditions, yes, but flowers or fruit of a deeper and truer tradition, involving the Christian spirit of the family, the Christian patriarchal authority of the father, and linked in turn to the great Catholic tradition of our race. For others, and they are the majority, tradition means simply a rigid, static routine, a sort of archaeological residue, long petrified at the bottom of people's hearts.

Simple etymology would protest such definitions. Tradition means transmission, bestowal. And since it is the transmission of a moral bequest by a living organism in a constant state of evolution, the reality must surely be that this moral bequest, which may well remain the same in its fundamentals, never ceases to be modified from generation to generation, and to be continually enriched with new elements. In other words, tradition means continuity, constant progress, continual enrichment; and therefore there can be no tradition but a living tradition. In the widest sense of the word, does it not mean simply the major characteristics and features of history? Tradition has been aptly defined as 'a nation's constants', its guidelines, its blueprint. The word connotes an intellectual design, an architectural plan by which a nation builds its history, and, faithful to the special impulse of its own nature, lives, creates, evolves, without ever breaking away from its fundamental pattern, remaining in harmony with its past, its ancestors, the very genius of its race.

How can one then overrate the role of tradition? Can one build the life and future of a country without paying the slightest attention to the foundations or the building stones, without even consulting the blueprints of its destiny? Such reckless behaviour is sometimes evinced by statesmen who consider knowledge or commonsense to be mere hindrances; or by a people afflicted with adventuresome or suicidal madness; it is never the hall-mark of true leaders of nations nor of true French, rational people. Is it not obvious, then, that to define the role of tradition is also to define the role of History? Who is capable of drawing out the 'constants', the guidelines, from the tangled profusion of fact? Who is capable of tracing their course in the scenery of the past as clearly as major routes on a touring map? What is the purpose of History? It helps a nation avoid deviations from the proper path, prevents it from building its life, its mores, its education along entirely wrong lines, protects it from hasty, improvised solutions to its economic, social or political problems, saves it from being a mere guinea pig in the hands of politicians, endows these political leaders with consistency of purpose and a capacity for leadership. These are the services we can expect of a country's History, not to mention a few others of similar insignificance!

148

But, you may ask, what are these constants in our French Canadian history? Can you show us the guidelines visible in our past? An easy task: our first constant is so obvious it springs immediately to mind. Our religious tradition, our Catholic faith, you say. Yes, and no. Catholicism has created and animated everything about us; very often it has undertaken the task of healing and restoring our people. In it, we see more than a great tradition. It transcends all our life, it invigorates all our being and, because it has played this supreme role, I hesitate to call it a tradition; it is rather the heart and soul of all our traditions. In any case, I intend to place my discussion strictly on the human and national level, and I say therefore that the first constant of our history has been our agricultural vocation. We are country men, born and bred on the land. All the founders of our country, from Champlain onward, all our governors and intendants, our kings, Richelieu, Colbert – all of them conceived of New France as an agricultural country, a country of farmers. Of course they had other ambitions for the colony, but first and foremost, they wanted to throw down sturdy roots and thus gain a solid footing on the soil of the Laurentian Valley. When Richelieu, echoing Champlain and the early priests, gave the Hundred Associates the task of doing missionary work among the Indians, the great minister insisted also on the support of a settlement of Catholic and French peasantry. In any case it is hard to imagine how the country could have been settled, except by a constant march forward of men of the stamp of Louis Hébert and Robert Giffard, pushing new clearings through the forest, building new farms beside the old, and dotting the land with steeples – almost the work of magicians!

At the same time, just note the almost split personality of these peasants or sons of peasants from Normandy, Perche, Anjou, Poitou, Saintonge, from Picardy or Champagne: as they set up pastoral realities, they dreamt of heroic deeds. Half their sons they gave to the cultivation of the soil, half to adventure. Founded as a missionary post, the colony was drawn by this apostolic mission away from the Laurentian Valley toward the Indian tribes living far to the west, the south, the south-west, and the north. Geography and the fur trade soon added their powerful attraction to this religious ideal. The expansion of the French colony, which had begun with Champlain, the missionaries, the employees and interpreters of the companies, which had gained new momentum and been regulated by Talon and Frontenac, was soon to spread, as you know, across the continent. Its advance was stopped only at the Gulf of Mexico, Hudson's Bay, the base of the Rockies, and the western slopes of the Alleghenies. Never perhaps had such a tiny handful of men encompassed such spaces. Never, in any case, had such a small people shown such vigour in disseminating its civilization and faith over such an extensive territory. Had the mother country seen fit to support them at this point, these Frenchmen would, without a doubt, have conquered and civilized two-thirds of the North American continent – an achievement without any parallel in colonial history.

The constant pattern of our early history thus emerges with great clarity; a strong farming settlement within a small domain; and surrounding this domain, satisfying an extraordinary need for action, for conquest, for missionary work, a vast unbounded territory for adventure, heroism and glory. All around the pastoral, the immense epic. "Whether we like it or not, we are marked by our race," I recently read in a work written by a young French Canadian. Yes, we are most strongly marked by this history, and by the heredity it has bestowed upon us. When I see these Frenchmen, who only yesterday set out to conquer an empire, forced today into the role of servants and labourers, and not even masters of their own Quebec reserve, I understand that our young people rebel against such a fate and swear by their fathers never to accept it!

Then there was 1760. We lost our empire, but we kept the stronghold of our agrarian position. Recoiled into our Laurentian soil, we girded our loins for an effort as moving and audacious as the conquest of America: our French survival. Following the Treaty of Paris, our forefathers took stock of their numbers and saw immediately that they were the most insignificant people on earth and, apparently, the most unstructured. Happily, they were strengthened by their Catholic faith which had taught them not to attach absolute value to material things but to live according to transcending ideals. Their culture, that of seventeenth-century France, had shaped their nature, making it strong and well-balanced. Their own history, on their own land, had marked their spirit with a grandiose vision and an exalting pride. Before the conquest they had relied on the support of their peasantry as they advanced to conquer a continent; now, retrenched behind those same peasant lines, what ambition they could still display! Incorporated into an empire with foreign laws, faith and language, which, at the outcome of the Seven Years' War, had risen to be the first power in Europe, a group of sixty-five thousand impoverished peasants formed this resolution: to remain themselves, to live their own lives, to protect their own flame and carry it high. It was to be a peasant's struggle, the struggle of a stocky, patient athlete, unaffected by moral or physical fatigue, who knows that with both feet planted on firm ground he will eventually win out against his opponent. Look at him: the guidelines of his history are again easy to discern. The only goal he set for himself was this: to escape from the grasp of the conqueror, to free himself a bit more each day, gradually increasing his autonomy and tending with all his might towards the dignity of a French destiny. Please note as well that this goal included the defence of his laws, his mores, his schools, and, above all, the defence of his language. But it included more: it aimed still higher. Its goal was full self-government, full political power: that sum of powers which enables a people to keep its own attributes and national character and to ensure above all an organic life, a complete fulfilment of material and spiritual potential. Wonderful, providential circumstances abetted the efforts of this small and audacious group. 1774 brought civil and religious freedom, 1791 the beginning of political freedom and, theoretically at least, the establishment of the province as a French state. During the fifty years that followed there was a continual struggle to obtain greater political freedom: having gained control of Parliament, we determined to gain control of the Government. Next in this endeavour came two tragic setbacks, the uprising of 1837 and the annexation of our province to Upper Canada in 1841. Not quite a year was to elapse, however, before the situation was remedied: we transformed the unitary state into a federal one and, in 1848, shared political power in a coalition government, the result of a colonial autonomy partly of our making. Finally, in 1867, we flung off the last shackles of 1841: Lower Canada regained its national and political identity; the state of 1791 was reconstituted with, this time, executive as well as legislative powers. That year, we might at last have witnessed the solemn triumph of all the efforts we had made since 1760 to free ourselves and fulfill our own destiny, to acquire the profit and joy of a destiny of our own. What then was lacking? More than ever we needed to keep our guidelines in sight. Why, at that decisive hour, did the authoritative voice of History choose to be silent? Instead of the shortsighted flunkies we were given, why did Providence not send us true leaders, men of sufficiently realistic and sound intellect to grasp the implications of the recent political evolution and above all to see the direction of our future, the only one allowed by our past and its constants? Had we been so fortunate, seventy years ago, we might well have insisted upon and obtained a French state, with policies distinctly French and national, and we would not be here at the end of June, 1937, questioning our fate in an atmosphere of setbacks and defeats. Instead, we would be consolidating our position and continuing along the ascending curve of our history.

# III

Let us now see how costly it can be for a people to deviate from the natural guidelines of its life. But pity the poor historian obliged to sketch such a dismal picture!

Firstly, we lost our agrarian position. I admit that we did retain our old agricultural territory. We even enlarged it in some respect. Still, the fact remains that we are no longer predominantly an agricultural country, a country of farmers. We are now hurtling towards the proletariat and no one knows how to apply the brakes. A disorder resulting from an incredible lack of foresight! This disease is not a trifling one; in the economic and social spheres it is one of the most serious that a people can experience. We have facilitated it by the debasement of our middle class, the very class which most nations regard as their best safeguard. Nor did the trouble occur overnight, as the result of some dire calamity. It spread slowly through our whole organism like a cancer. Its long and silent gestation was followed by a hideous eruption and it has now been gnawing at us for a century. The emigration of our people to the United States was a terrible, interminable hemorrhage caused by the same disease. Prior to 1848, when our lands were administered by a small committee in London, or prior to 1867, when we had only partial control of our policies, we could claim that others were responsible for our miseries. But after we became masters of our own government, not only did we not succeed in halting the evil, we even managed to aggravate it. In former times it was dire necessity that made our people uproot themselves; now, it is mere whim. Yet anyone can see what pariahs our countrymen have become in the pay of inhuman employers and an inhuman financial system; we all feel the harsh economic slavery weighing this province down. These observations, along with our past and our instincts, should indicate that we still retain a liberating power – the land. But, alas – and here the responsibility of our leaders becomes apparent – the farmers think of nothing but leaving that land!

Having lost or compromised our first strategic position, did we at least retain the others? What became of the mystique of our French destiny? I repeat: 1867 could have, and should have, served as the springboard for a renewed attempt to gain greater autonomy and an increasing fulfilment of our French being. However strange and imperfect the federal constitution, and however confused the national ideology of the Fathers of Confederation, nonetheless, 1867 did reconfirm two vital principles in our favour: provincialism and nationality. Political institutions were placed in our hands here in Quebec – incomplete, I admit, and badly defined. Nevertheless, I am convinced that a nation of virile, skilful and, above all, energetic men, could have obtained from these institutions whatever they desired. Such men – they do exist in this very province – would never have been hindered by constitutional texts or obstacles. But such activity required constant reference to the guidelines of our history and retention of a blueprint of our national life. This is elementary foresight, after all, and minimal political sense but were we guided by either? I acknowledge, moreover, that some kind of harmony and co-ordination had to be established between the central government and the provinces, but harmony to my mind does not mean the invariable subordination and sacrifice of one to the other. Did we make such distinctions? Instead of elaborating a frank and loyal provincialism, co-operating with others on every point except the inflexible one of our constitutional stand, we have generally tended to treat provincial matters as narrow and petty and to look to Ottawa rather than Quebec as the place where we could play our most brilliant role. We complain, nowadays, of not exerting any influence in the country as a whole and of occasionally meeting with deep contempt for our people. But what stress have *we* put on our French Canadian characteristics? It is not only in the drawing rooms of our Anglophile, bourgeois families that these characteristics are hard to find. For the majority of our so-called political leaders, the most fashionable and orthodox type of French Canadian is the one shorn of all his peculiarities, divested, like an old penny, of all his markings, squeezed by a procrustean bed – all so that we can elegantly dub him an unhyphenated Canadian. Why not admit it openly: our national policy since 1867 has not been to free ourselves as much as possible, but to bind ourselves more closely each day with no exit and no recourse. Then too, our greatest fear has no longer been to be less French Canadian, but to be too much so – when we have not gone so far as to apologize for being French at all! And now, after eighty years of attempting to efface ourselves, to fade into oblivion, we suddenly notice our eviction from all the federal civil services; some of us are alarmed, with cause, at the increasing incursions of federal power; provincial powers in general and ours in particular are said to be in danger. But history will record that we French Canadians more than any others laid the groundwork for this legislative union.

Was our error any the less at the provincial level? Did 1867 really provide a new and glorious milestone along the road towards our French emancipation? Who would dare make the claim without any cynicism that we are masters in our own province? Who would even claim that we are taking every possible step to gain that mastery? The retreat of our tiny people from its strategic position and, perhaps more than anything else, its state of confusion and internal anarchy on the national question, show us where we are today. Anyone who attempts a simple definition of our national doctrine should be pitied. Country, homeland, patriotism, nation: all words for which we are still seeking definitions in the dictionary. We may well believe in the existence of a homeland, but where would we situate it on a map? As for knowing whether we do or do not constitute a nation, it would be most unwise to put the question to a referendum. And here is another sign among many of the inconsistency and incoherence of our patriotism: the veritable plethora of so-called national flags and banners we fly in this day and age. No people in the world has as many flags as the French Canadians; as a result, no people has so few nor can so often fly someone else's flag. But what am I saying? We, a people? A nation? Come, come. A mere collection of groups.

Have we even managed to retain some of the sources of inspiration which sustained our fathers in their trials and poverty, allowing them to retain their pride? For example, what images, what memories have we retained of our great past, of that great epic created by the conquerors of America? The harsh truth is that our tiny people, so greatly in need of the stimulation it could derive from its historical greatness, knows practically nothing about it. Ask these inheritors of that splendid history to name a single one of the famous explorers of the American hinterland. You would search in vain through our schools, our convents, our colleges, to find a map showing the ancient settlements of French America. And I would plead with you to resist the temptation to ask the average French Canadian or even some of our professional people and politicians for a definition of the constant features of our history and the guiding laws of our life since 1760. Meanwhile, we have our pundits contemptuously reprimanding us for stirring up the past. Leave the dead to bury the dead, they advise. Stop imitating that silly legendary figure who died contemplating his own features in the looking glass of a stream. Unfortunately, as I listen to the echoes and complaints of this Congress, I fear there is quite another form of suicide threatening us at the moment.

I find it painful, as you can well imagine, to continue with this analysis. Once we had lost the memory of our past and our national aspirations, once our minds had been emptied of their inspiring visions of greatness, it was inevitable that we should fall under the spell of the dazzling, glamorous, Anglo-Saxon fortunes we could see displayed beside us. But, instead of maturely confronting the attraction as a spiritual enrichment, we were spell-bound in a most servile, slavish way. This infatuation made of our middle and our labouring classes, – indeed of all of us – a resigned and defeated people, mournful plagiarists. A confirmation of the tragic dilemma which, according to Gonzague de Reynold, faces all small nations and small countries: "For them there can be only two solutions," the great Swiss writer has commented. "Either they must live according to the original character conferred upon them by nature and history, or they inevitably will be drawn into drab servitude as satellites of the greater powers." "Drab servitude ... " How many signs there are warning us of this fatal metamorphosis! An alert and courageous man, Mr. Victor Barbeau, has demonstrated and proved that the French language has already sunk in our estimation to the rank of an inferior language: a capitulation which our country throws in our face. Like unnatural children besmearing their mother's portrait, we have disfigured the majestic features of New France. Quebec is doing its best to erase its own French character. And yet, we try to attract tourists, especially American tourists. Even if we were completely devoid of pride or national awareness, our interest would demand that we make the most of the original character of this province. We don't even have this amount of commonsense. Our psychological deficiencies are revealed once again in this further symptom: unlike all other nations endowed with a minimum of personality, we are impotent to create a synthesis of the various cultures surrounding us. We are unable to discriminate between the various customs and fashions which lie within our grasp. With passive receptivity we accept everything, imitate everything: arts, customs, fads, especially those most abhorrent to our Catholic conscience and our French commonsense.

Do we need a further yardstick to measure the extent of our deprivation? What has become of our ancestors' veritable passion for action, their desire to extend their influence to distant parts of the continent and thus expand the homeland, desires which are characteristic of all people who are morally strong and overflowing with life? This thirst for greatness and this need for an extended influence are not completely extinguished. I can discern signs of them in the extraordinary propensity of our young people for foreign missions. This apostolic surge is an act of faith, no doubt. But make no mistake, it is also a protest against the all too general mediocrity of our lives. In any case, it surely indicates what the old instinct of our ancestors could have accomplished on home ground. When the horrifying emigration of our people to the United States and other parts of Canada occurred, it opened up vast new fields for our activity. We could have followed these brothers whom we could not retain and brought to their exile the comfort of our memories and our fraternal feelings. Such a mission would have been spontaneously undertaken by a strong, or even an aware state. To be quite fair, our clergy and our religious communities, as well as a few patriots and some national societies, did fully understand their duty. But let us be honest and concede that, apart from these few examples, our behaviour towards our dispersed brothers has simply been abominable. Since we were incapable of unity, even in our own province, how could we possibly bring unity to those who had gone away? Only in their gravest hours of peril, after they had repeatedly called for help, did we finally listen to them. At other times, we merely provided them bad examples. We could at least have avoided those actions likely to scandalize our brothers in exile; we could have kept the faith here so that it should also be kept afar; we could have created here, in the heart of New France, a centre of intense life and civilization to shine forth upon the large French family of America. But all this, at least until recent times, has been the very least concern of our people and especially of our leaders. The fact that, at this very moment, French girls and boys in Saskatchewan or Alberta can ask their parents 'what is the province of Quebec,' as they might ask 'what is Greenland or Indo-China', reveals a great deal about the power of our civilization to radiate its light abroad. And so all around us we witness the miseries which result when nations forget their past and stray away from their guidelines: incoherence, disintegration, acceptance of mediocrity and servitude, the impossibility of a collective life, the triumph of every kind of individualism – all signs of ultimate doom. And yet perhaps not. In all this misery, one point of solidarity remains: political parties! At a time when the plague of Marxist class struggle is rightly denounced with such vehemence, I hope my political friends will forgive me if I am so bold as to say that party struggles – with all their stupid hatred and divisions, with the collective hysteria and distortion of conscience which they foment in French Canada – are as destructive for a nation as any class war. In any case, for a tiny people driven to tragic solutions, the substitution of party for country, party for nation, party mystique for national mystique may well mean death; it is certainly insufficient for life.

## IV

Two questions arise. Our whole history seemed to incline us towards pride and faithfulness. What happened? Who is to blame? And, secondly, can we be cured? As for attributing blame, why bother? History is not a court of retribution. I would rather consider the second question, for I am one of those who believe that we can be cured. We have not gathered here to intone a funeral dirge but to prepare a song of joy and triumph.

Nothing could be easier than to indicate the remedies. We have lost our socio-economic base as well as our historical base. The most urgent effort must be to recover them. The former will be restored by the reconstitution and maintenance of our peasantry. The agricultural vocation of our people seems obvious to me, certainly more obvious than being on relief! There has been much talk in recent years about human capital, about how much more valuable it is than other forms of capital. The time is ripe for our leaders to remember that no environment has been better suited to the production of a healthy and strong group of men attached to their family and national traditions than the fertile atmosphere of a rural life. We would remind those who might consider our policies of agriculture and colonization too expensive, that the improvement of our farming communities is the best insurance we could have against social upheaval. In all respects, French Canada's agrarian policy remains its most vital policy. No doubt it would be foolish to neglect a certain industrial predilection in this province. But we should make the attraction to the country as strong as the attraction to the city. The essential for a country is not to possess the largest industries or the largest cities. It is to possess health, which is the result of a balance between economy and society.

The first article of our programme, the foremost rule for all our leaders, could well be the following: to restore the dignity of the soil in the eyes of our rural communities; to place as many French Canadians as possible on every square mile of land; to reconquer all Quebec's land to the last arable mound; and hence to enforce the principle that not an inch of land can belong to the timber merchant, the American landlord, or the parasitical sportsman, before it can belong to the farmer's son.

The second remedy is equally urgent. When a nation is unhappy and disoriented because it has broken with its past, the first thing to be done is to weld it once more to its history. If only we could at last discover that we are French, and determine to remain so! Such a discovery would solve many of our problems, starting with the problem of our education. One thing is certain: our schools must have a national orientation. We cannot afford to be anything other than genuine, energetic Frenchmen. We are a tiny people confronting the American monster: we do not have the option of being French in a soft, dilettante sort of way. We cannot flirt with every passing fad: we have to be French through and through, intransigently, energetically, audaciously – otherwise we shall cease to be. But to make true French people no method has been found other than to raise them in a French way, in French schools, in a French atmosphere, guided by French ideals. This does not

157

mean that we should neglect or scorn other cultures; it simply means that second languages and cultures must not be given priority.

Our national orientation also raises the political question. Let me broach it openly on the assumption that a French priest has as much right to freedom of speech in this country as an English clergyman. The constant in our political and national realms, as I have repeated, and as is sufficiently obvious, has always been a passion for autonomy, a refusal of absorption, a striving – insofar as it was possible and legitimate – towards a truly French destiny. This means that we cannot accept any undue infringement of our authority, even from Ottawa. We are part of Confederation, but only as long as it remains a Federation. We accept co-operation for the common good of the country, but we feel that other provinces should also co-operate with us. And we maintain, furthermore, that we should co-operate only if it is as much to our profit as it is to others. What the older generation thinks of the matter is of little importance. I know what the younger generation thinks, and that is the generation which will count tomorrow. Do not ask them to choose between their French life, their French future, and a mere political regime. They are fully convinced that we did not enter Confederation to lead an impoverished existence but rather to find an enriched national and cultural life; not to be less French, but to be more French. For my part, I cannot see what constitutional texts, what moral or judicial obligations, what supreme reasons of state could possibly make us impose limits on the development of our French culture or our French ambitions. And consequently we refuse to sacrifice ourselves – or to be the only ones sacrificed – to support or strengthen Confederation. The purely supportive role of naive and servile Caryatids groaning under the weight of some shaky superstructure can never fulfill the ambitions of our national life!

Since we are so determined not to tolerate any infringement on our autonomy from Ottawa, it would be rather inconsistent if we imposed any on ourselves in our own province! Our fate is being decided here in Quebec. Here we have the task of fulfilling our destiny. It was for this that, in 1867, we freed ourselves from the clutches of Upper Canada; for this we brought about the establishment of the federal system and insured the political resurrection of French Canada. What conclusion can be drawn from these premises if not that French Canadian policies cannot be optional in this province, or merely opportunistic, but absolutely necessary; not policies of provocation but, for French Canada, natural and legitimate policies. If our history has a profound sense – and it has – our only legitimate and true destiny, the logical conclusion of all our efforts over the past hundred and seventy-seven years to free ourselves and live our own lives, the goal to which the ever ascending line of our history has been tending must be to create here in America that political and spiritual reality which is the most original masterpiece and the triumph of human efforts on this continent: an autonomous, Catholic and French state.

Moreover, I insist that the creation of such a state is vital for us. During the last few days there has been much talk of language, of its defence and renown. But we should be careful not to pay so much attention to language that we minimize the essential question – the entire national question. We must remember that we cannot graft an artificial love of language into the hearts of a tiny people. No love for a maternal tongue will withstand the force of our economic slavery. The essential task is to convince French Canadians that remaining French will not detract from their future prospects – quite the opposite, it will strengthen them. They must learn that only through faithfulness to their origin, history, culture and inborn strength will they be able to create the most favourable climate for developing their human and cultural personality and for acquiring the pride and dignity of a free people. Does the state have the right to neglect such a grave problem of national welfare? Can we expect the conditions I have just been discussing to arise spontaneously, without the intervention of the state and its power of co-ordination? The state has an absolute duty, a sacred role, to foster the material and moral conditions, the harmonious combination of economic, social and intellectual policies which will enable French Canadians, as authentic sons of the land, and as the overwhelming majority of the population of this province, to attain their human and national goals.

Proponents of *bonne entente* with the rest of Canada need have no fears. I do not forget that there are other people living beside us. I only hope that we, the Quebec minority, shall soon learn to look after our own affairs without having to ask permission of our neighbours. I am all in favour of co-operation, my Catholic sentiments in this respect being reinforced by long French tradition. But the kind of co-operation I want to see is a mutual, honest co-operation – not a trap for fools. Nor could I recommend co-operation at any price – that degrading policy of bowing and scraping before the mighty lion – but a co-operation founded on mutual respect and equality of rights. In fact, we have always practised this kind of co-operation, even when it was not reciprocated. We can therefore stop speaking about it as though it were our greatest need. Like free and proud people, we should instead adopt the attitude that we can occasionally even manage without it.

To those of our compatriots who are scandalized at the very mention of a French state, who are less concerned about the fate of their own people than the feelings of the English-speaking minority, I would say: "Please take note of the fact that French Canadians number 2,500,000 in Quebec, nearly five-sixths of the population of this province. Please remember that this country is the land of their fathers, that they have the right to live in it, that policies designed to let them enjoy that right can only upset those who are already upset by their very existence and will to survive." I would also say to them: "We merely claim the freedom to do in our own province what is done in all other provinces, and, indeed, to do it more generously. We have minorities outside Quebec. There are approximately 400,000 French Canadians in Ontario; Acadians make up a third of the population of New Brunswick. Would the advocates of *bonne entente* contend that it is chimerical to speak of fair treatment of minority groups in Canada or that Quebec should take lessons elsewhere in the art of being fair to everyone?"

To our compatriots of the other language and culture, I would make these remarks which I consider neither impertinent nor rash, far less unfair: "We are two nationalities, two cultures, destined to live side by side and to co-operate in the common interests of our province and our country. As English Canadians, you are proud of your origins, your history, your civilization; and, in order to better serve your country, you are determined to develop along the lines of your innate cultural pattern, to be English to the core. That is your right, and you are proud enough to claim it forcefully. I would certainly be the last person to blame you for doing so. On the other hand, we are just as proud of our origins, our past and our culture; and we maintain that our rights are as valid as yours. We too wish to develop along the lines of our innate cultural patterns, to be French to the core, not only for selfish reasons or through racist pride, but in order to contribute, just as you do, spiritual forces to the country. We are convinced, as you are, that this ideal and determination do not constitute a provocation or a challenge of any kind. *Honi soit qui mal y pense!*"

## V

Are we dreaming when we talk of returning to our traditions in order to fulfill our great dream for the future? Immediately a cry arises from our defeatists: "Too late! Your plan is too ambitious, the risks are far too great! How can we withstand the pressure of the entire continent? How can we maintain this little island undermined by erosion and beaten by the waves?" I know very well that the times are perilous and that there is not a moment to lose. When country people see trees displaying the wrong side of their leaves, they know a storm is approaching. We are a tree displaying the wrong side of its leaves. For nations as well as for trees, I know that there is a point beyond which a twisted limb can no longer be made straight. But we are Catholics and Catholicism has remained our guiding light. I have found evidence of God and His Providence throughout our history; They posited the very bases of our history and They habitually instill order and purpose in their works. Our fate is an exalted one, you say? I would answer that a Catholic people, no matter how small, cannot avoid the call to greatness. The obstacles seem fearful? Heroism can be our only state of security. Our faith will maintain us in such a state. Our Catholicism, when we learn to live it fully, will prevent us from dying in the shame of oblivion and capitulation.

But the dreadful depression, you insist. Dreadful indeed, but numerous great examples in today's world teach us that, for many nations, the depression has been the starting point of a vital renewal, a renaissance, followed by a march to glory. And the cycle has revolved with extraordinary rapidity. What was the good fortune, the grace that was given to these people? Men who were true leaders imposed a vision of glory on their country. Immediately these countries rose from their decline, shook off their haunting fascination with death to rediscover the pattern of their destiny and, with it, the passion for life and for renewal. Where did those leaders find such visions of glory? In the depths of their past, in their living traditions. Gonzague de Reynold has written of one of these fortunate nations, Portugal: "Any nation wishing to rise from a long decay must look back beyond that period of decline to the greatest, most glorious and fruitful era of its history. In that era it finds examples and, above all, reasons for hope: 'What I was I can still be'." To restore a discouraged people, sporadic reforms are not enough. What matters, above all, is to inspire it with ideal reasons for life, renew its living traditions, replace it within the profound guidelines of its history. The Italian Duce recently said: "Governing is not merely administering; it is providing a country with high ideals." The Belgian minister of finance similarly commented: "A government must be more than an administrator; it must be a leader, an inspirer." We are not therefore asking anything impossible or superhuman of our leaders when we say to them: "Provide us with a great ideal. Send an electric spark racing through our people, a powerful current of the kind that has not yet been nationalized – a current of moral electricity."

Please don't utter the defeatist reply: "Too late! Our people no longer care!" I shall defend our people with all my heart. Perhaps they have often appeared disappointingly inert but history has taught me that they are usually worthy of their leaders. Moreover, if an entire people is asleep, it must be because it is being lulled into this somnolent state. People who are only half awake themselves are scarcely in a position to blame our nation for its slumber. Too late? Let our leaders spend as much time doing something as they have spent doing nothing; let them pour as many millions, as much organization and propaganda – on the hustings, over the radio, in the newspapers – into a campaign of national revival as they have put into a sixty-year-old campaign to inspire us with the insane passions of politics; let them spend as much time enlightening and unifying us as they spent blinding and dividing us; then, let them speak of the general apathy of the people!

Too late? But, do you not see, do you not hear what is happening? Visions of glory are beginning to stir a rising generation. A new future already shines forth in the eyes of the more intelligent, determined, forward-looking of our youth. That is why I am among those who still have hope. Because there is God, because there is our history, because there is our youth, I still have hope. I share my hope with all our ancestors who never despaired, and with all those of our people who do not despair today; and this hope rises above my own time, above all discouragement. Whether one likes it or not, we *shall* have our French state: we shall have a young, strong, beautiful, radiant home, a spiritual, dynamic centre for the whole of French America. We shall have a country with its French nature stamped upon its visible features. The snobs, the advocates of *bonne entente*, the defeatists, all of them can protest as much as they like, crying: "You are the last generation of French Canadians ... " Along with our entire youth, I reply: "We are the generation of the living. You are the last generation of the dead."

# Doctrinal Groulx

## Our French Canadian and Catholic Youth

L. Groulx, "L'Ame de la jeunesse catholique canadienne-française," an article published in *La Revue de la Jeunesse de Paris* (January 1910) and reproduced in *Le Devoir,* February 12, 1910. Reprinted by permission of Mme J. Rémillard.

If I outline a few of the principal ideas of our young people and analyze some of the prouder feelings beating within their hearts, I believe I shall have defined our French Canadian, Catholic youth.

When on March 13th, 1904, our Catholic youth decided to form an Association, its predominant purpose was to affirm its whole and undivided Catholicism: "The first principle of the Association is absolute submission to the authority and guidance of the Church. Those who are repelled by our Catholic nature are not the elite upon whom we rely ... We believe that Catholicism – not a mitigated Catholicism which merely consists in believing a few truths and performing a few petty rituals, but the True Catholicism established by Christ for the good of mankind – holds the remedy to all the ills of our society and its individuals."

This frank and courageous creed came at a timely moment. However sincere and profound our Christian life, we cannot claim that it was entirely above reproof. The religious peace which had so long prevailed, an eroding liberalism, and the depressing atmosphere of politics, all these had shaken the faith and conscience of a good number of our people. A stranger examining our newspapers, our politics, our financial and commercial life, or our theatre, would not have to be extraordinarily perceptive to notice the falling temperature of our religious life. Our old moral laws were forced into strange compromises. The faith proclaimed so highly and openly in certain circles, was becoming increasingly speculative and traditional rather than being a faith actually lived and practised. In such an atmosphere, the profession of faith made by our youth thus acquired the tone and implications of a *Sursum Corda* and as such, could not pass unnoticed.

This was also the case when the Association defined the social nature of its Catholicism. An integral Catholicism could not disregard social problems. Our youth understood this, and formulated the second article of their creed accordingly. This article, again a most timely one, also seemed something of a novelty in a country where the action of the Church is hardly hampered, where its authority still meets with respect and obedience, but where the state has not perhaps always recognized what a force for progress the Catholic doctrine is, and where Catholics themselves have not always cared to extract the maximum social benefits from their Catholicism. On the closing night of the first Conference in 1904, the public figure chosen as their spokesman by our youth pointed out, in rather sharp terms, this great deficiency in our religious life: "On the whole we are quite ready, I believe, to acknowledge the place of religion in individual affairs; but we do not have the courage to proclaim the necessity of religion in public life, and the sway it should have over social matters."

Could one say more categorically to our younger generation: "Your ideas are well-suited to the times, and your insight into our national soul is profound?" These ideas, in any case, were not new. Nor was it the first time they had been formulated. But it was the first time an organized group had endeavoured to make them part of our French Canadian mentality.

Was their success commensurate with their efforts? Everyone knows what a gap can sometimes exist between a theoretical programme and its practical execution. However, let us take care not to judge the Association's delays too severely, without first looking at the atmosphere in which our French Canadian youth lives, an atmosphere free of battles and therefore lacking the tonic, the stimulating quality of an atmosphere of struggle. Does this mean that religious struggle does not exist in Canada? Not really: but it is sporadic, an underground sort of struggle. It is clear, then, that the young man who wishes to become a militant Catholic must first emancipate himself almost completely from his family atmosphere, from his college education, from what he hears preached to him and especially what he sees exemplified in the public men of his own nationality, from what is, in religious matters, a basic, incurable optimism: the doctrine of individual liberalism. It would therefore be too great a miracle to expect that our Catholic Association could so thoroughly renew the entire soul of the younger generation.

Unlike you Catholics of Europe we do not have that austere tenacity which asks questions and helps solve them by daily public debate. In Canada, there is a tacit agreement that religious problems are not raised, or if they are, one aspect only is discussed. For a long time now we have had no conflicts save a few short skirmishes over the education question, and a few diplomatic moves to resist the encroachments of the state. Hence the state of rather profound somnolence in which we find the great majority of our people, who scarcely stir at the occasional alarm. Hence also our lack of training in religious studies. All this would seem to lead to the conclusion that our young people do not leave college with strong religious convictions, or the firm desire to defend their convictions and perfect them. Our educators are beginning to face the truth in this matter. They are zealously attempting to give a more solid and durable form of religious education. Already this effort has produced results, and the generation now entering life seems to brandish its faith with greater pride than did its predecessors.

The integral Catholicism proposed by the Association (A.C.J.C.) has unquestionably been a prime factor in the new religious orientation we see in young people. One of the first plans of its founders was to engage the young in social action in order to attach their faith to their aspirations and to their passion for devotion. Surely religion would be more attractive to young people if it were not a religion of the boudoir or bedroom, as mediocre as the virtues it encourages, but the conquering Catholic faith, opening the wider horizons of apostolic work.

Apart from a few admirable projects, this social work has not yet, it must be admitted, exactly transformed the face of the country. This delay can no doubt be explained by many reasons, not the least of which is the extreme youth of most of our members. At the present time, the majority of them, or just about, are recruited in our colleges and seminaries. To this must be added the moderate nature of our social struggles, and the lack of adult projects which might provide training and a framework for the efforts of younger people. Then too, we must take into account the great dearth of sociological observation and documentation, as well as the precarious situation of this science which is the most realistic, the least "bookish" in the world. Small wonder then that people have preferred to stay within the serene regions of theory, awaiting action. In any case the waiting period can be both industrious and fertile, since social questions are on the agenda of all the study groups and are studied in depth and with remarkable practical sense. To be convinced of this one need only glance at the social programme of the Association or examine the plan of study and action outlined at the last Conference in Quebec by one of the first founders of the movement, abbé Emile Chartier.

However, we must not demand too much of our young people, whose energies are taken up with another question: the national problem. If you cast an eye over our newspapers and journals – both the thoughtful and the unthoughtful ones – every single one will tell you that we are, in the stereotyped phrase, "at a turning point in our history". The terrible abyss of militarism and English Imperialism into which selfish policies seem to be hurtling us is not the least of our terrors. How much more acutely worrying is the growth by leaps and bounds of a new population in the vast North Western section of Canada, a population alien to our faith, our nationality, our political ideals, and not unduly imbued, as we can already foresee, with respect for our federal pact. If during the last twenty years we have constantly been yielding our rights, what will happen to us, to our official language rights, to our provincial and religious liberties, when instead of being a third of Canada we are no longer but a thirtieth? Since the federal pact of 1867, we have been the equal associates of our Anglo-Saxon partners in Confederation. But it is quite clear that in a British country justice is not enough: pride and strength are also needed to impose respect for our nationality. Strength fails us; and as for pride, alas! How can we claim that our pride has not lost some of its old, superb intransigence? Not one of our statesmen would wish to betray openly the interests of his race, but too many, through political ambition, have preferred withdrawal to confrontation. If only that were all! But this tactic which can be of only passing value, has become a political gospel; perpetual and unilateral concession has been preached to our people as the only means of survival and of peace between the races. The influence of such monstrous theories, coming on top of the most cowardly defections, could only be profound and disastrous: the moral fibre of our nation was incredibly weakened. Political doctrines which would have been despised by the generation preceding us are now serenely accepted in our journals and newspapers. Thus the Canadian Senate was able to neglect the French language in flagrant violation of a custom which has lasted over forty years. And even here, in our French Quebec, the Legislative Council refused to allow our right to deal with our public utility companies in French. This open defiance of an entire province hardly met with more than mild protest.

It is to the Association's great credit that it was the first to display its disgust and revolt at such a scandalous state of affairs. Simultaneously, in matters concerning our national mission and our attitude to Confederation, the Association wished to revert to the traditional position advocated by our statesmen and patriots ever since the conquest: no concessions, no provocations, but the complete enjoyment of our rights, the loyal and precise execution of our treaties and our federal pact, the entire maintenance of our ethnic character, and frank and generous cooperation with other nationalities for the greater good of the country while awaiting the destiny Providence has reserved for the French race in America. This, at least, is the way the attitudes of our youth were defined by the man who was present during the first planning session of the Association and thus knew better than anyone the aims of its founders:

> The first intention of the Association was one of reaction. Reaction to our people's general indifference and apathy in the midst of the undeniable dangers threatening our faith and national life and in the face of even more menacing attacks by our brazen enemies; ... reaction against the daily race for petty interests, caused by both the decline of the public spirit beleaguered by so many conflicting doctrines, and the noticeable weakening of religious and national feeling. The Association also intended a dynamic return to tradition, to the national and religious pride which was formerly a law of our history.

Our history! Henceforth it was given priority in our study circles. In our colleges, the teaching of history was almost entirely renewed. And this new contact with our national tradition, with the magnificent dream of our forefathers, will lead, we hope, to a more comforting future. What is certain is that ever since the foundation of the Association, in spite of our politicians' efforts to enslave the young to their ideals, our younger generation has gone its own way, independent and free, its flags unfurled; "one may not like the flag, but one lets it pass ... "

\* \* \*

Such are the doctrines of our youth in the national, social and religious spheres. It remains to ascertain whether their courage is as strong as their ideal.

One fact which would be sure to strike a Catholic from France or Belgium attending one of our Conferences, is the way in which our young people express their faith and their religious conviction. It is possible that the young French Canadian's faith and piety are no less intense or deeply felt, but when he speaks about them in public he experiences a sort of over-refined modesty, a self-consciousness which involves him in tortuous circumlocution, and a kind of secular terminology. How far he is from that wonderful openness, that frank, clear simplicity your young people show when they so convincingly and movingly speak words such as piety, prayer, grace, communion, the Holy Virgin, Jesus Christ Our Lord. To our young people all this language seems to belong to an inner circle of mysticism and be appropriate only on the lips of a priest.

Where can we find the reasons for such a state of affairs? In the long ferment of secular thought so prevalent throughout our province? In the fact that the young French Canadian, being only a novice to apostolic endeavours, cannot yet plumb the depths of his faith and charity? In the love he bears the Church, which is perhaps a love of the intellect rather than of the heart? These may be partial answers: but the main reason lies elsewhere, beyond our control! In Canada the Church does not yet appear surrounded with the fascinating halo acquired through persecution or open combat. Our young Catholics lack the experience of fighting for their faith, of suffering for it. Only sacrifices in the service of a great cause can really extend and deepen the soul. If our young people do not have within their soul that exquisite flowering of idealism and generosity the young have in France or Belgium, it is because, unlike the latter, they have not been exposed to the purifying fire of battle and suffering.

It would nevertheless be rash to conclude that their work does not inspire them with the highest form of devotion. There is no beauty in the world more appealing than that of a young apostle, and we must say that our college students do indeed radiate this type of beauty. In the influence they exert on their companions, in the orientation of all their efforts – their conduct, their writings, their religious practices – towards a higher goal, in their growing awareness of the impact which their life has upon the moral life of the community, in all these ways they develop within themselves the prime virtues of any apostle: a social consciousness and the zeal for souls.

If to all this one adds the strongest, most pious, most ardent patriotism which has ever beat within the heart of the young, what can we not expect of them? The most visible characteristic of our French Canadian, Catholic youth is the fact that nothing is dearer to its heart than national sentiment. It may well be the case that for all French people in America the question of language is intimately linked to the question of faith. It may also be that the peril of the present hour threatens our national more than our religious sphere, since we detect other Catholic groups among the enemies massed against us. Let us skim over such complex and delicate problems without seeking to explore them too deeply. The fact remains that our patriotism is of such a pure, ethereal essence, its aims are so wide and so clearly linked with matters of faith that our youth can rightly rely upon this patriotism to promote a more perfect flowering of their Canadian soul and their religious conviction:

the chivalric ideal of nationalism will lead us to the devotion of apostles. Another fact remains: there are very few phenomena anywhere in the world at the present time which are as beautiful and moving as the phenomenon of this young French nation, hemmed round with millions of strangers, fighting for its survival against all historical odds, and nevertheless taking a firm oath not to die – not for profit or damnation but to keep the taper of its faith and its ideals burning brightly at the summit of the New World. It is not surprising therefore that such a cause should attract the ardent allegiance of our twenty-year-old patriots and not surprising either that they should elevate their cult of language and nationality into a religion.

What future can be foreseen for our youth? The future can belong to the young, on two conditions; they must intensify the quality of their life, and broaden their horizons. Already we can see that they are preoccupied with the quality of their lives, for closer attention is now being given to the personal formation of the Association's members. The series of retreats the Association had the honour of inaugurating in Canada will do much to help in this matter. For the same reason it will need to perfect its work methods and its study programmes in which order, logical progression, and synthesizing views are often sadly lacking, although what is perhaps lacking above all in these studies is greater contact with reality. In guarding against the perils of the sort of activity which is too external and too disorganized, it has perhaps fallen into the other extreme of neglecting action altogether – as if it were not an essential factor in the formation of apostles, or as if there were, over and above actual deeds, any other method of acquiring a true and clear vision of guiding and coordinating studies, and adjusting brilliant and generous theories through the application of sound common sense.

Let us admit it quite honestly: the blame does not entirely rest with our youth. In these study groups the problem was not that directors needed young people, but that young people needed directors. Many priests have not yet understood the necessity of this work, nor indeed have they perceived its beauty. However, it is only just beginning, and has at most reached the stage of building and consolidating.

This no doubt also accounts for the fact that, outside our colleges, it has made its way into a very small number of circles. It has not penetrated into the rural areas to any great extent. What a superb contribution we would have made to the realization of our national dream, if we could give this purest, most generous and most robust section of the population a more lively awareness of our nation's mission, its duties, and its resources! We would thus have channelled our freshest and richest energies into a great concerted effort.

The day it succeeds in doing this, the Catholic Association of French-Canadian Youth (A.C.J.C.) will become a major force in our province. And then whatever happens, even if it is extinguished like the rays of the setting sun, its work will have been beautiful, powerful and good. It will have provided an intoxicating ideal for several generation of young men. By inspiring them to devotion and to the fulfilment of their duties, it will have extended the reign of Christ on our French Canadian soil, and by the same token added to the "Cornelian capital" of the French race.

# The Clergy and Social Action

L. Groulx, letter to Father J.-P. Archambault, published in *L'Action française* 2 (February 1918), pp. 86-88. Reprinted by permission of Mme J. Rémillard.

My Dear Father,

I will not congratulate you on your latest brochure, *The Clergy and Social Action*. I will rather thank you for it, since it renders us such a courageous service. You remind us of timely truths, and do so briefly, without fuss, or vain erudition, but with that clarity of exposition so characteristic of your works. Your works even deserve to be reread – and that is surely, in our country, a great honour!

We must thank you for having disposed of so many pretexts for inaction. Although we are free from certain social problems in our province, social questions, you seem to say, are always with us. Always, everywhere, Catholics have the duty of proving the beneficence of their faith; and I am not aware that apathy or improvidence are Catholic virtues. Alas! Why must History so often show the sons of the Church marking time, always starting too late? Such a mistake would be doubly unpardonable in Canada, on the part of a young people with the whole of history as a teacher, a people which does not have to invent doctrines or activities but merely adapt to a concrete situation those already justified by experience.

Dear Father, you intend your brochure for the clergy; I would willingly see it addressed also to all young seminarians: they cannot afford to neglect the realities of the present or the near future, and they have the duty of adapting their life to the requirements of their country and their time. These young people need to learn that the priest must impose respect for himself not merely by the supernatural dignity of his character, but also by his energetic work and great devotion. They must be priests of the Universal Church, but they must also be priests of their province and their nationality. The Church does not exclude such particular concerns. On the contrary, it wishes the labourer to adapt himself to his work, his environment, to the particular souls which are in his care. Our young seminarians must not therefore detach themselves from the affairs of their country, from its needs, from the undertakings which will soon solicit their devotion. In their spare time, they should supplement the work of their teachers, who cannot do everything. Why prevent them from occasionally gazing through the window at the ripening harvests to study the field of their future endeavours?

You very properly emphasize that now is the time for precise duties, for action, for an end to delay. There are methods and attitudes which may have been appropriate yesterday, but will be worthless tomorrow. It would be sheer folly, for example, to try to stem the tide of certain working class movements with mere doctrines, without adding the benefits of Christian deeds. No, let us beware of the illusion that we can indefinitely make poor people choose between their faith and their material interests. If, through irreparable mistakes, Catholicism showed itself incapable of furnishing the solutions so urgently needed, there is no force on earth which would prevent the popular mass of the people from seeking those solutions elsewhere.

Perhaps, also, the young people in seminaries could be reminded that priests are held in great honour in this country; and that honour and privilege must correspond to indisputable merit and be justified by real usefulness. More than other people we must be careful not to appear indifferent to the "unmerited misfortunes" of the poor, and interested only in protecting our stipends.

The Canadian Church in the past has been able to adjust itself very well indeed to the needs of the people. And it is our firm hope, our certainty, that it will not shirk the undertakings of the future.

I therefore thank you for your brochure, Father, as I would thank you for a good deed. You are not simply engaged in Catholic action, but in the best kind of French action. The social work of our clergy could contribute much to the coordination of energies which we were discussing recently. Would it not be futile to be continuously losing ground on the social level while trying to achieve the awakening of our French consciousness? Therein lies, I am afraid, the great peril for the future: that the greatest crises in our national life coincide with a decline of religious thought and with an increase in distressing social problems; and that we remain powerless in the face of these superhuman tasks.

With cordial wishes,

Lionel Groulx, priest.

# The Economic Problem

L. Groulx, "Le problème économique,"*L'Action française* 4 (December 1920), pp. 558-565. Reprinted by permission of Mme J. Rémillard.

Those who have read Georges Valois's *L'Economie nouvelle* will remember the economist's assertion that doctrine played a major role in the reconstruction of France. "At the beginning of everything is the Word," he writes. "Events take the direction imposed upon them by the spirit ... If you wish to reconstruct or restore a nation, you must call upon the forces of the spirit."

The economist merely reminds us of a principle of basic wisdom. The spirit must always enlighten the will; knowledge must precede and guide action. No one should be more aware of this than our people, whose collective action has so long been directed by false leaders and spent in anarchical confusion without any definite goal in sight, without any over-all coordination.

There are many of us who consider that our old mistakes have lasted long enough and must not be repeated, particularly when the shocks we receive bring about unexpected transformations in our life. To come more directly to the point: what are we to do in the unknown situation suddenly thrust upon our nation by the economic problem? Time-honoured wisdom warns us that a young nation must beware of risky adventure; it must progress with certainty, never wasting any of its forces, or a single hour of its life. François-Xavier Garneau solemnly issued this warning at the end of his History: "Great nations are in a position to experiment with new theories ... but for us a part of our strength must come from our traditions." Alas, the lessons of history are such as to make us very cautious: wealth and opulence have almost invariably introduced a fatal germ into a nation's life. How could our Latin idealism not be fearful of the future, when every resource of the surrounding civilization is deployed to make us worship material power? Do we not daily witness the sad spectacle of so many of our compatriots whose acquisition of fortune has been accompanied by a decline in family life and a total or partial rejection of French and Catholic ideals?

And yet we cannot conceal the pressing fact: an economic war is being waged all around the world, a war without reprieve or armistice. It is being waged here among us, and against us. Whenever a part of our patrimony is lost; whenever it is badly administered so that it produces less than it could; whenever Quebec resources are productive for others instead of for us; whenever our capital and savings are drained away to foreigners; whenever we or one of our institutions succumb under the pressure of enemy competition: a battle is lost. This economic war is becoming more relentless, more brutal than ever in our province. "It could be claimed," the geographer Reclus once wrote, "that the development of humanity is written in advance in large characters on the plateaus, the valleys and the shorelines of our continents." These large characters are not usually overlooked by the great entrepreneurs of finance. Our province has far too much wealth not to attract the attention of the greedy. The problem is no longer whether resources will be exploited at all, but whether they will be exploited by us and for us, or by foreigners against us. We no longer have a choice: war has been declared, we have already lost ground and must therefore defend ourselves against the terrible, unbridled power of gold uncontrolled by principle or authority. We must choose either to seize mastery once again in our own home, or resign ourselves to be a nation of serfs forever.

Faced with this situation, is there anyone who would not immediately recognize the need for a general doctrine, or at least some guidelines to direct the efforts of our people and formulate a strategy for liberation? Is such an initiative not urgently needed? Do we not need above all to liberate our minds from false and dangerous ideologies? Provincialism is decried in Quebec and yet everywhere else in the country the material aspects of Confederation are discussed in terms of sectional and group interests. Our people keep repeating that business has nothing to do with patriotism, while the patriotism of business is being used as a weapon against us on every economic battlefield. To what extent are our leaders free of the errors of liberal economics and fatal *laissez-faire* theories? Too often they act as if some parts of our human activity could be detached from the sovereign rules of moral order, or as if the state did not have positive obligations in the economic sphere.

The special gravity of the situation has prompted *L'Action française* to take the initiative we are disclosing today. We have appealed to some of our friends who are specialists in economic matters, asking them to draw up a blueprint of action and defense: not a general, abstract plan, but a concrete, realistic one, resting on wide and sound doctrines designed to benefit more than just a few emperors of high finance, and based on our own way of life, our geographical situation, our ethnic heredity, and on the superior aspirations of our nationality. . . .

Our starting-point has been the assumption that French Canadians must at very least be masters within their own province. Unless they wish to be a subordinate nationality forever, or to give up territorial ownership, they must not allow others to administer their land and its wealth. We claim that the rights of conquest do not extend to the economic sphere, and that on this land which has belonged to their forefathers for three hundred years, French Canadians at least retain the rights and privileges of seniority. Consequently, Quebec's territory cannot be considered vacant territory to be auctioned away: it is a French territory which must be productive for French people. Does this mean that we must close the frontier and reject all foreign capital? No. But we must accept it as an aid, not as an instrument of disorder and domination. No motive or doctrine could possibly justify allowing this capital to acquire such a preponderant power that it gains absolute control over our economic and political life. Even if its influence does not extend quite so far, it would be naive to expect that foreign capitalists who have no roots in this province, who have no affinity with our institutions and our ideals, will not yield to the temptation of working for their own ends and individual ambitions, without worrying about the general good of a people they view merely as cheap labour, to be exploited. Surely, it was not merely to enrich other people that we kept the framework of our social institutions intact, that our ancestors passed on to us their admirable heritage of virtues and that our workers and their organizations offer the highest guarantees of morality and stability!

Our contributors were, however, asked to keep in mind interests more important than strictly national ones. As we have always maintained, a programme of economic action is closely linked to problems of a moral order. Economic activity is not an absolute; it should not absorb all a nation's energies, nor take priority in its thinking. A programme of this kind, if it is to be beneficial, healthy and realistic, must be a balanced one taking account of the relative importance of various activities. In this journal we have too often stressed the need for establishing priorities to forget the principle now, when it matters more than ever. What would be the point of conquering the economic struggle simply to find ourselves conquered by wealth? That is why one of the first articles in our inquiry, written by Mr. Antonio Perrault, will demonstrate that our economic efforts must be subordinated to intellectual and moral ends. This doctrinal theme will reappear throughout the other studies like a *leitmotif*, a guiding principle.

God preserve us from subordinating the spiritual to the material, thus deviating from our Latin pattern! It is a well known fact that we do not agree with those who consider progress and the Anglicizing of our education two sides of the same coin. Our contributors make it clear that they will advocate pride in our nation, confidence in our people, and the undertaking of successful efforts based on our essential qualities. Mr. Henri Laureys particularly intends to argue this case, in a justification of our higher commercial education which has remained so essentially French, thus constituting in recent years the best possible act of faith in the adequacy of our ethnic genius.

Our friends need have no fears: we wish to use our material wealth only as a foundation for intellectual and moral superiority. Some people may contend that a nation which aspires to the highest forms of life must provide itself with a certain basic material welfare; but how then can one prevent this material side from dominating?

Here indeed is the crux of the problem. To start with, however, please note that *L'Action française* is not launching a campaign to amass enormous fortunes, or achieve opulence. This is made sufficiently clear from our list of topics. Our appeal is for an organized collective effort in which everyone fulfills his duty at his own post; we invite all elements of society to collaborate in an effort to bring about the triumph of our communal independence and our individual welfare.

Certainly, publications must continue to provide directives. Our people needs direction at this point in its evolution as it did at every turning point in its past: it will always need guidance in the organization of its life. It will always be necessary to show a French and Catholic nation a "destiny higher than food, drink, hygiene, heating, mechanics, all the mediocre ambitions within which our democracy would imprison man's horizons," as Robert Vallery-Radot recently wrote. We must never cease believing and repeating that civilization expresses itself primarily in intellectual achievements, in pure and serious behaviour, in a blending of justice and social charity, in an acknowledged supremacy of superior goals. We must never cease proclaiming that a nation wastes its effort and its existence if it deviates from its vocation, from the life destined for it by Divine Providence. Such a premise should not be considered impractical by the architects of our material future. The author of *L'Economie nouvelle* would say to them: "Experience reveals that men and nations do not work for the prosperity of their country unless they are inspired by a vision of the future, which gives their action a further goal beyond the one of mere prosperity ... Men and nations desire an effort which lifts them above themselves; they want to believe that the action in which they are engaged is part of a larger movement towards universal order."

# Our Political Future

L. Groulx, "Notre avenir politique," *L'Action française* 7 (January 1922), pp. 4-25. Reprinted by permission of Mme J. Rémillard.

Twenty-two years ago now, Mr. Henri Bourassa, speculating on the enigma of our political future, uttered the following serious words:

> Contradictory influences – British imperialism and American imperialism – will pull us in opposite directions. Our country will be profoundly affected by these divergent strains. ... Can we develop enough internal strength to maintain an equilibrium and to conserve, for at least another century, the *status quo*? Or will we be torn from our present mooring and confronted with a new destiny? The answer lies only with Him who providentially controls the mysterious movement and causes of all human events. But whatever the future may have in store for French Canada, we have a duty to ourselves and to our nationality: the tolling bell must not surprise us; we must be prepared for anything.

Hasn't the time come to preach the duty of preparation even more insistently? In spite of the problems which both colonialism and federalism have caused us, not one of us advocates a rupture of the *status quo*. But perceptive individuals are not blind. The *status quo* is about to be broken, and without our help. This should give us cause for concern.

One thing is obvious: the circumstances of our political future can never be the same as those of the past. The most serious commentators all warn us: the world's centre of gravity is shifting. Without necessarily acknowledging that Europe is about to become "what it really is . . . a tiny excrescence of the Asiatic continent," it is nonetheless fairly obvious that world-wide changes are in the offing, to the detriment of Europe. Events like the Washington conference which forced European nations to consider the Pacific as a new Mediterranean are only a sign of the contemporary revolution. Only our colonial mentality allows us to look on, unmoved, at the vast pan-American movement which has developed since 1914. With our barely noticing, there was, for instance, a pan-American financial conference in Washington in 1915, a pan-American congress in Buenos Aires in 1916, a congress of the pan-American Federation of Labour in Baltimore in the same year, a Latin-American commercial exposition in New York in 1917 and in San Antonio (Texas) in 1918, a pan-American commercial congress and another financial one in 1919 and in 1920 in Washington. During the same time, a proposal suggested the creation of an American merchant marine to replace the European fleet in inter-American trade. Now under-sea cables are to join the two parts of the continent; telegraphic communications are to be co-ordinated; a great pan-American railway is to join New York and Buenos Aires. In brief, an economic and moral consortium is in preparation; a continental solidarity is emerging which could well work to our disadvantage. And yet Canada, a country at least as important as Argentina, will not even have played the role of a domestic in all these deliberations.

An even more astonishing revolution is taking place. While America has been busy becoming a major power, pushing the centre of human activity from the Atlantic to the Pacific, she has at the same time (thanks to her enormous material superiority stemming from the war) turned towards the old continent. She has reversed the old tide of influence from East to West. She has taken over the commerce which once enriched the ports of Europe; armed with merchandise, capital, battalions of businessmen and engineers, she has led an assault of exploitation on the old world. As a result, economists now sound the sorry note: "Europe, the mother of so many colonies, has become an American colony . . . all the wealth of Europe totters."

This vast revolution, this displacement of influence poses

many serious questions for our country. When the very foundation of the world is changing, how can our political life remain the same? What course should we follow: attach our destiny to the American continent or continue to uphold the exhausted giant? For, without a doubt, a powerful nation is staggering. Wasn't it only yesterday that the British Prime Minister, faced with the problems of Ireland and those of the Washington conference, cried in alarm: "We are at a turning point in the history of our splendid country." The inevitable freedom of Ireland is not the only blow to the Empire. Only a grant of gradual freedom can solve the problems of Egypt and of India, ending thereby the subordination of their interests to those of Great Britain. At the same time, London has had to abdicate her financial position to New York. And the sudden ascendancy of the Pacific, the shifting of trade routes, the substitution of the Panama for the Suez in Far Eastern trade, the strong competition from American and Japanese investors in the Dutch East Indies, in South Africa and in Australasia are all undermining the age-old supremacy of the British Isles.

Specialists in international politics all come to the same conclusion. Mr. Paul le Faivre declared quite bluntly that the England of Victoria, even of Edward VII is dead; no longer was it a majestic Empire, isolated but invulnerable, but rather an England on the brink of ruin. For others, it is the Pacific question which, pregnant with future struggles that will decide the mastery of the seas and the future of peoples and races, really threatens the cluster of Dominions around the mother country. Another specialist in international affairs, Mr. René Pinon of the *Revue des Deux-Mondes*, is convinced that the Japanese-American conflict can only lead to war. Such a war would undermine the entire political pattern of the Pacific; it would sap the moral cohesion, perhaps even the legal unity of the British Empire. And, continues Mr. Pinon, wouldn't the United States profit from the predictable divergencies within the Empire to establish herself as head of an Anglo-Saxon consortium, at least in the Pacific? Such an evolution may appear somewhat far-fetched. But would such an undertaking really contradict any of the traditions of American foreign policy? After all, a country which once used British imperialism to rid itself of French imperialism and subsequently French imperialism against English imperialism, would surely find it quite natural to make use of some of the remnants of the latter imperialism to establish its own hegemony in the Pacific and on the continent. And this is where our problem re-emerges. Does the *status quo* within the Empire really guarantee us a lasting and secure future? Stated bluntly, is British imperialism really anything more than an increasingly artificial organization of peoples, an outdated political formula, powerless in the face of reality?

Even more serious perhaps is the fact that the internal situation of Canada appears to us to be just as shaky. How many divergent forces tear at the Canadian Confederation! In the economic realm, the west noisily proclaims the principles of free trade while the east rivets its wealth to protectionist theories. The recent federal elections [Dec. 1921] have blatantly revealed this formidable antagonism. Racial rivalries, too, in spite of what one may hear, have lost none of their force. We are only just emerging from a period of hideous outbursts of hatred. True, calm does reign in the country now. But how many people really believe in the durability of the truce? Who would seriously contend that the present peace stems from fraternal sympathy between the Canadian races or from the majority's acquiescence in the pact of 1867? More likely the lull results from a realistic analysis of political and commercial interests, from a healthy fear inspired by the strength of Quebec. What is certain is that, in spite of the fleeting calm, the attitude of French Canadians towards the federal power and the Anglo-Saxon majority remains vigilant and uneasy. For the last twenty years, the French language has faced persistent haggling and niggardliness in all the federal services; surely this has constituted the most disloyal application of the federal pact. And in spite of all the expressions of good-will, we have yet to note any change for the better. In most of the provinces where English-speaking people are in a majority, the state has conformed to the pattern of all federations: it has used all means, including that of arbitrary force, in its penchant for uniformity. And arbitrary force has never been known for its generosity! The two races not only disagree on the letter and the spirit of the constitution of 1867, but also on the nature of Imperial relations. English Canadians are almost unanimously imperialists; French Canadians are adamant autonomists. And while this division reigns supreme in eastern Canada, there are other centrifugal forces at work. Geography alone plays havoc with the country. No doubt, "natural frontiers" no longer hold a mystical power over the minds of contemporary economists and politicians; there is scarcely a mountain or a river which bars the way to military or economic advances. In fact, all barriers may disappear with the advent of the airplane. Nonetheless, any state surely is in grave danger if it contains great stretches of unpopulated land. That northern desert created by the enormous gash of the Great Lakes marks an irreparable breach in Confederation. As if natural causes were not enough, the Federal Government has blindly allowed the most dangerous element to Canadian unity – Americans – to settle in the west. For many years prior to the war, as many as 40% of the immigrants who poured into the west came from the States. Given the racial and geographic differences, given the distinctive ways of life, no wonder Canada has developed two peoples, two societies, divided by the land and the ideal thereof.

Should we be surprised then if few people believe in the durability of the Canadian Confederation? Admittedly there are some historians and geographers who contend that federalism is the wave of the future. States of the future, they argue, will be more economically than politically oriented; in response to commercial and military needs, much larger groupings of people will emerge. But these same experts see no future in the cribbed colonial federalisms of America and Australasia. If, indeed, economics is to be the key to the state and hence undoubtedly to its borders, how can one really see anything lasting in these arbitrary formations? The engineer measured straight lines; he rarely took account of economics or geography. Ultimately such an arbitrary pigeon-holing of a country has to disappear. Already our own Edmond de Nevers in *L'Ame américaine* predicted a massive upheaval in the United States, with the survival of ethnic groups as the outcome. More recent observers agree with de Nevers, offering proof thereby that more than economics will enter into the new states of the future. Paul Bourget, for example, wrote in *Outre-mer* that the social problem in the United States was actually a problem of nationalities and that conflict among them was inevitable. Then, too, Mr. Emile Boutmy, in his *Eléments d'une psychologie du peuple américain*, stressed the seriousness of the Black problem in the southern states; he pointed out that many ethnic groups, such as the Irish, the German, the Swedish, still cling to their native land. Finally the German paper *Germania*, receiving its inspiration from Chancellor Wirth's party, proclaimed that German-Americans would soon demand self-determination. Then, continued the newspaper, all the world would see that 30% of the population of Wisconsin is German, 25% of the population of New York, Illinois, Iowa, and Missouri is also German. A political nation, reuniting all these German elements, will be the result.

There have been predictions in our country too, and especially in our province, of the break-up of Confederation. That such sentiments should appear in Quebec surely only increases their import. For what better premonition of rupture could there be than profound discord within a country? And who could be more disabused of their faith in the federal pact than Quebeckers? Let me quote just the latest of these predictions. The speaker was none other than Mr. Alexandre Taschereau, Prime Minister of Quebec, who pointed out to the congress of the *Fédération nationale Saint-Jean-Baptiste* last April 17 [1921] the seriousness of the present situation. "We have come to a fork in the road: the *status quo* or a break-up of Confederation; annexation to the United States or independence." Mr. Taschereau disclaimed any intention of rocking the boat; he dismissed both imperialism and annexation as unacceptable; he rather liked the idea of Canadian independence. And while he was very guarded in his views on the federal pact, he could not hide the warning contained in his remarks: "A vast transformation of the present system may yet occur when the eastern provinces begin to believe that the west is demanding just too much. Although I do not intend to talk politics, surely one cannot deny that the railway policy constitutes the most serious problem in Canada today. Nationalization of many of our railroads may well have saved the western provinces from bankruptcy, but it has also put an extremely heavy burden on the eastern provinces. Many people are wondering whether this policy may not presage a great breach of the federal pact."

There, then, is the almost certain conclusion to any analysis of contemporary geographic and political realities. A great many people are aware of it. But shouldn't we demand of those who have looked into the future some indication of what will replace the present system? Are we so lacking in intellectual vigour that we will submit to any and all changes, and entrust our future to our age-old lackadaisical empiricism?

We, of *L'Action française*, are determined to do our duty. We intend to warn our compatriots in Quebec before it is too late: with the crumbling of the present system, with the disintegration of Confederation, let us put an end to our old habits. We cannot continue our confined existence. Quebec must not abdicate her role in any future political organization of eastern Canada. For her there is no more serious problem. She must face every exigency, be it ever so probable. Since when did any people attach its future to a perhaps? And when a particular future appears inevitable, shouldn't one be prepared? We are convinced that, be it ever so strong, neither economic nor geographic determinism is the ruling force in history; human foresight and will are rather the prime movers. There is nothing passive or fatalistic about a people. As free beings, they create rather than accept their destiny. And it is as free beings that they are expected to collaborate with Providential designs. As moral beings, therefore, they must follow God's intentions; they must achieve a temporal destiny, an historical vocation through which they can attune their activities with those of God. What, besides, is politics except the art of anticipating and directing events instead of following them? And if the rupture of the federal state does indeed depend upon a series of uncontrollable events, then surely the organization of eastern Canada is in our hands, with, of course, the aid of God.

What concrete form will this new Canada take? Let me state a few premises. Anyone who is not blind will admit a connection between what one might term internal and external providence, between the inner core of a moral being (sign of a particular vocation) and the external circumstances in which he acts. Given this principle, then the very position of our nationality, the enormous domain which we occupy, stretching from beyond the Saguenay to beyond the Ottawa, is an indice of our special destiny. The French Canadians are not nomads, settling this vast region by chance. Rather they have kept and cultivated this land for three hundred years. By free choice and in accord with economic determinism and our spiritual affinities, we are rooted in this, our native land. It must be said that our territory, the ultimate condition for the existence of any state, does have some arbitrary, artificial contours; but we counteract them with the cohesion of our people. History as much as geography has moulded us. For on this land there lives a people of French nationality, one of the most homogeneous peoples on earth. Any perceptive person recognizes therein a healthy originality. Besides, this people has proved its moral and ethnic strength by achieving what even foreigners call "the miracle of survival." Then too, this people professes the Catholic faith and even exports its religious vitality to all the other provinces of Canada, to many parts of the United States and into the missionary fields of Africa and Asia. Such a people, maintaining its traditions and occupying a country larger than many European states, may indeed one day constitute the only Catholic people in America north of the Mexican border. Through these facts one can discern a future plan, sketched in all likelihood by Providence. Doesn't our future, therefore, already appear brighter?

One can bring even more precision to these initial postulates. If in fact there is room for a Catholic and French state in North America, if indeed the supernatural vocation of such a state designates a particular, superior role, then surely certain rigorous conditions must be met. The first of these conditions is that the French Canadian people maintain its special soul, the soul which forms apostolic aptitudes, which incarnates civilization. We must, in other words, avoid any contact, any constraint which could kill or wound this soul. We must use all our strength to achieve the political and moral conditions necessary for the survival and the flowering of our particular personality, our special characteristics. But, once again, where can we find these conditions except in a political formulation towards which every nationality desirous of controlling its own existence is progressing? For a people, just as for an individual, being is more than simply existing. To be is to have total integrity, to control all one's faculties, to expand one's moral fibre. "For a people," wrote Paul Bourget, "being is more than breathing, eating and drinking. One only truly is when one is totally independent, thinking by himself, making his way by himself, formulating his own thoughts, in a word, completely free."

Should we pursue this analysis even further? Is it time to conclude? Let us rather continue to the very end. Let us penetrate the ancient dreams of our ancestors to see if they don't have some lessons for us. What answer can we evoke from our history? Ever since that far-away time when we became conscious of our ethnic identity, our native land and our nationality, the idea of French independence has never ceased to haunt the spirit of our race. At the time of the conquest, our forefathers had to choose their allegiance; they were so few and so poor that one dare not accuse them of abdicating. And yet, as if by instinct, they followed the dictates of their blood and survived. So much so that right up to the American revolution and the arrival of the Loyalists, which revived the old hopes of British domination, the governors themselves recognized our future as a French entity. One can only surmise, in the following years, the worry and annoyance in the minds of administrators evoked by the contemporary expression "Canadian nation." Then came the rebellion. For the patriots, the old dream suddenly took concrete form in Robert Nelson's project for a republic. Another document, more depressing but equally revealing, attests to the persistence of the dream. In that deplorable article in *Le Canadien* in 1839 when Etienne Parent recommended national resignation, he nonetheless couldn't help evoking the old dream: "There were some, and I was among them, who believed that French Canadians, with the assistance and favour of England, could preserve and enhance their nationality to such an extent that they might one day form an independent nation." Parent did go on to say that he believed the old aspiration to be the most supreme blindness and folly now that destiny had spoken. But we know the outcome of destiny's sentence. The Act of Union of 1841 eliminated French Canada as a distinct political entity; it imposed a legislative union on us with the intention of swamping us numerically. And yet, as early as 1842, Louis-Hippolyte LaFontaine tore the imperial document to shreds by agreeing to co-operate with the new government and by urging his Upper Canadian allies to accept the principle of a federal alliance. And the old dream continues to live. It reappeared at the time of Confederation and more recently during the fanatical campaigns of wartime.

Whenever a storm blows up and the nationality senses danger, the idea of independence bursts forth. It appears now in a speech, now in a popular demonstration, now in a book like *L'Avenir du peuple canadien-français* by Edmond de Nevers or like *Pour la Patrie* by Jules-Paul Tardivel.

These illustrations of collective psychology are all the more important for us, since there is nothing artificial about them. They stem neither from pride, nor from megalomania, nor even, as in other countries, from a tiny elite of intellectuals and propagandists. Rather they are the spontaneous manifestation of a national life, the soul of a particular existence. And our ancestors, by their very being, were quite incapable of renouncing their aspiration. How indeed do the historians account for the emergence of various states? Differences of family and social institutions, differences of geography, ethnic difference – these are the true natural divisions between states. What, in fact, could be simpler, more normal? Surely there is nothing mysterious about the fact that political entities are based as much on moral and social as on material survival. Whenever a sensitive and aware human group fears for its existence, it acts instinctively to protect itself. It tears away the oppressing tutelage; with an effort stronger than will power, it seeks security; it forms a state. That is the lesson of history. Just look at the world during the last fifty years: everywhere different nationalities have aspired to their emancipation because everywhere empires and large federations have attempted to crush them.

The solution to our problem is now in sight. Need we add, in passing, that the right of national self-determination is not the fundamental basis of our solution. We simply demand the elementary right of preparation for all contingencies, of choosing, with the aid of God, our own destiny. Quite bluntly, the constancy of our dream of political independence has resulted from the constancy of the threat to our French existence. As the latter continues, so will the former. Aware of these blunt facts, we intend to add our stamp of approval to the will of our ancestors and, with them, in the event of the breakup of Confederation, we would like to see the establishment in eastern Canada, of a French state.

This particular format for our political future has been carefully considered, lengthily weighed. For almost a year, responsible individuals, aware of the arduous task and yet anxious to be of service, have scrupulously investigated the question. These men suffer from no illusions; they ask only one thing of the intellectuals of their country: that they look at the scheme with at least as much loyalty and seriousness as the initiators put into it. We are fully aware of the numerous and powerful obstacles to the realization of our scheme. But we must, in all truthfulness, admit that none of these obstacles appeared to us insurmountable. For example, it is easy to foresee the legitimate fears that such a scheme will arouse in the minds of our brothers in the far provinces who have been attached to us through the federal tie. Let them however be reassured. We do not imply any abandonment of our compatriots in the west. We have stated it firmly right from the beginning: we are not precipitating a separation; we will simply accept that which necessity and the hazards of history impose upon us. Besides, separation does not necessarily imply hostile or even closed borders. Both our duty and our interest will ensure the continuance of ties with our former associates. Then too, our compatriots know that the present political arrangement has nothing to do with our loyal friendship for them, our sincere desire to share their lives. These feelings stem from a much more spontaneous solidarity, a much more profound brotherhood, both of which, as we shall see, can only grow along with the national personality of Quebec.

In the practical realm, a number of thorny problems also arise. Independence means the entry of a distinct entity on the international scene. No state can do without allies and we must look to those who share our spiritual affinities and our interests. There would be no point in having a people suddenly come to life only to have them succumb to a more oppressive dependence because of the proximity of an overpowerful neighbour or of the feebleness of their means of survival. A state cannot count simply on its spiritual cohesion, the strength of its traditions, the community of language and religion or even a long, difficult existence. Every state is attached to a part of the globe which is its territory. It will be up to specialists to map the territory. They will have to find some system more rational than that of a series of pigeon-holes for determining the contours of the states of tomorrow.

However, there will be, in the French State on the Saint Lawrence, ethnic minorities whose rights must be preserved. When Quebec is looking for a guarantor of freedom, she has only to turn to her own traditions. Finally a people does not achieve independence unless it acquires dignity and strength, unless it creates the essential instruments of its new existence. The future is going to demand of our race an enormous effort of co-operation and will. There must be a fervent moral and intellectual preparation for the future. Our collaborators intend to trace just such a plan of action.

Obviously we do not wish to jump tremulously into hasty solutions. We believe we are respecting human contingencies and God preserve us from presuming upon the designs of his

Providence. What does the future hold in store? Possibly we may have to undertake intermediary steps before reaching our supreme goal – perhaps a temporary period of Canadian independence, maybe even American annexation, or possibly a smaller federation. Common sense tells us not to precipitate matters, but to make the most of all circumstances leading to the final success. The essential thing at the moment is to rivet the aspirations of our French community to the political ideal, to the ultimate stage which can be none other than our essential goal. To be ourselves, absolutely ourselves, to constitute, as soon as Providence intends, an independent French state – such must be, from now on, the hope that guides our efforts, the flame that never dies. This dream can no longer develop in the shadows, in coteries of initiates; the flame must burst forth. The Princess Louise of Bavaria recently remarked in her beautiful book *Autour des trônes que j'ai vus tomber*, "For a long time the king harboured the secret conviction that in order to survive, Belgium required some great purpose." Let us admit it: we need some great hope to lift us to the heights. Only for the lack of this great purpose did so much anarchy disperse our strength, so much apathy devour us, so many bastions fall during the last fifty years. The great purpose which 1867 provided never really caught the imagination of our race. For any people that wishes to live a strong and co-ordinated life must recognize a worthy ideal behind each of its activities.

For our part we have sought inspiration from the past and the present, we have calculated the merits and the hopes of our ancestors and now we confront French Quebec with the destiny of which we believe her to be worthy. In particular do we offer this destiny to the youth of our race, the thoughtful young people, architects and builders of great things. If this ideal suits them, let them accept it as their guiding light, let them not be late for their rendezvous with destiny.

# To *L'Echo*, Collège d'Edmonton

L. Groulx, draft of a letter to *L'Echo*, Collège d'Edmonton and to abbé Sabourin of Saint-Boniface [May 1923?], from Groulx papers, Fondation Lionel Groulx, Montreal. Reprinted by permission.

Dear Friend,

We understand that the attitude of *L'Action française* to our political future has been worrying our best friends in the West.

From a few words recently spoken in Montreal by Mgr. Béliveau and Mgr. Prud'homme, we gather that these anxieties are now acute; we would therefore like to try to dispel them.

Many misunderstandings would, I believe, be avoided if the precise views of *L'Action française* on this major problem were kept in mind. We have never preached separatism "by dynamite"; we have never resolved to impose it by violence. Rather, we ask our compatriots to take proper precautions in the face of a separatism which seems inevitable and to which we have long been pushed. To our knowledge, no one has ever refuted our demonstration of the instability of the Canadian Confederation. Even Mr. Henri Bourassa, according to *Le Devoir* of December 23, 1921, only gave Confederation a probable life span of 20 to 30 years; and he does not seem to have repudiated the words attributed to him by his own newspaper, on this serious question of our future.

You will admit that 20 or 30, or even 50 or 75 years – for we estimate a longer time·lapse than Mr. Bourassa before the definitive split – is a fairly short period in the life of a nation which must, more than others, be far-sighted. We understand how such a political dead-line can induce misgivings. We ourselves do not accept it light-heartedly. But how can your fears or ours improve the situation?

As for us, we are convinced that it is in the interests of everyone that Quebec decide its future by itself. We believe, furthermore, that our project of forming a French State does not in any way mean that we shall abandon our duties towards the French groups scattered throughout the country. Within 50 or 60 years the French population will be dominant in eastern Canada – a fact which is certainly not unknown to the higher political or university circles of Toronto. Indeed it is quite probable that proposals for *bonne entente* between the nationalities – that infallible soporific for our good-natured people – are not entirely unrelated to this sort of anxiety. Our fate will then rest entirely in our hands, that is if we do not allow ourselves to be surprised or outflanked by our enemies who are prepared to stoop to any means, even American annexation, rather than abandon their determination to dominate. If the Canadian Confederation disintegrates, it is obvious that the master of the situation in the eastern provinces will be the group best prepared for this eventuality, the group which has already gathered its forces behind a clear and precise plan and has thus in a sense prepared the framework for the future. Would it be better, for us and our minority groups, to leave our people to indolence and traditional pragmatism, to rely on chance and improvisation to settle such a serious matter, running thereby the risk of being dominated once again by a minority of politicians and financiers or of being dragged by the English element into the American abyss?

Does our formula for the future really have such disastrous implications for our brothers in the West? They will readily admit, I believe, that the present system of political federalism has given them little or no support for their school rights and for the defense of their French character. They must know, as well, the aversion Quebec has to the federal power of disallowance, in which we see a threat to our own institutions. The only help our French groups have ever received has come from what I would call a "national federalism". Racial solidarity – at least whatever racial solidarity has survived our political federalism – has made us turn from time to time to the Western Prairies. Unquestionably, the concept of a French State would immediately strengthen the internal life of Quebec. It could not do otherwise, if it is indeed true that a nation always gains from reducing the essence of its patriotism into a clear formula, and if it is also true that each step taken towards a more complete individuality increases its moral fibre. Mgr. Béliveau and Mgr. Prud'homme both expressed it quite clearly: the best support for our Western groups is a strong Quebec.

A strong Quebec: that is exactly what we intend to build, with the help of God. I might add that in formulating this plan, we have thought of our brothers as much as we have thought of ourselves. It seemed to us that once Quebec had reconstituted a true national consciousness, she would respond more quickly to the appeal of racial solidarity. We are also convinced that when a French State borders on the western shores of Lake Superior, it will be just as easy for us to help the French in the West as it is today to help the Franco-Americans of New England.

And that, dear Friend, is the way we formulate and understand the problem. Until such time as it is demonstrated to us that the peril does not exist or is not as critical as we think, or, even if it is real, that the best plan would nevertheless be to wait and do nothing – until such time, can our present attitude really be condemned?

It would have been far easier for us to float along with everyone else on the tide of events. But we believe that other duties are imposed upon us, for the sake of our compatriots. As for you, don't you think that you should find expressions other than "destructive" and "revolutionary" to apply to men who have had the courage to seek a legitimate solution and who are aware as they propose this solution that they are not thereby undermining any of their duties?

# The National Problem

L. Groulx, "Le problème national," *L'Almanach de la langue française*, 1924, pp. 50-52. Reprinted by permission of Mme J. Rémillard.

*L'Action française* attempts to deal with the national problem in a comprehensive and rational manner.

It is careful not to reduce the problem to the defense of our language. Defending our mother tongue is a task which must not be abandoned; language is one of the prime factors of nationality; the national character or soul is maintained primarily through language, – its internal philosophy, its inheritance and transmission of intellectual and moral traditions.

But language by itself does not make nationality, nor is language an independent power. All the various elements in a nation support one another. Just as culture and moral values are conditions of material progress so too this progress is a condition of spiritual survival. Our national problem thus concerns our whole life; to express the problem accurately we must include all the elements which constitute the normal life of a nation.

Here in our province, the greatest obstacle to this normal life is the weakness of our collective soul, the anemia of that internal principle which ensures that a living being acts, defends, and improves itself.

The clearest symptom of our vital inadequacy is our inability to defend ourselves. We do not even have skills possessed by the most rudimentary living organism: we cannot distinguish between what can safely be assimilated and what cannot. Plays, films, newspapers, customs, foreign clubs, neutral societies, we accept them all without considering whether they can be adapted to our mentality and without taking account of the poison they might contain. Every day our federal services, public utility companies, or simple bureaucrats treat us as if we were an inferior race; a small elite reacts, while the masses remain indifferent, accepting the insult or becoming indignant with their own defenders.

Similarly, we are unable to perform those actions which would develop and strengthen our national life. We need to keep our own patrimony for ourselves, and we sell it to foreigners. We need to accumulate our savings, our resources, for ourselves, and we scatter them abroad to build the fortune of our rivals. We need to retain our population, and our people are drained away to other countries. We need to hold on to the land, attach ourselves to the healthy life which created the vigour of our forefathers, and we crowd insanely into cities where we are decimated by infant mortality and where the level of morality falls sharply.

We need to strengthen ourselves internally, therefore, and as quickly as possible. We must give our nationality a vigorous and proud soul; we need to strengthen the principles which motivate action even more than we need the actions themselves.

*L'Action française* proposes to achieve these goals, firstly, by the teaching of our national history. History provides not only a link with the past, but also a link between the descendants of a given people. History, even more than blood, generates ethnic feeling and makes it vigorous. Racial spirit is created between people who discover that they have a common ancestry; solidarity soon turns to pride when the greatness of this ancestry is realized. For a people to defend its nationality and its culture it must first be aware of their value.

That is a first condition, but there is another one: the nation must have hope for the future. The glory of a history, the nobility of a culture, by themselves are rather ineffectual stimulants if they cannot prevent a nation from dying. Simple common sense tells us that the effort must be proportionate to the value of the goal. A nation will fight for its survival only if that survival seems certain. Then too, do not expect a people to put heart and soul into securing a life which is merely that of an inferior nation, perpetually dominated and never achieving a full, independent personality.

There are very grave symptoms which reveal the instability of the Canadian Confederation. That is why *L'Action française* feels justified in giving its readers hope that a French State may be created in Eastern Canada. The dream is one which can come true if we are determined enough and capable of waiting for it. Besides, it has the supreme advantage of being closely linked to the greatest aspiration of our ancestors, and of providing all our efforts with a goal to stimulate and coordinate them.

To these already powerful motives, *L'Action française* adds another one which it regards as a strict duty for our Quebec group: the duty of living and being strong in order to support the entire French fact in America. Finally, because we are Catholics above all and wish to direct all our efforts towards a supreme goal, the editors of *L'Action française* remind French Canadians that they must make use of their inherent qualities, of the admirable aptitudes of a Latin people, in order to remain in the service of God – an apostle which, although young, has a magnificent destiny before it.

That is the national problem.

When our people has acquired racial spirit and pride, when it is conscious of struggling for a worth-while future, when it is imbued with the greatness of its apostolic vocation, then truly will it harbour a vigorous soul. It will spontaneously react against poisons; it will build its economic, intellectual, social, and political life in accordance with the laws of its nature and its destiny; like an elder brother it will defend younger French groups; it will be determined to maintain its French and Catholic integrity. The principles we propose could become, if our people wished it, the guiding light; they are simply the two or three key ideas which, as Brunetière said, succeed in "breathing life into the concept of a homeland."

# Mr. Bourassa's Lecture Series

L. Groulx, "Les Conférences de M. Bourassa," an anonymous article in *L'Action nationale* V, 5 (May 1935), pp. 257-265. Reprinted by permission of Mme J. Rémillard.

A series of highly inappropriate lectures was recently given in Montreal. No doubt the best thing would be to let them pass into oblivion, were it not that the reputation of the speaker has endowed them with an aura of sensation. Our intention is not to refute the shifting ideas which confused fact and fancy almost to the point of incomprehension. There are certain points, however, which we would like to make clear and which Mr. Bourassa should know, the first being his own large share of responsibility in the modest awakening of that nationalism which so terrifies him.

Ours was a generation of men in their thirties, forties, or fifties, which was passionately enthusiastic about Mr. Bourassa and his ideas. That man had the marvellous ability to rouse people. He also had the rare opportunity of being, two or three times in his life, the spokesman for an entire nationality, proclaiming in moments of crisis its unshakeable hope and determination. In him we had a true leader, and he promised us guidelines. Our small people experienced a brief renaissance. A wretched prisoner of the gloomy past, we suddenly felt between 1910 and 1920, that we might be released from the ball and chain of our perpetual misery. Alas, we were soon deceived. When, ten or fifteen years ago, Mr. Bourassa's strange evolution began, a few men consoled themselves with the thought that he could never harm us as much as he had previously benefited us. Would those men say the same thing today? The fact remains, of course, that he did a lot of good: for that we shall always be grateful. But the fact also remains that he has done us a lot of harm; and for that harm, which we feel as a wound in our spirit and even our flesh, we can only grant him Christian pardon and infinite pity.

There came a time when he and a few others in whom we had believed and placed our trust suddenly turned their backs on their past, on their own ideas. To complete the shocking scene, they presented us with the spectacle of former associates and companions quarrelling violently among themselves, flinging invective at each other, firing at their enemies as best they could from the safety of their own entrenched positions. For the men of our generation, it was the tragic massacre of an ideal. May younger generations forgive us for the element of bitterness and pessimism that was consequently imbedded in our soul. Disoriented and disorganized, abandoned without compass or guide, an entire generation fell into discouragement and insignificance. Politicians were quick to take control once again, and they did so in their customary way. Our people began to decline. They would be declining still if another generation, the very young, had not refused to accept such a dishonourable fate. This generation reacted, sometimes roughly; it was only too happy to bully our would-be undertakers. But we must be brave enough to face the facts: the man primarily responsible for this new growth of nationalism in French Canada, is the Bourassa of 1922, the man who trampled upon the ideals of a generation.

*　*　*

When we contemplate this man's final evolution, how can we help but feel infinite sadness? He is still too intelligent not to admit that in the terrible environment in which we live, an ethnic group as weak as ours cannot survive unless it constantly defends its character, unless its patriotism is constantly active and on the alert, unless, in a word, it is prepared to commit itself to what is commonly called nationalism – but a healthy and legitimate nationalism. He must also know that whereas Catholicism safeguards spiritual values by imposing a scale of priorities on our duties, it does not command us to neglect or despise any of them. Yet it is these first stirrings of nationalism and of our determination to defend ourselves that Mr. Bourassa feels called upon to condemn. At the very moment our nation attempts to surface for air, he decides to stamp on it and send it back to the bottom of the abyss. Unless he has lost all his former judgment, which was great, he cannot be unaware that his compatriots have never before in their entire history been so demoralized, so given to despair. Yet he warns a humiliated people against racist pride; he accuses a nation without the slightest national consciousness of excessive nationalism. Because a younger generation has wearied of the taste of defeat, because it begins to shake itself out of slumber, our former leader is quick to shriek: "Beware! You might be committing a sin!" We believe we can discern the origins of these policies, this invitation to perpetual slumber, this concern lest we wake, this inducement to lead narrow lives, like docile sheep fleeced without a murmur, never disturbing others even when those others have ravaged us. Some time ago a great politician, Mr. Bourassa's first leader, preached exactly these policies. After his break with his master, the disciple used to enjoy demonstrating the extraordinary, pernicious influence of his former leader by recalling in vehement diatribes how the advocate of appeasement and "conciliation" had succeeded in winning even his political adversaries over to his philosophy. The former leader now has his revenge. Mr. Laurier's most brilliant conquest is a posthumous one: he has succeeded in regaining Mr. Bourassa's allegiance.

Mr. Bourassa had a special grudge against our old journal, *L'Action française*. He castigated it for preaching "separatism." Leaving aside, for the moment, the degree of inaccuracy, indeed of sheer fantasy, contained in the reproach when it is formulated in such a black-and-white way, we would like merely to recall one text and one fact. The first article of "Our Political Future" in which we raised the question of a French State in Eastern Canada, appeared in *L'Action française* in January 1922. Since Confederation was in danger of falling to pieces, we argued, would it not be appropriate to make plans for that eventuality? Only a few weeks before, on December 21st, 1921, a banquet had been held in Quebec. The time was immediately after the federal election. Lavergne had been defeated. His friends were honouring the defeated candidate at this public occasion. During the banquet one of the speakers uttered these words:

> Confederation has existed, at least potentially. I do not know whether it will last twenty or thirty years, but some day it is bound to dissolve ... When they annexed an immense Western territory sure to be penetrated by American influence, the Fathers of Confederation made a fatal mistake. They placed an adder within the country's cradle. Increasingly, our life is bound to be dominated by rivalry between West and East. Because of

Confederation, we must determine a clear programme of action; we must see to our own interests, to our own reconstruction. The English have tried to use Confederation to subjugate us; they have not wanted an equal association with us. Let us therefore seek our support elsewhere . . .

These words were uttered by none other than Mr. Bourassa. We quote from his newspaper, *Le Devoir*, of December 23rd, 1921, p. 2, column 2. No doubt Mr. Bourassa will protest, like so many public figures, that he was misunderstood, or misquoted. There are only two possibilities: either he did say what he is reported to have said at the Lavergne banquet, in which case how can sentiments that were quite legitimate when he spoke them be transformed into criminal heresies when published in *L'Action française*? Or he was in fact misquoted, in which case why did he, the editor of a newspaper with pretentions to authority and leadership, never repudiate the report of his speech in *Le Devoir*, especially if he considers these ideas so serious, so unorthodox? In addition, we quoted his words in the concluding article of our inquiry in 1922, and reproduced them in the volume published separately: *Notre Avenir Politique*. Mr. Bourassa condemned our inquiry. But has he ever repudiated his speech at the Lavergne banquet?

*   *   *

Mr. Bourassa must face the facts: he is no longer a leader in this country, nor will he ever be. A few young fools – certainly not members of the Catholic Association of French Canadian Youth, whatever rumour says – may dance attendance upon him, but youth on the whole no longer follows him, nor can it follow him. To be a leader, a man must have at least a minimum of precision and consistency in his philosophy. How can youth believe in this man, when his ideas have undergone such a dismal evolution? How could youth not feel shocked when it sees him praised, adulated, proposed as an example by men who were formerly his enemies, the worst politicians who have had the most lamentable effect upon our life? Furthermore, is it not a most peculiar failing to confuse everything as he does, to the extent of discovering racist pride in a small nation rather inclined to lack confidence in itself, and oppressed by a host of contemptuous denigrators? To be the leader of a generation, a man must be able to speak with hope of the future, to provide clear ideas, and firm, intoxicating goals to inspire and coordinate action. But the former leader has scattered his old doctrines to the winds, without replacing them with anything new. For a small nation afflicted with suicidal tendencies and in great need of stimulants, this would-be leader can only prescribe tranquillizers. Mr. Bourassa would be well advised to leave us alone. If no other considerations can move him, respect for his past and for his white hair should make him keep quiet or change his tune. The good he has done us in the past does not give him the right to keep on harming us now forever. It is not within his power to check the surge of a younger generation which, defying the pessimists tolling their requiem bells, is determined to proclaim its faith in life, determined to live.

Abbé Groulx, speaking to a group of young lawyers in Quebec, said, last February 9th: "We must not be afraid of taking a stand. There is no nationalism in the world more legitimate or more orthodox than ours. Nothing in the absolute dictates of our faith, nothing in the strictest Catholicism obliges us to renounce the Quebec Act, the constitution of 1791, the great reforms of 1842 and 1849, and our more complete emancipation of 1867." This speech by abbé Groulx has been printed in a brochure, which carries the *imprimatur* of the Archbishop of Quebec on its title page. Such orthodoxy is at very least worth that of the new, self-styled, "Father of the Church."

# To Pierre Chaloult

L. Groulx, letter to Pierre Chaloult, editor of *La Nation*, Quebec, February 22, 1936. Reprinted by permission of Mme J. Rémillard.

Thank you for what is surely a most sympathetic article. Have you interpreted my ideas accurately? I believe that on the whole I can answer: yes. It would be difficult for me to deny that our future has always appeared to me to lie in an independent French Canada. As early as 1904, as my *Adolescent's Crusade* indicates, I was proposing this political and national ideal to the young students at Valleyfield. I have always seen it as the natural outcome of our life. All sorts of reasons prevent me from believing that our present Canada will last very long. To achieve the ideal, however, have I ever advocated a hasty rupture of Confederation? That is another question. It has always seemed to me that Confederation was gradually disintegrating with the passage of time, and that nothing could save it from this fate. But you will have noted that the inquiry in *L'Action française* (1921, 1922) which reinvigorated the idea of an independent French Canada, suggested the ideal within the framework of a very definite hypothesis: the hypothesis that the Canadian country would be dismembered, which seemed at the time probable and indeed imminent. None of our contributors, to do them justice, suggested provoking such a split.

What I have always wanted above all, and still want – and I believe that if my writings and speeches bear witness to any one thing, they must bear witness to this continuing desire – is a French Canada in which French Canadians could entirely fufill themselves. Can such a French Canada exist within the framework of Confederation? I must admit that I am not sure; but the blame seems to lie not with the institution but with the men. And when I say "men," I mean us. You know as well as I do that at least two other ethnic groups in Canada would never have allowed the federal constitution, however imperfect, to become an instrument to crush or humiliate their nationality and their solemnly guaranteed rights. Is it still possible to redeem the situation? Anyone would be quite justified in feeling some scepticism! The experience of the past sixty-eight years, alas, seems to demonstrate that it is futile to hope that our representatives in Ottawa will show more courage, more national awareness, more concern for the interests of their province and their compatriots than they have shown so far.

Well then, you ask, do you conclude that separatism is the answer? I refuse to provoke it or precipitate it. In our present state of moral depression, or rather of moral and national nihilism, to rush headlong into such an adventure would simply mean changing our master and our chains. Our present misfortune is national rather than political. I have often said that the great problem for French Canadians is that there are no French Canadians. The most urgent task for our province, the task to which all men of good will should rally, is to work for our *spiritual renewal*. I mean "spiritual" in the widest sense of the word. Through schools and all other possible means, let us produce a generation which is entirely 100% French Canadian. This is within our power. These true French Canadians will normalize our life in Ottawa and in Quebec. Not only will they redress distorted values; they will be of a calibre to prepare another future for us, a future we shall be able to enter without fear, because, through our vitality, we shall already have created within our province the institutions necessary for a viable state.

I am aware that this way of seeing things, or if you like this programme of action, does not always meet with the approval of some thoughtful young men. They wish to go faster. The best and indeed the only way of developing true French Canadians, they maintain, is to inspire them with a national ideal which is a true intellectual force, which corresponds to their natural destiny. Let us propose to them the creation of an independent

French Canada. A persistent struggle for this objective would rapidly re-establish our life on a more rational foundation; it would reform our political situation in both Ottawa and Quebec. And then, either Confederation would have become an acceptable framework for us, or we should have shattered it by the very force of our aspirations.

I must confess that this other plan has its attractions. It contains a large measure of truth. In any case, I do not disapprove of it. The Cardinal has allowed you free discussion on the subject. I can do no less. I would merely point out that in either case our nation cannot avoid the need for a national renewal. That is where I would start. I think it practical to create the ability and the feeling, to reform the soul, before proceeding to action. I am furthermore convinced that the future will be ours on condition that we ourselves systematically work towards it.

With my best wishes,

Lionel Groulx, Priest.

# Groulx on Groulx

## My Childhood

L. Groulx, "Mon enfance," *Mes Mémoires* (Montreal, Les Editions Fides, 1970), Vol. I, pp. 21-29. Reprinted by permission.

In an environment governed by the rhythms of rural life, I spent my childhood. Childhood! Now, at the age of seventy-three, I remember scenes bathed in a golden haze of enchanting poetry. Am I romanticizing, distorting images through the rosy lens of memory? My childhood always seemed idyllic to me: I really think it was. In my thoughts it was already surrounded by that golden haze during my first years at college, on days when nostalgia gnawed at my heart. I think I had a truly happy childhood. My parents were severe, though never harsh. We were poor, yet so little was needed to fulfill all our greatest wishes! In my *Rapaillages*, I must confess I did fictionalize to some extent. I sometimes romanticized people or things. I attributed to my grandmother actions which had really been my mother's, and vice versa. I synchronized events. Still, most of the facts in that book are quite authentic. What I wished to capture primarily was the atmosphere and the colour of this small corner of the country, the flavour of the narrow world in which I spent my first years. All that I believe I described exactly.

I have said we were poor. We had no games, no toys, not even a ball or a bat. My little sisters had only the dolls they made themselves: dolls with some rough shape for a head, but no hair or eyes, dressed from scraps of old clothes. My elder brother and I shared a single pair of skates, a steel blade encased within a wooden sole. We never had a sled, except the homemade one used for carting firewood. Yet what blissful hours we spent sliding on it, the sharp wind whipping our faces as we swooped down the snowy river bank that sloped away from our father's house. Our ingenuity made up for the lack of toys. As you can well imagine, the inspiration for our games came from the rural environment, from the objects and sights which met our childish gaze. My parents sometimes took us to the regional exhibitions at parish or county fairs. There we watched, wide-eyed, as the prize winning animals were paraded by. From this we brought back the idea of spending hours cutting out pictures of farm animals from any newspaper or illustrated magazine we came across. Elaborate displays began parading across the kitchen table and bench. We were holding our own fair. How proudly each child defended his own collection, how hotly each prize was contested! At other times, we transformed simple pieces of wood into horses or machinery and recreated harvest scenes with mighty roars to imitate the thresher. Our budding architectural or engineering instincts were exercised on the construction of huts. Who can say what mysterious impulse in children is satisfied by this form of play? Almost invariably we chose to build these huts so that they could not be seen from the house, behind a building, a wall, or a wood pile. We would crawl through the low doorway and spend hours crouched in rather uncomfortable positions, savouring the full delight of this special retreat. For little rustics who rarely left the radius of their paternal home, the hut represented all the joys of evasion. We would often ask Mother for a piece of bread and butter just for the pleasure of eating it in our little hut. Such snacks – rarely did we even have jam – became the rarest, the most exquisite of delicacies.

The monotony of the passing days was also broken by the various seasonal events of the farm. Any one who has not been a farmer's son during the period 1880-1890 can hardly imagine what an event, for a small child who was a joyful prisoner within his narrow horizon, was the birth of some new animal, a little calf, or chicks, piglets, lambs, and above all a new foal! These are very small delights. Yet what a pleasure it was to venture forth in the morning and discover a mother hen coming back through the tall wet grass, clucking a little anxiously, a little guiltily too perhaps, for she had hidden away to brood, and surrounded by a lively flock of chicks, agile and wild as baby partridges. The birth of an animal, especially if it were a horse or a cow, meant that a newcomer, a new personality entered the life of the farm. He would be given a name: he would have his own story. In those days horses still had a great deal of prestige as man's inseparable work companions, and the birth of a foal was an exciting event for the entire neighbourhood. Neighbours came round to see the wonder. Each of them would have his comment and prediction to make about the newborn: he would grow to be a good work horse because of his solid hams and large build; he would be a fine trotter, a good riding horse, because of his lively eye and fine legs; he would be chestnut, black, dappled, or grey, because of the colour of the hair around his eyes.

There was another event in our farm life which we youngsters always found highly impressive. We would be in the fields
one day, perhaps even in a neighbour's fields, or coming back
from school, when a loud noise would suddenly ring out from
our home. It was the familiar sound of a bugle, which we called
a loudspeaker, and we knew it meant: "A new swarm of bees
has emerged. Come quickly!" Off we would go at a gallop. As
we came nearer we could hear other noises: the wild, rhythmic
beat of a staccato tom-tom, a sound also very familiar to our
ears. At home, as soon as she laid aside the bugle, Mother busily
gathered her troops about her. She also gathered all her kitchen
implements, iron or tin, and distributed sticks for the children
to beat the pots and pans with all their might. Just as in the time
of Virgil! What fun it was, making that delectable racket! Our
tom-toms drowned out all other sounds, whether of church
bells or nature's own orchestra, and we were completely
convinced that our magnificent jazz before its time would
persuade the cloud of tiny insects dancing wildly in the
shimmering air to settle somewhere in the garden, upon a
scented bough of apple or plum blossom. Father arrived. I can
still see him, enveloped in his special costume for the occasion,
his hands and arms covered in white cotton. Had we been more
learned we would have thought him some Arab priest in the
middle of his sacred rites. The young bees, apparently, had been
waiting for this apparition all along. Instantly, a black cloud
appeared on some branch. The cloud thickened, elongating
itself into a cone. The young bees were regrouping as they
awaited their new hive. Father held it between his hands. To
attract the frivolous insects, he had coated the inside of the little
square house with syrup or sugar. Within a few minutes the
new swarm had taken refuge within it. Later, at college, I would
translate from Virgil's *Georgics* the long poem about bees. How
delighted I was to find therein my own childhood memories!
How mysterious they seemed to us, these industrious insects,
performing their marvellous tasks within the close security of
their little house! Like the enchanting Latin poem, we were not
far from thinking them the bearers of a spark from the divine
soul:

> *His quidam signis, atque haec exempla secuti,*
> *Esse apibus partem divinae mentis et haustus*
> *Aetherios dixere . . .*

On summer days, our greatest delight was provided by the
beach in front of our house where a narrow strip of sand
sparkled beneath the sun. You could walk out into the water

for a long way before it became deep, so that it was quite a safe place to play. What happy hours we spent there on the days that the north wind or the west wind left our inlet alone, our short pants rolled as high as they would go, and the sand cool under our bare feet. Like all children, our greatest pleasure was to paddle in the water. We collected shells, discovered crayfish or snails lurking under rocks, and scooped into our hands or jars the minnows darting in shoals between our legs. Our games on the beach occasionally became more complicated, more adventurous. We had many uncles or cousins who travelled, living in the village of Sainte-Anne de Bellevue, on the other side of the Bay of Vaudreuil. They were barge captains for the Murphy and Davidson Company and would travel, during the navigation season, between Ottawa and Montreal, and sometimes further, transporting wood for the large saw mills in Hull. A familiar sight when we were children was a fleet of these barges, which we called "taux" (tows), sailing in pairs past the Ile-aux-Tourtres, or on the Deux-Montagnes Lake, heavily laden and towed laboriously by tugs whose steady "puff, puff" we could always recognize in the distance. These travelling relatives often came to visit, especially in winter, and would relate long tales of their adventures. Hardly surprising, then, that on our own beach we sometimes played at being travellers ourselves. The old buckets that were relics from sugar-making were transformed into small craft for the occasion, and long sea-going expeditions organized along the quiet beach. Our knowledge of geography being entirely rudimentary, the itineraries we planned were often surprising, to say the least. Laden with precious cargo of pebbles or sand, sometimes rigged with sails, small vessels in procession would slowly set out for the big cities along the Great Lakes. To be quite honest, we drastically simplified the geography of the country. Sometimes, I must confess, the Ottawa River joined the Saint Lawrence in the most amazing places! What point would there have been in conformity to maps, when the very attraction of the game lay in the lure of remote, unexplored territories lying at the end of these deliberately long voyages? The sails of the tiny vessels soon filled out. We followed them. Unfortunately we had not reckoned on the treachery of the elements, the sudden gusts from the north or south. A shudder would race along the surface, a sudden wave appear, and these adventurous ships on their way to distant ports laden with their precious merchandise and even more precious childish dreams, would suddenly capsize and drift upside down with sails broken and battered, tossed by the waves like chips of wood. Thus did we learn the meaning of disaster and catastrophe.

So many memories flood my mind, surfacing there like long-forgotten melodies. I merely have to choose. For example, how many holiday hours we spent playing school! Being the eldest and recognized as the most learned, I naturally stepped into the role of the schoolmaster with my younger brothers and sisters as pupils. I was a stern master. Rules of silence and discipline were strictly enforced. My former pupils recall that both reprimands and punishments were meted out very liberally. With a happy presumption, I was trying out my youthful authority.

Childhood memories come back pell-mell; now I recall long winter evenings in the *rabat*. When we children huddled together on mattresses redolent of fresh straw, how mysterious and disquieting was the howling storm that gusted down the chimney, making flames of the stove dance upon the walls! Sometimes a shadow would pass by with muffled steps. It was Father or Mother, soundlessly going their rounds, inspecting the fire, the pipes, the chimney, doing everything they could to protect our childhood security. I have mentioned our *rabat*. The *rabat* was a kind of folding sofa built entirely of wood. During the day it served as a seat in the largest room in the house. At night the top came down to reveal the mattresses, blankets, and pillows of the children's beds. To be exact, during our childhood we progressed through three kinds of bed. First the cradle, placed beside the parental bed, within Mother's reach. When a newborn awoke or wailed, it was thus very easy to rock the cradle gently, chasing away the nightmares and quickly sending him to sleep again. Whenever the Indians brought another child – in those days babies came from the Indian reservation at Oka – the newcomer would take possession of the cradle. Its previous occupant would migrate to what we called the *cassette*, a small high cot placed at the foot of our parents' bed. When yet another newborn arrived – it happened fairly frequently – a double migration would take place: the occupant of the *cassette* would graduate to the *rabat*, which could accommodate four children lying feet to feet, and the occupant of the cradle would move into the *cassette*. In our home there were two *rabats*, one for the boys and one for the girls.

Among the childhood souvenirs I most happily recall is that of awakening on New Year's Day. When I reached a certain age, around 7, my mother required my services on Christmas Eve and New Year's Eve. My little sisters were still too young for the task, and so she asked my help with all the baking, the preparing of pastries and meats for those festive occasions. This was a task I adored, for it meant being up while the household slumbered and it thus conferred a certain distinction upon me, singling me out from my brothers and sisters. How I loved that delectable smell of stews, *tourtières* [meat pies], and donuts! I also enjoyed supervising the fire, making sure it remained at just the right temperature, a job which I felt to be a most responsible one. On New Year's Eve, my mother kept me with her until almost midnight. But as soon as the hour had struck, she would say: "Now off to bed. The Child Jesus is on his way. If you want Him to leave you anything, you must be in bed, and sound asleep. And don't forget to hang up your stocking!" In my day children believed in the visit of the Child Jesus on New Year's Day. Sordid commercial interests had not yet chased that radiant vision from our childish imaginations. The Child Jesus did not bring very much: his gifts were tailored to the state of the family's purse and the modest desires of children in those days. But at the first break of dawn the next morning, how eagerly we sprang from our beds and ran to the dangling stockings. The toe was swollen with a small parcel. What bliss! How ecstatic we could be at finding a handful of mixed sweets, with sometimes the added treat of an orange! A festive din filled the house. Soon all the children were up: our first movement was to throw ourselves into our mother's arms, the second to kneel in a row for the paternal blessing. Deeply moved, his voice filled with emotion, the head of the family would repeat the same formula over the head of each of his children: "Yes, my child, I bless you, and may God bless you as well!" An entire day of almost unmixed happiness was about to begin.

I would boldly repeat that within our grey house at Les Chenaux there lived a very happy family. We sprang from two paternal lines. My mother, having become a widow six weeks after my birth in 1878, soon re-married. Her second husband, Guillaume Emond, adopted the children from her first marriage as his own. Between us there was always the most perfect harmony, an indissoluble, fraternal kinship like the tie that used to bind sheaves of wheat. Before we were separated by college and marriage, there were five boys and five girls, two groups of almost the same age. What wonderful times we had when we came back from college for the holidays and the whole family was together again! How we loved to tease each other! My elder brother Albert was past master at this art. During meals, our parents witnessed these skirmishes with a great affectation of neutrality, but even they could not help bursting out sometimes in uncontrollable laughter.

As we grew up, one death came to sadden our family life: a younger sister, Imelda, died quite suddenly at the age of thirteen, from an infection resulting from a vaccination. I was then in my first year of *Philosophie** at Sainte-Thérèse, and came home for the funeral. The bereavement was a revelation

*The second-last year of the eight-year classical college programme.

to us all of the depth of our fraternal bonds. For me especially it was a great shock. This little girl had been very dear to me. Then too, this death was linked in my mind to another loss which I could barely remember, yet which had left indelible traces of melancholy imprinted upon my childish character. When I was hardly three years old, death had carried away three members of the family: our eldest sister, a brother, Julien, my immediate elder, and another little girl who was not quite one year old, the first-born of my mother's second marriage. Within the space of eight days, a merciless epidemic of diphtheria had taken them all. From five children only two were left, my brother Albert and myself. I have no memory of my brother Julien. But an old family album preserved a chrome photograph of my eldest sister, dead at 8 years of age. That picture engraved the deepest impressions on my young mind. My mother so often spoke of her first-born, telling me how much the dear child had helped her. She described my sister as an affectionate child, and very pretty. How often she described the solicitous care with which my eldest sister had surrounded me after our Father's death! I thus acquired a great affection for my dead sister, and a kind of nostalgic regret. I would frequently pore over her picture, trying to seize the expression of her young face, as if to plunge deep into her soul and penetrate its mystery. Even today I cannot say how deeply deprived I was by the loss of this sisterly affection, for I was then a sentimental child, who often felt lonely even amongst the members of his family. My excessive and almost uncontrollable sensitivity was a great torment to me in adolescence. This was an inheritance, perhaps, from my mother who, when she was carrying me, was pining with loneliness for her husband, away during the winter months in the lumber camps along the Ottawa or in the paint factories of the United States.

# The Vicarage at Mile End

L. Groulx, "Au presbytère du Mile End," Mes Mémoires (Montreal, Les Editions Fides, 1970), Vol. I, pp. 273-4; 275-79. Reprinted by permission.

In 1917, an event occurred which seemed of slight importance and yet was to have a profound influence upon my life. Ever since my arrival in Montreal, seventeen or eighteen months before, I had been living at the vicarage of Saint-Jean-Baptiste.

I have related the conditions of my life there, conditions incompatible with my teaching which alone was more than sufficient to absorb all my time. One day I spoke about it with the Auxiliary Bishop of Montreal, Mgr. Gauthier: "Let me be a simple curate," I said, "or a simple professor." I was not, I repeat, reluctant to undertake my duties in the parish. But I had neither the health nor the time to cope with the double task which had been set for me. Indeed, if a historian truly appreciates his discipline, can he really devote himself to anything but history? One man knew of my situation and found it deplorable: abbé Philippe Perrier. I must say that as early as 1915, I had wanted to go and live with him. Instead, I was sent to Saint-Jean-Baptiste, I do not know exactly why, unless it was to withdraw me from the influence of a priest frowned upon in some high circles. One day early in 1917, I received a phone call from abbé Perrier: "There is a room free here; if you wish to take it, it is at your disposal." That very day I requested and obtained permission to change lodgings. At that period I barely knew the dear priest. At the *Grand Séminaire* in Montreal, he had taught me canon law in my fourth year – a year lasting four months. Since then we had occasionally met at various conferences. He was ten years older than I. This extremely intelligent man, imbued with a strong sense of apostolic duty, had an impassioned love for young people. He was acutely interested in all the events of our national and religious life. As early as 1915, he was among the most eminent members of the clergy in Montreal and in French Canada generally. For these reasons, I had long felt an admiration bordering on worship for that magnificent priest. He received me with open arms. "I was aware of your situation," he was kind enough to say, "I was in a similar position at one time in my life. I shall ask nothing of you. The most you will be required to do is to sing one high mass every morning. For that you may choose whatever time best suits you and your work. That hour will then remain always the same. All I want is to help you work." . . .

THE NATIONALIST SCHOOL

Joining abbé Perrier's vicarage had a particular influence upon my life: it carried me straight into the heart of the nationalist movement. The *curé*, although openly a patriot, had none of the characteristic traits of a politician priest. Nevertheless, he sympathized heart and soul with the group of men – they could even be called a school – which was then working to bring about a national revival in French Canada. It happened that the principal leaders of the movement lived in the *curé's* parish, or close by. Henri Bourassa was a parishioner of *La Mâlaine* (this was our pronunciation of "Mile End") as were Paul-Emile

Lamarche, Antonio Perrault, Doctor Gauvreau, Jean-Baptiste Prince and Louis Verschelden. Omer Héroux lived on the periphery of the parish and also, I believe, Georges Pelletier. The *curé* extended his warm hospitality to all these men. His vicarage was also a gathering place for the priests, brothers, and even members of the episcopal hierarchy in more or less close sympathy with the nationalist creed. When they were passing through Montreal, men such as Father Charles Charlebois, Father Rodrigue Villeneuve, abbé Georges Courchesne, the Bishop of Rimouski Mgr. Léonard, the Archbishop of Saint-Boniface Mgr. Arthur Béliveau, the Bishop of Gaspé Mgr. F.-X. Ross and a few others would always stop at the Mile End vicarage. In some ecclesiastical circles, as a result, the vicarage was facetiously, or even sarcastically re-christened "the Bishopric of the North." After the retirement of the seriously ill Mgr. Bruchési, many bishops who did not take to the icy manners of his successor began to show a clear preference for the "Bishopric of the North."

I have lingered on a description of this environment because I wish to demonstrate clearly the influence it had on my development. There have been so many attempts to probe into the origins of what is called my system of thought, and my concept of history! I need hardly say that when I arrived at abbé Perrier's vicarage in 1917, I was already a nationalist, and had long been one, like the *curé* himself. I was a nationalist like any normal French Canadian, or, if you prefer, like any member of a minority group exposed to the perils of assimilation and consequently obliged to preserve the essential elements of its culture. Surely that is the essence of nationalism. Is it such a crime? Unfortunately, by the most extraordinary of aberrations, nationalism in French Canada has been so severely distorted that it has finally been stigmatized as an ideological monstrosity, a kind of sin. A virtue for Anglo-Canadians becomes a disgraceful vice for French Canadians, limiting and narrow. Let a people think of itself, turn inward to look after its own affairs, and it displays the most shameful and archaic selfishness! As if the greatest nations were not occasionally obliged to turn inward and attach themselves more firmly to the basic ideas of their civilization! As if cultivating self-awareness meant enclosing oneself in a cocoon! I believe I understood the thinking of my contemporaries. We saw nationalist doctrines as the vital synthesis for our small people. No doubt these doctrines were secular, human theories, designed to preserve human values. But our group of nationalists at the beginning of the century also remembered that civilization is an organic entity based, essentially, upon a spiritual choice. Starting from this premise, they believed and professed that the future of their nationality lay in the attaining of a dynamic equilibrium between material and spiritual forces. A synthesis, to use the word again, in which human and temporal values remain in their proper position, without attempting to be transcendent. This does not, as has so often been claimed, make religion and the Church subordinate to the homeland, the nationality, or the language; it means rather that earthly and temporal aims are vigorously coordinated according to spiritual values and directed towards higher goals for man, his nation, and the world. Our group always maintained that the first duty of any nation is to ensure its own health. We did not wish or seek anything else.

I would add that fifty years ago nationalist doctrines seemed even more attractive to us because they posited a complete renewal of our political life and a decisive return to our own historical line of development. They swept away the clichés and idiotic values in which the old parties wanted to keep us trapped. On the provincial level, being a nationalist meant advocating the nationalization of our political and economic life; it meant organizing all sectors of society in a reconstruction of our homeland. On the Canadian level, it meant returning to the effort which, ever since the Conquest, had never ceased leading us towards the goal of complete emancipation from all forms of colonialism. These aims, even more than the fiery eloquence of a Bourassa, made the new doctrine attractive to our generation. A young people, a generation of young men, is easily captivated by the fascinating hope of leading the province and the country into adulthood, shaking off all humiliating yokes. The time inevitably comes when a people feels that it has attained the age of majority, when it can walk without crutches. From that day on it can barely tolerate the domination of foreign gold or the sight of a foreign flag flying over its soil. These doctrines and feelings were, I know, upsetting for many people stuck in their ruts and old-fashioned loyalties. So many men of that older generation around 1900 felt their colonial status to be something definite, fixed forever. Why did we want to aspire to autonomy, and especially to an independence regarded as almost a religious or political heresy? In thick and heavy theses, members of the clergy attempted to shore up the crumbling pillars of the empire, as distraught as Saint Augustine observing the fall of the Roman Empire. The nationalist school itself, around 1910, couched the final stage of the evolution in very discreet language. But to what straws the old school of politicians clung! When I was passing through Paris in 1931, Canadian students there told me of the dismay expressed by that brave man, Thomas Chapais. The venerable senator was on his way home from Geneva, where he had represented

Canada at a session of the League of Nations. 1931 was the year of the Statute of Westminster, surely a rather innocuous document. But Chapais could hardly contain his alarm at this serious evolution of the British Empire. "Where are we heading?" he had cried to the students, his arms raised in a gesture of despair. A most revealing exclamation! If as late as 1931 intelligent politicians could still think such thoughts, what were other people thinking?

I will not deny that the nationalist school had other attractions as far as I was concerned. Within it I met some of the best intellects and most noble characters of my time. Their influence marked my life, and, to a certain extent, my teaching. I saw and understood what these intellectual circles were awaiting. This stimulant spurred me on, and made me realize even more clearly the austere responsibilities of my profession as a historian. Not that the thought ever entered my mind to subordinate this profession to any school or group whatsoever. But I can say in all sincerity that I do not consider history to be an impassive muse. To be a historian I cannot, indeed must not, strip myself of my Catholic and French Canadian nature. To my mind this would be depriving myself of my own original being, of the very essence of my personality. Even if I were to desire it, such a deprivation would be impossible. One can only divest oneself of one's personality by ceasing to exist, by being literally a nobody.

# L'Action française: An Appraisal

L. Groulx, "Jugement sur l'oeuvre," *Mes Mémoires* (Montreal, Les Editions Fides, 1971), Vol. II, pp. 380-383. Reprinted by permission.

*L'Action française* had now lived its span. What would remain of that flurried and exhausting work? Had I simply wasted ten years of my life? No matter how modest his post, a man who accepts to keep watch and sound the alarm for his people must also accept being isolated and misunderstood. Sometimes, of course, he may be told he is doing a useful and even necessary job. He may be praised for his great insight, for striking at the right moment, for sowing seeds in fertile ground. Is this really the case, and what does he know of it anyway? Absorbed in his task, he scatters his ideas, his appeals, sometimes even his anguished cries to the four winds. Will he ever know if his voice has been heard or how many of his people have been reached, shaken, improved, or inspired to action by it?

A watchman's post, a lighthouse keeper's post. How often, when I was a child fishing by night on the shores of Deux-Montagnes Lake, I raised my eyes to gaze upon one of those lights, the lonely lighthouse at the tip of Ile Cadieux, in the very center of the lake. That mysterious light attracted my thoughts, conjuring up my first visions. Ever since that time, I have often dreamed of lighthouses perched on promontories, or on cliff-tops, in the middle of lakes or far out to sea. What do they know of the men they save from shipwreck, the ships whose course they help correct? What do they know of the poets and dreamers whose thoughts flutter around their wind-swept and fog-bound luminous eye like gorgeous night butterflies?

What has remained of *L'Action française*? When I try to define the orginality of our movement, it seems to me that it was to gather into a more precise, more substantial synthesis those ideas scattered helter-skelter by Bourassa, by *Le Devoir*, by the entire nationalist group. Then too we helped these ideas live, move and inspire events by placing at their disposal almost every means of propaganda. At times I was passionately interested in this movement, despite all the failures and disappointments. How hard, how difficult, to rouse a nation from its apathy when it has been dislocated by conquest and poisoned by its own people, especially its politicians, those obsequious servants of the conquerors: traitors – perhaps unwitting – but nevertheless prepared to sacrifice everything, like a herd of wretched sycophants, for the petty glory of a single man, or for party profit.

Not without regret did I separate myself from *L'Action française*. I could not see it die without much sorrow. How would it be replaced? It was impossible for me to forget those ten years during which a group of men had so generously and freely given the best of themselves. Among many other happy memories, could I ever forget those evenings when, following our sometimes heated discussions in the building on Rue Saint-Denis, I would walk back to the vicarage at Mile End, alone with Antonio Perrault? Of the entire group, Perrault was the man with whom I felt in closest agreement on all our problems. It would be getting late, and along the almost deserted street we could compare notes in perfect privacy, exchanging thoughts and feelings. How dear to us was our small homeland! How far we were from cynicism or from the haughty contempt shown by today's young people, who are so terribly lost and bewildered. For us, our small, French and Catholic country represented a rich reality, a living, possible belief in the achievement of a noble, a truly great culture. In spite of its hardships, our small nation did indeed exist: the conqueror's descendants found it so awkward and embarrassing; the ogre of assimilation sought to strangle and devour even its tiniest manifestations. Yes, we believed in the future of French Canada. During those long evening walks, I remember how much comfort and joy we derived from our slightest victory. I remember too how strongly a slide backwards, a loss of ground, an unfortunate act or word, the cowardice of some politician, would hurt and disgust us. Ah, those conversations in almost complete solitude, in the middle of the night, when the large city around us was busy with its amusements, or already asleep! How easily those talks could have inspired us with doubts about our activities! Had we wasted our time, chasing after illusions? But no – was it simply another illusion? – when we arrived home and were just about to say goodnight, Perrault and I almost always felt more buoyant than ever, filled with firmer hope and conviction.

In spite of everything, I feel I can truly say that my generation reacted energetically, obstinately refusing to adopt attitudes of resignation. One night in June 1927, on a historic pilgrimage to the banks of the Saint-Maurice, I undertook to describe this reaction, this attitude so characteristic of the men of my time. To end the chapter, I would like to quote that description, taken from volume XVIII of *L'Action française* (110-112):

> When our generation began its life, around 1900, it immediately reacted against the preceding generation, a generation of negative politicians who made the entire life of the nation revolve about the sterile gossip of the public place. Our reaction was perhaps excessive, too strongly motivated by blunt contempt for the men and the period we abhorred. Still, it carried its own remedy for its excesses, since it added to this contempt for the past and the men it considered responsible for that past, a strong determination to organize the future, beginning immediately with positive policies. Our generation criticized the nation's deviation from its destiny, not merely through sterile recrimination, but in order to recognize more clearly the principles from which we had deviated. If an over-all view of the doctrines sustaining the various groups and schools of the time were taken, it would be seen that in every case the policies were clear and decisive: in the moral and religious realm, a greater understanding of the role of the Church, of the social nature of its doctrine, of the supreme goals it imposes upon a people; a deeper and more conscious pride in our nation's supernatural vocation and the duties consequent upon it. In the political realm, to remove the haze that clouded the nature of our tie to the Empire and to examine that tie in the

cold light of national principles and interests; to fulfil the purpose
of 1867 by wresting the provinces and Quebec in particular from
an all-invading federalism. In the national realm, to stem the tide
of national abdication; to defeat those feeble doctrines of
prudence and tolerance which simply disguised our failures; to
discover and prescribe the tonic for our national soul, to renew
its sense of history and to reveal the value of its heredity and its
rights.

That is what a generation of young men thought and
attempted to do twenty-five years ago.


# On the Fiftieth Anniversary of my Priesthood

L. Groulx, "Au soir de mon cinquantenaire de sacerdoce," a speech
delivered at a banquet in his honour, Montreal, November 21, 1953.
*Pour Bâtir* (Montreal, Editions de L'Action nationale, 1953), pp. 208-
216. Reprinted by permission of Mme J. Rémillard.

I did not want any celebration to mark my fiftieth anniversary.
At first I opposed the idea most vigorously. Over the past six
months, however, I have discovered what subtle and cunning
strategies can be used to undermine even the firmest determination. Let this be a warning to old men who linger longer than
necessary and still have illusions about the prestige of the
ancient. Could it be that one could grow old without accumu-
lating excessive wisdom?
      That was precisely the apprehension that, some forty-five
years ago, on the twenty-fifth anniversary of the Parisian newspaper, *La croix*, I heard Canon Desgranges expressing to his
friend, abbé Solange-Bodin, curé of Menilmontant, who was
then in the full vigour of his youth: "My friend," Canon
Desgranges began his word of thanks to the young speaker,
"you already have far too much wisdom. What will you be like
later on, when you have grown old and asthmatic, paralytic,
rheumatic, – even, who knows, an honorary Canon . . . ?"
      Still, we must assume that wisdom is serviceable at any age.
For example, as I look along this table of honour, I see a great
many people gathered to endorse the past fifty years, among
them my Archbishop, a Cardinal of the Holy Church. The sight

would turn anyone's head, would make any man foolhardy, especially a man with strong tendencies already in that direction. Wisdom counsels humility, reminding me that usually only those people whose credit rating is low require so much endorsement.

Some people will think it strange to celebrate a jubilee with a day of study which, I was told, was at first to be called "a day of national recollection," inspired by the gravity of economic problems in our province. True, fiftieth anniversaries are called golden jubilees, but everyone knows that the gold mentioned is purely symbolic and not very useful in our modern purses. It is equally true that not long ago, a daring writer described Jesus of Nazareth as the "precursor of the big businessman of the modern city." The thought does not exactly reassure me. A few years ago, I was very struck by a directive sent to his clergy by Cardinal Suhard, the Archbishop of Paris: "The priest is a redemptor, not a temporal Messiah ... He must not strip the supernatural quality from his message or reduce the words and power of God to a philosophy of humanism or infinite progress."

I recalled then, with some uneasiness, the numerous, very secular enterprises in which I had taken part. I was editor of *L'Action française*, for example, for nearly ten years; in that capacity I organized an inquiry into economic problems, in 1920, for which I wrote the leading article and the conclusion. In 1936 I gave a talk on "Economic and National Issues" to the Junior Chamber of Commerce of Montreal and, three days later, to an association of young lawyers in Quebec. I taught at the School for Higher Commercial Studies at a time when any self-respecting professor was supposed to have encyclopaedic knowledge: I therefore taught not only the History of Canada and Universal History, but also the History of Commerce from the beginning of the world to the present day. In the spring of 1916 I went on a lecture tour of all the colleges and seminaries of the province to introduce the School for Higher Commercial Studies to graduating students and inform them about opportunities for new economic careers. And I could go on ...

Doubtless I could plead extenuating circumstances. Who sent me to the School for Higher Commercial Studies? Who asked me to undertake the lecture tour? One of my ecclesiastical superiors at the time, the Rector of the University, Mgr. Gaspard Dauth. Similarly, the stand taken by *L'Action française* as an avant-garde journal of national action was also well-known. Who pressed me to take on the editorship? My colleagues of the period, and particularly my good friend Mr. Antonio Perrault will remember how reluctant I was to do so. Ecclesiastical permission was required before I could assume the function, and I stated firmly that I would not seek this authorization myself, convinced that it would be politely refused. Mr. Perrault undertook the task, and, to my utter amazement, came back victorious. A few days later Mgr. Bruchési remarked to me: "Accept. In this sort of intellectual undertaking, I think it most appropriate that priests mingle with the laity." This was all very well, but did it not present me with opportunities for all kinds of rash action?

In fact, were my ecclesiastical superiors really at fault? The priest must of course be a spokesman for the word of God here on earth; he must concern himself with the mass, the sacraments, the most sublime forms of divine activity in this world. This is the priest's role and he must fulfil it. That does not mean that he is a statue on a pedestal. His ministry carries him into the thick of human affairs. That great leader of the Church, Cardinal Suhard, reminded his Parisian clergy of this fact in the document I mentioned before: "The priest is failing in his vocation if he limits his efforts to the salvation of souls; for his parish does not include only souls, but problems, structures, a given time and a given place in the earthly city . . . and so while clericalism in all its forms must be repudiated, for it involves a confusion of jurisdictions, the collective salvation and human improvement of the city are imposed upon the priest as a duty."

My conscience was also relieved when one day I read this extract from a letter written by the Sacred Congregation to Mgr. Liénart, the future Cardinal of Lille: "In our present day and age, no member of the clergy should imagine that such work (that of the worker-priest) is foreign to his ministry, simply because it is carried out in the economic realm, for it is precisely in that realm that the eternal salvation of souls is imperilled." This lucid directive indicates the priorities which the priest should bear in mind when approaching secular issues. You will hardly be surprised, therefore, that when you spoke to me about this study session and asked me what aspect of our collective life we should emphasize, I immediately answered: all aspects. Not one single problem but all, because they are all interrelated and affect one another. Convinced of the rather obvious fact that the life of a nation is a living synthesis, "an active metaphysic", to use a famous phrase, I can truthfully say that I never thought of the French Canadian problem except in these terms and in this context. When, long ago in the days of our *Action française*, I tried to define our policies – that was in January 1921 – I wrote: "Our policies can be stated in one brief formula: We wish to reconstruct a full French life for ourselves." A few years ago – in 1941 – I was asked to speak to a hundred students gathered together by one of them, a man who became my excellent friend, the learned

Dr. Jacques Genest. He asked me in what area we should primarily try to excel. My reply is in *Parole à des étudiants*: "We should excel in everything. We need great politicians, great lawyers, great doctors, great engineers, great writers, great poets, great artists, great philosophers, great theologians, great saints." And I added, for the women students who were also present: "In addition we need great schoolmistresses, great nuns, great mothers, great women." The other day I reread by chance the programme for *A National Revolution* outlined by Marshal Pétain immediately after his accession to power. How happy I was to discover a similar regard for synthesis, and thus to acquire a bit of Pétain's high authority. With France lying wounded almost unto death, the Marshal said: "We want a strong state fortified by the spiritual values and natural associations of home and workshop; we want strong families reinforced by reforms in education and inheritance laws; we want a strong labour force by means of corporative organization; we want laws which will free us from the rule of politicians and the domination of money; we want intellectual and moral reforms which will replace mere facility by a sense of effort, the danger of idleness by the dignity of work, the neglect of youth by an upbringing in hope and faith, contagious selfishness by the primacy of the homeland."

We must be concerned with synthesis. Not however, to the extent of refusing to give our undivided attention to one particular issue. A human organism is a synthesis. It is important that all its various functions be organized harmoniously. Must we therefore refuse to devote particular care to a diseased organ which could compromise the health of the entire body? These are the reasons which have made me turn frequently, and perhaps more frequently in recent years, to economic problems. I have been obsessed with them because their entanglement with our highest spiritual interests makes of them a major problem. Given the enormous extent to which the planet is now being exploited, no one in any country in the world can escape the implications of economic problems. Why should we with our almost frenetic rate of industrial development expect to escape them? We say that language is the guardian of the faith, and rightly so. But I maintain that in French Canada we also need an economic life to be guardian of our language and culture and consequently of our faith. Call it what you like, servitude can never be a healthy or normal condition for a nation. A people which has become in large part a proletarian mass – you know what I mean – cannot be forced to learn a second language just to earn its daily bread and still be proud of its maternal tongue. If our population retains only a sentimental attachment to its culture, denying that it has any practical value, this culture must inevitably become that of an elite – and we may well ask what elite, and for how long? I would even be so bold as to ask how a proletarian population can maintain its faith, knowing full well that the vistas of great material success, the displays of strength and wealth, the exercise of authority, are all denied to people of its faith. Such a problem, such a threat to all our institutions is very serious indeed. I know that I am touching on extremely delicate questions, not easy to solve. But I believe that a nation and its culture need a vital minimum to survive. I would certainly like to know how we can survive if we do not face these problems squarely and courageously! History has at least taught me one thing: a nation can subsist and keep the power to renew itself as long as it retains its own type of personality; but as soon as this type is destroyed, spiritual anaemia sets in, which will inevitably lead to physical anaemia: the nation is doomed. Nations are not immortal, certainly; but is it normal for them to die before they have even lived?

Here I shall stop: these observations are no doubt rather severe for a festive occasion. When so many rash optimists were trying to lull us to sleep, I may have rung alarm bells too often and too indiscreetly. I consoled myself, and do so now, with the thought that doing some good for one's compatriots does not always mean giving them pleasure. That is why I have chosen this way of thanking you for the many moving tributes you have just offered me. Could I in the past, can I now take any other course of action? In the areas we have been discussing, the role of the clergy is not to teach technical or strategic methods of liberation. Its role is to prepare the reform of the temporal order by working from within, by reforming men's souls. The role of the priest is to be a priest: to prepare the moral state which in turn prepares liberation. More than has been the case in the past, the priest's main role in schools, colleges, and universities should be to form liberators with well-trained minds and sturdy hearts.

All the rest – and it is a great deal – belongs to you, forms part of your role as laymen. The frontispiece to the great report by Timor Mende entitled  L'Inde sous l'orage  has a picture of an Indian crouched with his head between his hands, extreme tension written on his anguished features. I wish that, faced with the problems of our country, we shared some of that anxiety. You have examined our problem today in all its complexity, trying to achieve a synthesis of its various facets. You wish to find a solution by faithfully keeping in mind this global view, giving the economic issue its rightful due but no more. You seek wide-ranging, durable, constructive solutions, not merely defensive strategies which, like miniature Maginot lines, are easily distorted. Perhaps you have even realized that if we want to get anywhere the first step is to start. It is obvious that we need a new psychological incentive to start us off. We need more than a simple pat – we need a great push. Shall I say what the problem really is? We are too old, and too weary for our age. Our thoughts are no longer young. Our hope is no longer young. Our art, our literature are no longer young. We some-times acclaim works which are no more than pale reflections of the most decadent overseas productions. We need vitamins, we need a bit of shaking up. But who can do this, who can give us this exalting inspiration, if not an elite of courageous and far-sighted leaders?

I remember a lecture I heard in Paris in 1922, in which the speaker attempted to answer this question: "How did the Russians manage to form an army which was able to repulse the German offensive of 1917?" The reply was that their young soldiers had first been taught modern military tactics; then, two hours a day had been set aside for specialists to inspire these young men with an impassioned love of the Bolshevist mysti-que. First a modern, up-to-date strategy, then a vital mystique! Let this be an example to us. Let us modernize our tactics, without forgetting the essential mystique. Then, if you scale the heights of sentiments that move the hearts of men and entire nations, you will discover that to fashion a collective will, a decisive awakening, nothing can move our small French-Canadian and Catholic people more than the firm ambition to preserve its culture, its civilization, and its faith. Then will there be hope in French Canada.

# In Defense of the Nationalism of my Generation

L. Groulx, "Le chanoine Groulx fait l'apologie du nationalisme de ceux de sa génération," a speech to the Federation of Saint-Jean-Baptiste, Saint-Hyacinthe, May 30, 1959. Le Devoir, June 5, 6, 1959. Reprinted by permission of Mme J. Rémillard.

If I wanted to gauge the strength and the audacity of your Federation, I would only have to point to your digging up and reprinting that old work of mine, Directives. Twenty-two years old it is, somewhat shrivelled to say the least, and yet with what obstinacy and confidence you have revitalized it! A veritable *tour de force* that any gardener would envy!

Thank you for this unsolicited, generous mark of esteem. Certainly, if I listened to some young people, I would be haunted by the thought that despite all my hard work, my life has been utterly wasted. My generation, it is claimed, completely misunderstood the most serious of our national problems: political autonomy for example, or the relationship between social and national issues, between nationalism and humanism, etc., etc. I myself extolled our ancestors too much, exaggerated our history and thus incited our people to rest complacently upon their laurels: I lulled them into a false and dangerous sense of security. Please believe me, I do not say these things to complain. Old age teaches modesty. At my age, life, however long and full it may have seemed, is but a handful of dust scattered by the wind.

Still, simple regard for the truth prompts me to ask whether any of our nationalists ever preached autonomy for its own sake, as though it could be an end and not a means? It was always considered a means, nothing more, a means by which a people and its essential institutions could fulfill themselves in complete freedom. What were our reasons for wishing to shake off the yoke and be masters in our own home? None other than the one formulated, more than 30 years ago by the man speaking to you now, in the following brief motto: "Freedom for fulfillment." Did our nationalism blind us to other realities, to other vital aspects of our life, for example the social aspect? I know that a young professor, at least 54 years ago, in 1905, published in the *Revue ecclésiastique de Valleyfield* two articles under this title: "The Preparation of Youth for its Social Role," articles reproduced almost integrally in the A.C.J.C. journal *Le Semeur*, and widely commented upon at the time. We old-timers should not forget that ours was after all the generation which created Catholic and national trade unions for our workers – institutions which seemed to us at the time liberating ones for the working classes, since they gave workers the noblest social doctrines, those which believers still think are in closest harmony with the most generous humanism and which manifest the greatest concern for the condition of the labouring classes. The same generation, if I am not mistaken, also founded the agricultural union movement – the *Union Catholique des Cultivateurs* which was to have such a bright future. It was again this generation of nationalists – the same men unless I am deceived – which demanded family allowances, organized the widespread dissemination of popular savings banks, and determined to cover the province with co-operatives of all kinds because it saw in them a powerful means of achieving economic emancipation. It was that generation which, responding to episcopal directives, dared to dream of setting up solid corporative structures; it began the annual *Semaines Sociales* to study social questions; it urged and founded faculties of social science in each of our universities. Cynics may pour scorn on some of these undertakings because they did not fulfill their early promise. Sincere people, however, must admit that the list of works I have just outlined does not demonstrate much of a divorce between our social and national interests. We all hope, of course, that the efforts of the younger generation in this field will produce results which will surpass those of earlier generations; we must have faith in the future and criticism can sometimes be creative. Meanwhile, since modesty is always appropriate, we could try to be more generous towards our elders instead of being so eager to push them over the edge of the grave.

Allow me to return to the subject once more. Nationalism was always something more than mere words for us, more than an aggressive, negative formula, more than the swaggering threats of an adolescent letting off a bit of steam. How often have we said, and repeated, that a nation's life is a vital synthesis in which all problems are interdependent; that these problems can only be solved within this total perspective; and that it is important consequently to plan action on all levels! The nationalism we dreamed of and lived was inspired by a living, an exalting humanism. We were attached to French culture, ours and that of France; we preached devotion to it. For my part, I tried to place before the eyes of my compatriots some of the glories of their past and this past honestly seemed to me as I described it, not at all despicable or insignificant as people today take pleasure in painting it. Above all, we recommended a living, unshakeable faith in our Catholicism, a filial attachment to the Church. All of this we did because we saw in our history, in our French culture, in our religious faith, in the divine Church, authentic means of attaining what I once described in rather an ambitious phrase as a fine and robust humanity. I am only too willing to acknowledge that we were men of our time, of the twenties and thirties. We were not prophets, not supermen, not in advance of our own time. But, to give due credit to a generation which I believe I knew to some extent, I refuse to think that it was as narrow and petty in spirit, as ridiculous and clumsy in action as people today so condescendingly claim.

Enough of this defence, which will convince none of the short-sighted people for whom the history of the world begins in 1930. Let us consider instead, if you will, an inquiry which was recently held in *Le Devoir*. Apart from a few diatribes which smack too strongly of schoolboys or adolescents not yet fully emancipated, a great deal of this inquiry merits our attention. One word has particularly irritated our new breed of intellectuals: the word "survival". It was no longer enough to survive, we were told, now we had to *live*, as though there were some opposition between the two. You will no doubt have noticed that all the contributors to this inquiry are agreed on one point: survival is a continuing problem for us. They even concede that it is an anguishing problem in our present context and one which will continue to plague us for some time to come. However, there is one most comforting aspect in this inquiry: in the present period of black philosophy, black novels, black poetry, black art, black history – and God knows these pessimistic fashions have reached our shores! – in such a period, even the most cautious contributors do not counsel pessimism or despair. They maintain that there are strong reasons for hope. However serious they might think our ills and disasters, they nevertheless consider that we are not beyond recovery. Alleluia!

But even better, they believe that recovery is possible through education, through the kind of education and teaching we backward souls used to call "national education." Furthermore, it would appear from this inquiry that education of this kind could be dispensed without a complete upheaval of our pedagogical and classical traditions. Certainly there are strong criticisms made of our universities and colleges. In the latter, education is obviously lagging behind, instead of being redesigned to meet the needs of the sons of a people engaged in a struggle for its life. I myself did not hesitate to note this defect recently. A misunderstanding no doubt exists, but I prefer not to linger on this point, confident that superior authorities will not fail to remedy it.

We might also note one delicate point touched upon by the inquiry: the role of the clergy in our national life, and even the role of Catholicism and the Church. On this point too, the more intelligent contributors have not thought it wise to advocate building our life outside the faith, or separating the national sphere from the religious. Nor do they really believe, despite the rumours, in a complete divorce on the national level between our people and the Church.

Our religious authorities, it is claimed in some even quite respectable circles, no longer care about the fate of our small nation. The authorities have decided to concern themselves with their strictly spiritual mission and, in order not to compromise this mission, will maintain a position of cold and strict neutrality in cultural and temporal controversies. I need hardly tell you that I have neither the intention nor the authority to defend the clergy. But I believe I am familiar with the thinking of some of the more important of our religious leaders. No doubt they would immediately claim that their mission is, first and foremost, of a spiritual nature. And nothing obliges them, even the absence of an active laity, to take on cultural or political responsibilities. But they will also tell you that a spiritual mission cannot dissociate itself entirely from earthly and temporal matters.

The Church is not an extra-terrestial institution. A continuation of Christ, it is incarnated in all the people among whom it lives; it espouses their miseries just as it espouses the values of their culture and civilization. The eternal salvation of individuals and peoples – as the Church has long known and taught – cannot be dissociated from their economic, social, and cultural condition. How indeed could the Church be indifferent to elements which constitute a basis of support for the faith?

I am convinced that our religious leaders today would willingly endorse the declaration our former Bishops made in 1850, during the Union period: "True patriotism," these Bishops reminded their faithful, "is inseparable from true faith." And they added: "Since the clergy is the guardian of the people entrusted to its care, it must direct them in ways which will lead to their temporal happiness. It is a doubly sacred duty we fulfil when we ensure terrestrial abundance for our people in their native land, and simultaneously provide them with the comfort of their fathers' religious beliefs."

You will find a rather similar declaration in the recent letter written by the Bishops of Quebec about a certain television programme in which the bounds of decency were not maintained. Our present-day Bishops forcefully called for respect of "Christian principles and religious convictions of which our nation is so justifiably proud, and which it rightly considers essential to society, and inseparable from our civilization and culture." The Church knows perfectly well, in addition, that by espousing the cause of French Canadians, it is not harming anyone, not declaring war upon anyone. It is simply accepting its role and adapting itself to it. After all, a French Canadian should not have to beg for his right to exist in his own country; he should not have to make apologies for his traditions and his culture.

May I remind you, at this point, that it was we French Canadians who in 1864 and 1867, insisted on the federal nature of the new state. Without us, without our enormous bridge between Upper Canada and the Maritimes, Confederation would not have been possible.

Without us, what would have become of the Canada dreamed of by the Fathers of Confederation? Possibly the federal idea might have won out some day. But how much trouble would it have occasioned when we consider the resistance of all the provinces, except Ontario, to their entry into Confederation? That is why we have the right to be blunt – a privileged right, I might say, to demand all the attributes of a sovereign Quebec, so that we may survive and live. For the same reasons, our religious leaders do not have to appeal to any but the ordinary rights of citizens in order to take an interest in the national rights of the faithful.

Besides, there are very special and powerful motives, of which the clergy are well aware, and which compel them to undertake more than their spiritual mission. From the very origins of French Canada, the Church, almost alone, had to assume the functions of teaching and education. It still retains a notable part of this function. It plays a role on the Council of Public Education, in our universities, our colleges, our convents, as well as in most of our schools. When the clergy accepted the duty of teaching and educating an entire nation, was it not also accepting the duty of forming the whole man – that is not only his religious and moral formation, but also his intellectual, national and civic formation? As schoolmasters to a nation our clergy is linked forever to the fate of French Canada. This is a role of the utmost importance which, to my knowledge, they have no intention of relinquishing.

The very spiritual mission of the clergy requires it to prepare French Canadians for their tasks, for the demands of their particular time and place – to make of them worthy witnesses of the faith. Let us therefore place our trust in the leaders of our Church. They know the interdependence of the spiritual and the temporal. Since they are guardians of human values in French Canada, how could they become accomplices of policies designed to uproot our people? How could they support those mundane philosophies of despair and surrender which are all too fashionable nowadays? Particularly when one does not abandon sacred duties unless one is preparing to resign many other functions as well. All of which means that our great educators would be betraying whatever is sacred in their mission if they did not make of us citizens and Christians of the highest quality.

There is thus no divorce at all between the clergy and the French Canadian nation. No divorce, either, contrary to the wishes of some people, between our national life and Catholicism. Not even for the rather peculiar reason sometimes given of making ourselves more open to non-Catholics – as if Catholicism engendered hard hearts and narrow minds! Are we believers or are we not? If we are, we do not need to learn that a baptized people can only banish its faith or the rules and inspirations of its faith from its public life through the most disastrous of errors. Have we forgotten what marvellous uplifting powers the divine grace of Christ can confer upon us, powers which daily inspire our most courageous achievements?

Just yesterday, the new Apostolic Delegate praised French Canadian missionaries for the ease with which they adapted to the various peoples among whom they exercise their ministry. What has given these sons of our nation their warm, open heart and understanding nature, if not the charity which derives from their faith? Have we forgotten that what Catholicism accomplishes in our individual lives, it can also accomplish in our national life? It is indeed the strongest of catalysts, the purifying and organizing principle, the incomparable factor ensuring balance between all the elements of a civilization. I once wrote: "We shall be Catholics, or we shall be nothing at all." And since we must use every human or superhuman power at our command to solve the enormous problems that have long confronted us, why not keep at least the means of being something?

Yes, my dear friends, we are a people of Catholic faith and French culture. This I consider to be a verifiable, an almost tangible truth. North of Mexico we are the only Catholic nation organized within its own state and occupying a territory comparable in size to that of many great countries. It could be our destiny to encourage the growth upon this old soil of Quebec of a civilization, modest perhaps, but truly original, a Latin flower in the heart of an English garden. Its values would be those of the most orthodox and strict Christian civilizations: it would be an homage from grateful sons to their Mother Church. As I speak to you of such aims, am I being carried away into the realms of whimsy or fiction? Quite the contrary: all this, it seems to me, simply derives from what we are, from what Providence has willed us to be.

Gentlemen, you are seeking an undertaking, an idea capable of attracting and guiding a whole generation. I must admit that I would simply fail to understand a young generation which did not respond to such a marvellous prospect for the future. It would be even more baffling if educators and advocates of nationalism did not try to impress a disoriented and uprooted generation with the promise of so enviable a destiny.

Let me confide in you: it is these perspectives which have animated my life, sustaining me through efforts which often seemed overwhelming. They will keep my incurable optimism intact, I hope, right to the end. In the exalting atmosphere of this ambition, the men of my generation spent their youth. I only wish that it be passed on to you as well.

I do not wish to conceal the fact that to achieve such a future we shall need much intelligence and much courage. New generations will have to relieve the old at the post. From time to time we shall need men of genius to govern us. Yet it is not a mediocre ambition for a nation to have within its soul a design of greatness and nobility. You, who are leaders of men, must remember that such long-term hopes, mere folly in the eyes of the world, are reserved for men of faith.

# My Concept of History

L. Groulx, "Ma conception de l'histoire," a speech delivered over CBC television, December 22, 1959. *L'Action nationale* (April 1960), pp. 603-617. Reprinted by permission of Mme J. Rémillard.

I am often asked about my concept of history. This is not simply a matter of technique, or methods of work. In a similar circumstance, Marc Bloch wrote, "Here you have the historian called to account for his work. Not without a few qualms will he venture to do so." Nevertheless, the curiosity is a legitimate one, if this concept is the key to a work of history, revealing its inspiration, its structure, even its bias, for there are people determined to find one whether it exists or not. I shall confess straight away that this concept was not a spontaneous creation of my mind. No fairy godmother produced it with a wave of the wand. Forgive the rather presumptuous comparison, but I am not very impressed by the story of Minerva springing fully armed from Jupiter's brow. As is well known, I came rather late to history. My previous training had prepared me for teaching literature in a college, and this I in fact did for a period of some ten years. In September 1915, when Mgr. Bruchési appointed me upon very short notice to the Chair of Canadian History – a Chair which had been vacant for fifty years – at what was then called Laval University of Montreal, I had no practical training in my new profession. It is true that at the University of Fribourg where I was studying languages, I had sat in on the courses given by a great Mediaevalist, Father Mandonnet, o.p. At Valleyfield College I had written a small textbook of Canadian history for my students. To improve it I had done a few months of research in the Archives in Ottawa. This flimsy training was all the preparation I had for my new task as a University Professor of History!

In great haste I sought enlightenment on the notion or

concept of history and on methods of work. Where did I look? I consulted the manual of methodology then in current use, a book by Langlois and Seignobos (5th Edition, Paris, 1897). "The perfect textbook," it has been described, "for an erudite positivist," and already the object of much criticism. Men of my generation remember, for example, the passionate campaigns the young contributors to the Paris *Action française* waged against "the Sorbonne crew." They also recall Péguy's vehement denunciations, in *L'Argent* and *L'Argent suite*. Where would the Seignobos method have led me? To a dangerous misconception of the historian's role as an entirely passive one: the observing of a few rules and models so as to record the past with "mechanical faithfulness." I also ran the risk of being saddled with a singularly unintelligent concept of the historical method as a kind of "tool, a machine in which raw documents are fed through a funnel and spewed out at the other end in a continuous, fine stream of historical knowledge." (Marrou). Such a theory leads straight to mere erudition, to the kind of history so strongly denounced nowadays, the "history of events": great events, great people, wars, political turmoil, diplomatic negotiations, a few catastrophes, and so on.

This methodology was much criticized, as I have mentioned, and there were reactions against it. These reactions were to take a very brilliant form between 1940 and 1950, under the guidance of three remarkable theorists of history: Marc Bloch, whose *Apologie pour l'histoire: ou Métier d'historien* (*The Historian's Craft*) appeared in 1941, Lucien Febvre whose *Combats pour l'histoire* appeared in 1953, although his *Propos* for the Ecole Normale Supérieure dates from 1942, and Henri-Irénée Marrou, the author of *De la connaissance historique* (*The Meaning of History*), 1954.

What concept of history was put forth by these theorists? For the three of them, history is the science of mankind, or rather of men. Let us see what each one of them says about it. Here is Marc Bloch:

> Long ago we were taught by our masters, men like Michelet and Fustel de Coulanges, to recognize that the object of history is, by its very nature, Man. Better still: individual men. History must penetrate behind the visible features of the landscape, behind tools and machinery, behind what seem the coldest documents and the institutions most remote from their founders, to seize the men themselves. The historian who does not manage to do so will never be more than an erudite drone. A good historian is like the giant in the fairy tale: whenever he smells human flesh he knows his prey is near.
>
> (*Métier d'historien*, "Cahier des annales", No. 3)

Here now is Lucien Febvre:

> History, the science of Man (with a capital M), the science of our human past. Not a science of things or concepts ... There can be no History but that of Man, for this is history in the widest sense of the word ... History, a science of Man: then you can have *facts*, yes, but *human facts*. The task of the historian: rediscover the facts, the events, and interpret them ... *Documents*, yes, but *human documents*. And the words of which they are made up. *Documents*, undoubtedly, but *all the documents*. Not only those documents in archives, to which people attach such privileged importance ... Documents, obviously, but not only documents ...
>
> (*Combats pour l'histoire*, 12-13)

And finally, H.-Irénée Marrou:

> The object of history is the complexity of reality, of man ... History will be true if it succeeds in discovering man's reality in all its richness.
>
> (*De la connaissance historique*, 131)

I would first like to point out that my own historical works lie very definitely between the two schools. *Nos luttes constitutionnelles* (the substance of my first lectures) dates from 1915-1916. The four volumes of *L'Histoire du Canada français depuis la découverte*, the synthesis of my lectures and studies, date from 1950-52. Where have I defined my concept of history? In the few prefaces I wrote for some of my volumes, in my notes for small classes at the University of Montreal, and, of course, in my works themselves. Where did I obtain this concept? Did I borrow it from Fustel de Coulanges, or from Godefroi Kurth, the masters I studied most extensively at the very beginning of my career as a historian? Did I counter-balance the Seignobos textbook with my timely reading of *Travail scientifique* by Father Funck? One discovery which of course pleases me is that my own concept, drawn up and almost completely formulated forty years ago, is amazingly close to that presented by the new school. Take, for example, these extracts from the Preface to *Naissance d'une race*, which appeared in 1919:

> I kept in mind that true history must merge into psychology. It would not be worth undertaking such long and arduous research to find the facts and events of ancient eras if they did not in the end reveal a certain frame of mind, a form of humanity. ...
>
> In the vast accumulation of facts, the ones which are of particular interest to me are those which mark the evolution of a human type, and which consequently have psychological significance or value.

Here is another equally explicit text from the Preface to *Lendemains de conquête*, published in 1920:

> It [history] is not simply an inferior kind of display in an archaeological exhibition, or a museum of great names and famous dates, the bare bones of history. The task of the historian is to assemble the debris from the past and organize it so as to infuse its former life into it again; it is to resurrect what remains the highest element of the past: I mean the psychology of various periods, the soul of successive generations, all that human dust clamouring to live again. That is what makes history worth writing. (pp. 7-8)

Finally, from a small brochure on Jeanne Mance written in 1944, I take the following phrase:

> The supreme joy of the historian will always be to pierce through the complexity of innumerable facts to recover and study the souls of men. (p. 13)

The object of history, therefore, is Man, "all that human dust" as it appeared to the novice historian I was then. I would gladly echo a phrase of Mauriac's from *Mémoires intérieures*: "I belong to a generation which believed in man." By "Man" I mean – and this could be the second element in my concept of history – not abstract Man, but concrete Man who must be glimpsed and picked out from the immense context in which he moves, from the network of powers and influences enveloping him; Man with his innumerable ways of behaving, Man in his geographical, economic, political, social, cultural, moral and religious environment.

Since I am concerned with concrete Man, it has also been my belief that one has to take into account the role of the great man, the leader, the strong personality who in any field, whether it be theology, philosophy, politics, art, or literature, creates great, and sometimes tragic, upheavals: Those awesome heroes who precipitate the normal development of history.

Beyond the great man, however, I have always looked to another supreme leader of history: God, his divine Providence. True, this divine action is not always easy to discern. But as believers, we know that our faith prevents us from considering God an impassive witness to our human drama. He pursues his own works, through the will of men or despite it. This divine action could be compared to the diffused light in the stretches of blue sky that form the background of those famous paintings, a light whose source remains hidden yet which deepens the perspective and brings into sharper relief the characters, gestures, and objects in the foreground of the canvas. In addition, we have the presence of the Church, the visible Church which continues here on earth the work of the Son of God. We observe that through its doctrine, its almost unrivalled intellectual power, its morality, its sacramental dynamism, it has the opportunity, at very least, of influencing men's actions, institutions, private and public customs, and often of magnifying them with great splendour. We know as well that civilizations are mortal, and that their death results not merely from natural, irremediable causes, but from the voluntary introduction of a deadly virus into their blood stream.

There are all the elements of my concept of history. To verify them, simply consult my notes for my small classes. How often have I reminded my students that the life of any people can be defined as a vital synthesis! History, I have always taught, is made up of complex factors, the constant interaction of cause and effect; history is not simply a compilation of facts; it has its own internal logic, its pattern of development which must be discovered. Events, I also said, do not merely follow one another, they form a chain: they are produced by and in turn produce other events. The historian's delicate and difficult task is to unravel the complex of causes and assign each of them its true role. A difficult task, but so fascinating, one of the most fascinating of all tasks undertaken by the human intellect. As proof of what I have just said, allow me to quote this passage from the first volume of my *Histoire du Canada français*:

> The history of men carries its own logic. Events are not merely juxtaposed or compiled. They do not sprout like mushrooms, if indeed mushrooms do sprout without cause. In history everything is cause and effect. The present is not merely the chronological sequel of the past; it is the product of the past; between the present and the past there is a continuous and filial relation. It is this relation, this link which the mind seeks through instinct or inner compulsion that I would like to make visible. In other words I would like to draw from their tangled and yet fused interplay the causes, all the causes if possible, of the curves and evolutions in the life of our small people.

That this was indeed my concept of history and not merely an artificial pattern will I think be sufficiently obvious in my historical works. From the very first, I never discussed a period without ending with a review, or rather a drawing together of the various historical factors, whether political, economic, social, cultural, or religious. I am aware that Lucien Febvre is set against the "pigeon-holing" of history. "There is no such thing as economic or social history," he says. "There is only history, in its unity." Nor is it desirable to have those "aspects" of history stuck on at the end of books, like appendices, as we find for example in Voltaire's *Siècle de Louis XIV* and *Siècle de Louis XV*.

No doubt this is right, if it means that various elements should not predominate but remain rather the warp of history's fabric. Does this mean that it is forbidden to examine various factors one by one to see their role more clearly? Why should it be desirable for the historian to forget the limits of the human mind, to forget that the mind is obliged to proceed by analysis, by dividing in order to define and understand?

Ferdinand Brunetière held that *L'Histoire des Variations des Eglises protestantes* was Bossuet's masterpiece; he even considered it "the most beautiful book in the French language." Critics lauded the great writer to the skies for his ability to handle two factors simultaneously: the discussion of doctrine and the narration of events. Very good. But what praise would then be deserved by that miraculous historian who could relate, with the same mastery and order, not only a chapter of religious history, but the integral, complex history of an entire civilization? Must we seek perfection to that utopian extent? Will the historian ever be born with the breadth and dexterity of mind to weave together without ever mixing the numerous strands which make up the life of a people? In history, some mending has to be done. This darning is surely as inevitable as those last touches which the artist gives to his painting, those few vigorous brush strokes applied to certain areas to emphasize the integrity of the whole composition.

One prime question remains to be tackled. In such theories, however orthodox, what becomes of historical objectivity, by which I mean the capturing of reality in one's reconstitution of the past? Do we have techniques which would allow us to attain the whole of this reality, sometimes long evaporated? There is one dream which we can immediately dismiss from our minds: in history, can we really ever speak of absolute objectivity?

Recent theorists have certainly done much to rehabilitate the reputation of historians. They have reminded us that historians cannot simply be improvised: to be a historian requires certain gifts which technical skill can and must perfect but cannot create. History, they further maintain, is subordinated to the historian, to the qualities of his mind and his technical training: history depends more on the historian than on documents. What is a document without an historian to discover and interpret it? The historian, said Marrou, is neither "a bookworm, nor a filing cabinet." The same theorists, however, have also underlined the historian's limits. He should know everything, since his intention is to investigate the whole of man's past, and all aspects of life in the past. But can he know everything? He must deal with the endless increase of historical material continually being deposited in various archives. Contrary to Mr. Seignobos' naive assumption, it is quite wrong to suppose that all historical documents have now been collected and their bulk will diminish with the passage of time. At what point in his research can the historian ever be sure that no important document has slipped through his net? He must also pick his way through the overlapping concentric waves created by so many events, and through the almost inextricable tangle of cause and effect, grappling with mysterious causes, often impenetrably hidden away in the depths of the consciousness of the great and small actors of history. No observer can, at any given moment, grasp the whole of the present. How could a historian grasp, *objectively*, the whole of the past? History, as Fustel de Coulanges once said, "is the most difficult of all sciences."

With Marrou, then, one arrives at this modest conclusion: in history, nothing but a very relative objectivity is possible; absolute objectivity is impossible, and so are complete possession and resurrection of the past; only approximations or partial reconstructions are feasible. We must be resigned to being forever ignorant of certain aspects of the past. These aspects are as elusive, I would say, as certain galaxies whose mystery we shall never penetrate. It is not within the power of a historian to reach complete certainty: he must be content with the merely probable. "Historical knowledge resting on the notion of documentation is only a second-hand experience of reality through an intermediate party." It is therefore not "susceptible to proof," it "is not a science, properly speaking, but a learning based on trust." (Marrou, *passim*, 133-135, 143.) In other words, we may speak if we like of historical *knowledge* but should be careful of the rather inappropriate term historical *science*. The reason is that in history there is no absolute determinism. History exists only in the singular; it may occasionally repeat itself, but never in exactly the same way.

After all that am I still questioned about my own attitude to this problem of objectivity, especially to problems of Canadian history? I have never had any pretension to neutrality, indifference, insensibility or impeccability. I aspired only to impartiality. I have carried on my career as a historian without divesting myself of what each individual calls his personality. I am not one of those naive or pretentious people who thinks it possible or desirable for a historian to deprive himself of his personality. On the contrary, I have always thought that a historian must bring the whole of his being, all his faculties, all his strength, to bear upon his work. He has nothing superfluous which he must discard. I fail to see why the accident – if it is an accident – of being Catholic and French Canadian should prevent a man from being truthful and just, or expose him more than does the Anglo-Protestant mentality, for example, to the pitfalls of subjectivity. I am not aware that French reason or Catholic sentiment have any innate tendency towards injustice or the distortion of facts. Pushing this theory of eliminating one's personality to its logical conclusion would result in the absurd proposition that only a perfect atheist or a man without a country could be a historian.

On this point as well, unless I am mistaken, the new theorists support my view. I will simply quote Marrou: " . . . a historian is not an abstract individual as defined in the context of liberal thinking, but a committed being, rooted through all the fibres of his being to the human environment in which he belongs – the social, political, national, cultural environment – which has made him what he is, and which is benefited by everything he does" (*Op. cit.*, 278). All that is required of him is that he take care not to be trapped within his own mentality, "which is borrowed on the whole from the mentality common to his environment and his own time" (*Ibid*, 151).

Ferdinand Brunetière once congratulated the Protestant Rébelliau on the unbiased manner in which he had judged *L'Histoire des Variations*. Rébelliau even forgave Bossuet for the touches of acerbity in his lively style. Brunetière wrote:

> If, instead of Bossuet, one preferred some ideal, imaginary historian whose apparent impartiality would in reality be mere indifference to the questions discussed, that would be . . . I won't say a mockery, although I think it. Where is such a historian, and what is his name? . . . the fact is that there is no such historian, and never could be, because history would be the lowest employment for the human mind if it consisted merely of satisfying a platonic curiosity . . .
>
> People complain that Bossuet, while relating the history of Protestant sects, passes judgment on Protestantism. Why do they not chastise him for having dared broach the subject at all! . . . To rebuke him for his partiality . . . is simply to rebuke him for not being a Protestant himself (*Bossuet*, Paris, 1913, 73-75).

Finally, I turn to questions of form. How should history be written? On this point, I shall again be frank. I have always thought that there is no theory or method, however exacting, which obliges the historian to write badly, to be boring or unreadable. I have always believed that any effort to express one's thought well can only add to the precision of that thought; such an effort indeed can only be an aid to objectivity. Before setting about the actual writing of his work, what harm can it

do to the historian to shake off some of the archival dust clinging to his fingers? History must be soberly written but it does
not have to be entirely dry! It is more than mere erudition. Shall
I note that on this matter as well my opinion receives the
support of history's new technicians?

It is often in the attempt to express itself that knowledge takes
a step forward, achieving decisive progress ... Our scientific
history would not have fallen so low in the public esteem and its
function would not have been usurped by all kinds of caricatures
(romantic or anecdotal literature, or servile propaganda) if serious
workers had not so completely neglected their public, being
content to churn out books that were simply the undigested
contents of their filing cabinets, rudis indigestaque moles. Too
many publications are not history, but simply a semi-refined
heap, the raw material for history.

The same Marrou adds:

To perform this task well, to really fulfil his function
completely, the historian must also be a great writer. As can easily
be demonstrated, all great historians have been great literary
artists as well. (Marrou, Op. cit., 281-283, 285).

In history, I do not even object to those "portraits" which
some find so repelling. Not, of course, those descriptions which
are nothing more than a brilliant performance, an exercise in
literary virtuosity. Not the description for its own sake but as
a function of historical knowledge. Why not? The historian is
required to describe the landscape, the setting in which the
history of a nation unfolds. Why forbid him from describing
Man, the great creator of history? Man is the object of history.
Why then prevent the historian from attempting to grasp him,
in his physical being and in his psychological depths? How
many events, great or small, had their first germination in the
deepest corner of the human conscience, in that mysterious
world where the great struggle is waged between good and evil,
between duty and the passions! Consider, for example, how
minutely Marrou describes Jules Ferry and his background
when he discusses this statesman's accession to power in the
French Government of 1880. (Marrou, Op. cit., 57.)

It is therefore very difficult to understand and accept the
almost Olympian disdain expressed by French Canadian critics
for history and historians. It would seem that the development
and progress of Letters is only judged by works of the imagination: poetry and novels. Only poets and novelists, apparently,
are creative artists. As for history, it is relegated to a

second-class rank in the realm of literature! Is this an acceptable judgment? If the genesis of historical works and the skill
required by the historian's craft were better known, it might
well be that this second-class citizen would also be granted the
status of a creative artist. "History is man's torment," I once
wrote. What kind of a task is it to reconstitute the life of a man,
the life of a people, with nothing but dusty archives, the dry
bones of the past? The historian is more than a builder, he is
a restorer; instead of building with new, fresh materials, he
builds with ruins, with the vestigial remains of a shadowy past.
When we consider the vast learning required of an historian,
the mental effort demanded by a complicated technique, the
difficult work implied in the organic reconstruction of a life
which has sometimes been forgotten for centuries, what intellectual undertaking demands more of the human mind?

Let us turn a final time to one of the great theorists of history:

> ... *historical reality* does not exist, ready-made and waiting for
> science to reproduce it faithfully: history is the product of the
> creative effort by which a historian establishes a tie between
> the past he is conjuring up and the present which is his own ...
>
> We could transpose to history the Pascalian theme of the
> double infinite ... I shall not carry the idea any further – enough
> for us to have glimpsed the dizzying heights ...
>
> If such is the task implicit in this kind of history, what intellect
> could declare itself equal to it? We reply: if such a mind exists,
> it is that of our Lord God, whose uncreated wisdom is in itself an
> intelligent Spirit, subtle, agile, penetrating, clear, trenchant,
> incoercible, solid, sure, capable of anything, dominating every-
> thing, penetrating everything ... (Marrou, *Op. cit.*, 55, 58).

That is my concept of history. Have I always remained faithful to it? Let those people reply who believe in the historian's
impeccability. Or those fortunate, if not very modest, people
who believe that they themselves have never deviated from the
line of conduct they set for themselves. A "concept" is a general
inspiration for the mind; it is not an internal dictatorship, far
less a straight-jacket.

Have my poor works been sufficiently clear and truthful to
increase our knowledge of the past? A pioneer in all senses of
the word – faced with the penury and hardship of pioneering
workers – did I even manage to provide a modest testimony to
my environment, my own time? Did I contribute a single milestone to historiography in French Canada? I would wish it
without exactly expecting it. I have not done everything; I have
not even done much. I hope that I shall be forgiven my intentions, which were always to do a great deal and to do it well.

# Last Will and Testament

L. Groulx, "Extrait du testament du chanoine Lionel Groulx, "*Revue d'histoire de l'Amérique française* XXI, I (June 1967), frontispiece. Reprinted by permission of L'Institut d'histoire de l'Amérique française.

To my friends and relatives I leave this brief message: as a priest, I spent but little time ministering to souls. It was one of the regrets of my life. I consoled myself by remembering that I had chosen neither my career nor my duty. I accepted the choice that was made for me by my ecclesiastical superiors. Another of my consolations was the knowledge that I had worked for the survival of French Canada: a small country and a small people which, because of its Catholicism, always seemed to me the greatest spiritual entity in North America. From this, my abiding point of view, I think it will not be difficult to make sense of everything I said, wrote, or did, or even to understand the passion with which I did it. In view of these motives and this inspiration for my actions, may God forgive me and grant me mercy.

When a man has not accomplished everything he would have wished during his life, he must at least make good use of his death. In all simplicity, I offer mine for the Church, for the causes I have loved and would have wished to serve better. Through the grace of God, I have long accepted my death on the day and hour of His choosing. God grant me to accept it from His hand as a supreme offering: my last mass as a priest.

I earnestly recommend my soul to the prayers of my relatives, my friends, and all those who have kindly assured me that they learned some good from me. As a young seminarian, studying the page of theology which referred to it, I took the "heroic vow". I expressed it in due and proper form. I never repudiated it. Perhaps this will be seen as a reason for not forgetting me too rapidly.

# Québécois on Groulx

## A Narrow Little Sect

"La petite secte," part of an editorial from Le Soleil, October 21, 1927.

To judge by its writings, L'Action française has the most impressive collection of narrow minds in the country. Perfect little toy-like minds they are, tiny, delicate, and incapable of coping with two ideas at a time; minds which imprison all thought between thick walls of prejudice; minds like fine mesh sieves through which anything large, deep, or powerful passes only to emerge minute, superficial and petty. Pretty, convoluted, compartmentalized, like a row of mass-produced baubles, these minds even have the most admirable gift of infallibility, as well as obduracy and a truly wonderful incomprehension of the simplest things. L'Action française is an ingenious device to let people prattle and prate, adopting positively Olympian attitudes, interpreting the secret designs of Providence itself, governing the whole of mankind, doing everything except that which requires simple common sense.

## Blind Prejudice

"Aveuglement sectaire", part of an editorial from Le Soleil, October 24, 1927.

When one reads the whining complaints of these infants pretending to be grown-ups, one realizes that they have never really understood the precise and profound meaning of the word "colonization". In their view, perfect colonization would be sitting in the forest with the mosquitoes. Colonization is quite another matter: it does not mean simply settling pioneers deprived of everything upon new lands, but also encouraging the growth of commerce, industry, all the activities of civilization. Building factories and towns at the same time as the settler sows his wheat on his freshly cleared lands, so that he may hope to sell his crop in neighbouring markets: that is colonization. Anyone who understands the word in any other sense is simply engaging in Utopian fantasy.

Utopian fantasy! Is *L'Action française* anything else? While these men are busy fluttering around the question of an independent French state on the banks of the Saint Lawrence, and bludgeoning the best French elements of the province with their unjust criticism, the world goes on without them, and in spite of them. One day they might happen to notice that not all men are perverse enough to bow down to their opinions and as a result may well decide to leave this small planet, shaking its dust from their feet as they embark for the moon, where there are immense tracts of land as yet uncolonized by the Taschereau government.

# Mr. Lionel Groulx, Prime Minister

"M. Lionel Groulx, Premier Ministre," an article in *Le Jour*, September 16, 1937.

A SECRET PLAN DRAWN UP BY THE NEW NATIONALIST PARTY

We are informed by reliable sources that a political party which has the support of many young people in Quebec is at this moment attempting to persuade abbé Lionel Groulx, the apostle of separatism, to accept in principle the idea of becoming Prime Minister of French Canada.

The Hamel-Grégoire-Chaloult faction, which represents a reactionary element tinged with statism, that is, a modernized extreme-right, has taken the initiative in creating a French state which, by fair means or foul, would establish our nationality as a dominant force not only in politics, by breaking the federal pact, but also in commerce, industry, finance, and even in our mode of thought.

As a first step, abbé Groulx would stand as a candidate in the next provincial elections. This might present a few difficulties. The higher echelons of the clergy would have strong objections, especially in light of the recent speech of Cardinal Villeneuve, indicating his desire to dissociate the superior interests of the

Church from all forms of political intrigue.

To this objection it is replied that there is no absolute incompatibility between being a priest and participating in public life, even as a Member of Parliament or Minister.

In this connection an eminent Member of the new Nationalist Party recently listed a number of priests who have had brilliant political careers, from Richelieu and Mazarin to Lacordaire during the French Romantic period, to Mgr. Seipel quite recently in Austria and to abbés Brémont and Lambert, the latter an enthusiastic supporter of Doriot in France, and many others!

With these precedents in mind, some French Canadians wish to invite certain members of the clergy to participate actively in the political life of the province. This step is even more urgent, it is thought in some ultra-nationalist circles, because of the importance of imposing on our compatriots, not only an exclusively French Canadian way of life, but also a corporative regime and a fascist administration.

What are abbé Groulx's chances of success? Until now this racist leader has been able to count on the support of a few directors of some young people's associations. People who are over thirty-five and less susceptible to thoughtless enthusiasms are almost solidly against any exploitation of regional nationalism. They simply refuse to be fenced in.

The Hamel-Grégoire-Chaloult faction pins its hopes for success on students and youth organizations. In a recent speech Mr. Philippe Hamel suggested that youth would find inspiration for all its activities in the talk given by abbé Groulx at the French Language Congress. During the Congress, the apostle of separatism exclaimed: "Whether one likes it or not we *shall have our French state!* We shall have a young, strong, beautiful, radiant home, a spiritual, dynamic centre for the whole of French America. We shall have a country with its French nature stamped upon its visible features."

It is the poetry of such language which has attracted abbé Groulx's following: he appeals not to young people's reason, but to their emotions. Through such appeals he has also succeeded in detaching quite a number of our compatriots from the true Canadian nation which stretches from the Atlantic to the Pacific, and which, if it abandoned these sterile "racial" struggles, could become one of the great civilizations of the world. 'Tis a pity.

No one doubts abbé Groulx's competence. Although he has never had any administrative experience, he is intelligent, honest, and an eloquent speaker. If such qualities are sufficient to show our nation how to place its capital in the most productive enterprises, well, so much the better!

# The Spiritual Father of Modern Quebec

Claude Ryan, "Le père spirituel du Québec moderne," Le Devoir, May 24, 1967. Reprinted by permission.

Once or twice I wrote that I did not subscribe to some of abbé Groulx's views on the religious events of the times, or that the historian had been too severe in his judgment of the generation which grew into adulthood immediately after the war. But these few reservations have never prevented me from recognizing the decisive role played by Groulx in the evolution of modern Quebec.

In our period of extremely rapid change, the influence of one man or one work rarely carries over a single generation. Men rapidly forget yesterday's enthusiasms. They are forever pursuing new myths, new idols. In contrast, and it is a tribute to the greatness of the man and his work, the influence of Groulx marked three different generations. Because of this, he will go down in history as the spiritual father of modern Quebec.

There is no doubt about the influence Groulx had on men who are now over fifty. In that generation, almost every man who worked for the benefit of French Canadians was a disciple and admirer of Groulx. As young men they had read his articles and listened avidly to his lectures and speeches. From him they received a particular vision – of man, of society, of French Canadians, of their past and future – which was to mark their entire career.

All the activities undertaken by this generation – political movements with nationalist leanings, campaigns for provincial autonomy or for political emancipation, efforts to make our politics more honest, developments in education, original contributions in the social and economic spheres – all these were first influenced and inspired by abbé Groulx. Men like Jean Drapeau, André Laurendeau, Jacques Genest, Richard Arès, François-Albert Angers and many others were, in their youth, disciples of abbé Groulx. Later on, as they went their separate ways in very different careers, they revealed through their work and attitudes the profoundly constructive nature of Groulx's thought. What he sought to do all his life was to show the French Canadian nation its own character, make it conscious of its tragic situation and its original destiny, and inspire it with confidence in its own genius.

Mr. Groulx also saw, very early, that the destiny of the French

Canadian people had to revolve around one fact: the State of Quebec.

This was perhaps his most vital and decisive contribution to the renaissance which was to occur much later. He had long studied the historical evolution of the Canadian Confederation. For years he had compiled eloquent data on the economic alienation of his compatriots. His work very soon led him – as early as the 'twenties – to the conclusion that the State of Quebec would be an essential pivot for the future of which he dreamed. Thirty years later, events were to prove him right.

* * *

During the years between 1940 and 1960, the influence of Groulx suffered an eclipse.

That period was one of Catholic Action, of a surge in the social sciences, in trade unions and co-operative movements. In its haste to destroy the much too strict union of the temporal and spiritual spheres, the generation which emerged from the Depression and the War entirely rejected the guides of the preceding generation.

Louis Saint-Laurent was then in power in Ottawa, and Maurice Duplessis in Quebec. Many believed that nothing more could be expected from traditional nationalism, that the ways of the future had to be sought in entirely new paths. During this period, movements of Catholic Action developed, strongly universal and social in nature, severing thereby the traditional alliance between nationalism and religion. New disciplines emerged to shatter the rather monolithic intellectual patterns of the past. All confessional ties were withdrawn from several social institutions, notably trade unions.

Gérard Pelletier once wrote that this generation had no tutor. What he meant was that they did not recognize any supreme guide in their own midst. For never before, perhaps, had any generation accepted with such enthusiasm the guidance of masters from France and elsewhere. In this sense we can say that Groulx's influence was definitely on the wane. It continued to be felt in some very important circles, notably in the History Department of the University of Montreal, at Le Devoir, and in several economic institutions of French Canada. But it was no longer "the" great influence it had been. Mr. Groulx felt this most painfully, and it explains some of the rather harsh complaints he made from time to time about what he called the "Action Catholique" generation. He rebuked several men of this generation for having opted for the universal by leaping thoughtlessly over national matters. After joining Le Devoir, I myself was forced to concede that the complaint was not quite so ill-founded as I had cheerfully assumed in 1950.

* * *

The period of the "quiet revolution" produced a very interesting synthesis.

Between 1960 and 1966, we witnessed for the first time a meeting between the dreams of democratic modernity entertained by younger men, and the old national ideal which abbé Groulx had never ceased to advocate. Men who until then had been extremely cautious about the Groulx brand of nationalism became ardent proponents of a strong development of the State of Quebec.

Men who had been thought entirely dominated by one single nationalistic ideal demonstrated that they were definitely not indifferent to the social dimensions of problems, or the requirements of the most exacting disciplines.

Nearly everyone who took part in this gigantic effort to modernize the province discovered that they owed something to Lionel Groulx, that they had a great deal in common with him. The scientifically-minded, forgetting their former prejudices, discovered by re-reading Groulx's works and especially by taking note of his important work with the *Revue d'histoire de l'Amérique française*, that he had preceded them all in their chosen field. Men of action, all for a while convinced of the urgent need for a renaissance in Quebec, also realized that Groulx's work was penetrated with love for the people and for democracy, that it had long contained the germ for this great inspiring project of our contemporary history.

One aspect of our recent history profoundly disturbed Lionel Groulx. He had always considered the religious factor an essential element of French Canadians' vocation; now he witnessed with painful impotence the shattering of the spiritual unity of our people. He wanted the cultural, political and economic spheres to expand in a dynamic symbiosis with the values of Catholicism. Instead, he had to witness symptoms of rupture which could not fail to disturb him.

This was indeed a significant phenomenon: dozens of young people rejecting – although perhaps not all as irrevocably as they would have us believe – Groulx's religious heritage, and yet proclaiming their full support for his historic vision of French Canada's destiny.

These young people were quite willing to recognize that the man had a certain quality or "style", had always stood with his head high and had been first to discern the form of political orientation which corresponded to their most profound desire.

Abbé Groulx thus had the joy of seeing, at the end of a very long career, that he had become a kind of spiritual hyphen linking three different generations of French Canadians. In certain circles people continued to debate his ideas. But during his lifetime he had already attained a kind of discreet halo which surrounded him everywhere and was not granted, to our knowledge, to any other modern French Canadian. Those who had formerly been faithful to him remained so, even increasing their respect. Those who thought they had rejected him discovered that they were in fact close to him. Those who were too young to have known him well, set about reading his works with enthusiasm.

Through a rather peculiar paradox, this priest whose heart remained so ardently apostolic to the end, has not had a marked influence on the evolution of the Church, to which he remained strongly attached. Under the pressure of present-day events, the Church has in fact irrevocably adopted movements of *aggiornamento* that abbé Groulx would often have wished less rapid, more subtle.

Yet without ever engaging in partisan politics, without ever abandoning the spiritual perspective which colours his entire work, Groulx had a decisive influence on the temporal destiny of his people. He was, in brief, the spiritual father of modern Quebec. Everything noteworthy, everything novel on the Quebec scene has carried the imprint of Groulx's thought.

It would appear as well that anything of importance in the next few years must also trace the general lines of what Groulx said and above all of what he was.

# In Memoriam

Jean-Pierre Wallot, "In memoriam," *Le Progrès de Valleyfield*, May 31, 1967. Reprinted by permission of the author.

Motionless in front of the coffin, each person stood for a long moment. Then, with veneration, he lightly touched the hands of the deceased. Last week this scene was repeated hundreds and thousands of times. Canon Groulx seemed even more alive in his coffin. He drew all the leaders of the country, regardless of political party or affiliation. French Canada – and particularly our region – had lost the man who was perhaps its most illustrious son, certainly the only man to have belonged to the entire nation. This man of frail appearance, whose stature made him as tall as our greatest trees, so proud and simple, such a vigorous intellect – he appeared even more formidable in death.

Disciples and detractors were reconciled in their common observation that we had indeed lost a dear friend, and what is more, a giant, a great man.

Shall we speak of the historian? Certain big newspapers seemed to imply that a vast reappraisal of Groulx's works would now be made. None knew better than Groulx himself the fate of a historian, which is to write for his own generation, to respond to its queries and its demands. In the nature of things, a historical work is soon dated. Not only are new documents discovered, but interpretations change, along with men and their times. Groulx was forced to train himself through long, hard work. During his long career he studied and elucidated innumerable problems, opening new paths for others to pursue. He himself repudiated certain works of his youth. Yet an important part of his historical work has survived and will endure: firstly as a scientific contribution, and secondly as a milestone, a historiographical point of reference for others. Finally, Groulx awakened the nation's interest in history. To recognize one's own history is to perceive oneself as a distinct entity, to know oneself.

Groulx, however, was not content merely to write our history and teach it – he was the first Professor of Canadian History at the University of Montreal in 1915. Beyond words, he wanted concrete action to strengthen the roots of our "tiny people" threatened with assimilation by Anglo-Saxon America. Around him and his name, study and action circles, journals and various undertakings sprang up. His numerous lectures, public writings and personal advice influenced three generations of French Canadians. The essential part of his message – the existence of the French Canadian nation, its particular destiny, the appeal to excellence, the necessity of a strong Quebec as the central pivot for the development of French Canada – this message he preached unceasingly until it finally penetrated the consciousness of people and began to be fulfilled in the "quiet revolution" we have witnessed since Paul Sauvé.

A historian, a man of action, an incomparable stylist, Groulx was also a priest with passionate zeal. In his view, as in that of a great number of Quebec people, the painful and difficult destiny of French Canadians could not be separated from the impenetrable designs of Providence. French and Catholic: two adjectives which were always coupled in his vocabulary, whenever he spoke of French Canada. This union which is recorded in the origins of the French colony, has never been completely broken, not even in the past decade. No doubt our society is becoming more secular. But it remains penetrated with the ideals of the Church, one of its great founding forces. Evincing the legitimate freedom within this Church, our "national historian" did not hesitate to criticize the first efforts of the Catholic Action movement to achieve "Internationalism" while ignoring the essential point of departure, the nation itself. In the same spirit he fought for academic freedom within the university.

Quite apart from all these varied facets, it was primarily the man himself whom people found enchanting: his simplicity, his warmth, his humour, his unshakeable loyalty to great ideals at all levels, his unwearying labour, and the quality which was a synthesis of all the others, his fantastic gifts as a teacher. Mr. Groulx was a "Professor", a "Master" in the truest sense of the words. In intimate conversation or in a lecture, his personal magnetism enveloped his listener, his eloquence flared up and inspired his audience. He knew how to convince, that is, how to serve truth and present it clearly in flawless language. The Deputy Minister for Cultural Affairs summed it all up in one word when he said that Canon Groulx had "style." But a very particular style, which did not at all depend upon social prestige, or upon vanity or show. The style of a simple man, born of rustic people, born for a great destiny, that of creating his people's conscience and will. "We loved him dearly," André Laurendeau has written. That is the fairest comment, one to which anyone who knew him would wish to subscribe.

# Lionel Groulx

Jean Hamelin, "Lionel Groulx," *Culture* 28 (1967), pp. 167-168. Reprinted by permission of the author.

Readers will have learned with profound sorrow of the death of Canon Lionel Groulx. With him vanished the last representative of a generation of pioneers, often self-taught as well, who from Edmond de Nevers to Esdras Minville laid the foundations of intellectual and scientific life in French Canada. Léon Gérin initiated us to the study of sociology; Bouchette, Montpetit, Minville to economics, Marie-Victorin to natural science, while Groulx devoted himself to history, although he had undertaken advanced studies in philosophy and theology.

Of course, Groulx had predecessors (Garneau, David, Sulte,

Turcotte) as well as rivals (Chapais, abbé Maheux). Yet he distinguished himself from them in more ways than one. By his concept of history, to start with. Groulx wanted to reconstruct the past in its entirety, not limit himself to one aspect, whether political or religious, or to any one period. No doubt he was influenced by the *Revue Synthèse* and the great masters of French historiography: Michelet, Fustel de Coulanges, Febvre. This meant undertaking a gigantic task, well beyond the capacity of a single man. Groulx was well aware of this, but he tried to trace the main outlines of such a historical work and contribute a few erudite bricks to complete the structure he could only plan.

Groulx also distinguished himself by his sense of mission. He wanted men of his generation to become more conscious of their national personality, of the distinct culture which was theirs, from which would emerge our collective will to live, and in which should be rooted our institutions and our laws. There is nothing very new in this, for at that period we were often reminded of our French and Catholic vocation in North America. But Groulx renewed the theme and enriched it by his great genius and his zeal for work. André Laurendeau has already quoted this opinion which Groulx confided to him: "My central intention at *L'Action française* was to engage in a doctrinal campaign to draw my compatriots away from a narrow mystique of language. What was needed was to show French Canadians that theirs was the problem of life itself: an organic, synthetic problem." Did this not add a dimension – and what a valuable dimension – to a well-worn theme? Groulx therefore related the evolution of the French Canadian people: how it was formed slowly in the seventeenth and eighteenth centuries, defined in the nineteenth, and is now so slow in affirming and developing itself in the twentieth. He describes this evolution with considerable pathos, and this is scarcely surprising. Part of the generation which had witnessed the hanging of Riel, the education struggles, and the outbursts of Mercier, he naturally expressed the evolution of his homeland in dramatic terms. The deeply moving tones of Groulx marked the rising generation of the 'twenties. Victor Barbeau, who described himself as a traveller without either luggage or compass, admits that it was Groulx who gave him his naturalization papers and his love of the homeland.

One last feature distinguished Groulx from his predecessors. He never lived in an ivory tower, he never set up a water-tight separation between his historical work and his national or political work. Within him there cohabited a man of research and a man of action in constant and mutually profitable dialogue. Constitutional and sociological problems encountered by the man of action furnished the historian with themes for research and subjects for courses; the values underpinning civilization, which were discovered by the historian, justified the aims of the man of action.

Physically, Groulx outlived his own work. His long retirement allowed him to enrich and perfect his historical work, yet it prevented his work from being subjected to healthy discussion. Through a sense of respect and veneration, new generations of historians were reluctant to commence the debate. This will no longer be delayed, for Groulx himself always maintained that everything must be discussed and everything questioned.

# Lionel Groulx, National Historian

Michel Brunet, "Lionel Groulx, historien national," *Canadian Historical Review* XLVIII, 3 (September 1967), pp. 299-305. Reprinted by permission of the author and the University of Toronto Press.

The sudden death of Canon Lionel Groulx on Tuesday morning, May 23, 1967, at his country home in Vaudreuil, on the very day he was to attend a party to mark the publication of his latest book, *Constantes de vie*, came as a surprise to all who knew him. And how many there are who did know him! The reception was held anyway, and some six hundred guests assembled in the lounges of the Fides Publishing Company to pay tribute to the great man who had just passed away.

Only then did people remember that Lionel Groulx was eighty-nine years old; he was born on the 13th of January, 1878. His dynamic personality, the frequency of his publications, his regular presence at several public events, his frequent interventions in contemporary debates between French- and English-speaking Canadians, a recent television programme during which he had recalled his major memories, the last annual meeting of the *Institut d'histoire de l'Amérique française*, his remarkable and widely commented participation in a colloquium on history held in the Youth Pavillion at Expo 67 a fortnight before, all these had led people to think that he was still the master historian that three successive generations of readers and students had known. Each of us still saw him as we had when we were twenty, when he had revealed our own nature to us, and aroused in us options which have influenced the present direction of our collectivity. This is why we thought of him as eternally young. In the lounges of Fides, guests whose ages ranged from twenty to seventy-five spoke of him as a man belonging to their own generation.

What a unique and amazing career was Lionel Groulx's! It is comparable to that of George Bancroft whose historical work forged the unity of the American nation. The historian Allan Nevins quite rightly claimed that Abraham Lincoln and his generation undertook and completed the task of saving the Union in 1861-1865 because the teachings of Bancroft had given them faith in themselves and in the destiny of the United States. Lionel Groulx, spiritual heir of François-Xavier Garneau who was a contemporary of Bancroft, completed the mission which circumstances had thrust upon the first national historian of French Canada.

Groulx was the son of country people with little education, people who were even rather suspicious of those whose ambition was to pursue their studies – they had so often been deceived by fancy talkers! Inspired by an admirable mother who detected an exceptional talent in him, he had to accept heavy sacrifices in order to go to school. He was thus formed in an environment whose values could only be those of a traditional rural society, yet from the very beginning of his career Groulx obviously belonged to the twentieth century. In 1906, in some truly revolutionary articles, he denounced a system of education which was not preparing young French Canadians for the tasks of an industrial and urban age. His writings shocked the timorous souls who were then in a powerful majority and earned him some profound antipathy. These hostile reactions did not in the least deter him. He never feared controversy and always believed in the freedom of the intellectual and the researcher. He was a great defender of academic freedom in French Canada. As an admirer of the precursors of social Catholicism in France, he wanted to prove that a Catholic education can produce men conscious of their new social responsibilities and ready to assume them in a society which would never return to the pre-industrial age. His students at the Seminary of Valleyfield, where he taught from 1903 to 1906 and from 1909 to 1915, were all marked by this rouser of men; the veneration they had for him reveals the immense gratitude they felt for an educator who had opened new horizons to them.

Groulx's ambition to engage in intellectual action and his anxiety to achieve concrete results led him to historical studies. When he had to teach a course in Canadian history at his college, he was, quite understandably, astonished to discover that the students had hitherto used textbooks, summaries, and chronological tables designed for primary schools. One of the summaries was even a translation of a book used in the English language schools of Quebec and Ontario. At that time, the advanced state of assimilation which spokesmen for the French Canadian collectivity delighted in had spontaneously produced *the one* textbook, the textbook of the dominant group. For the benefit of those people who are unaware of the degree of servility manifested in official circles in those days, let me just recall one example: candidates for the Prince of Wales' Prize, awarded by Laval University for the best essay written by a graduating Arts student, were asked one year to compose the speech given by a Member of the General Court in Massachussetts proposing a military expedition to wipe out New France! Faced with such a situation, Lionel Groulx decided to put together a course of national history himself, for his students at the Seminary of Valleyfield. A new path was opening before him.

Having noticed how little his compatriots knew about their history, particularly the country's constitutional evolution since the Conquest, Henri Bourassa wrote in *Le Devoir* deploring the serious neglect of history in the classical colleges and at the University. Bourassa's remarks provoked considerable reaction, and a great deal of discussion. Lionel Groulx and a few other college professors, among whom was Emile Chartier, later to become Dean of the Faculty of Letters and Vice-Rector of the University of Montreal, informed the editor of *Le Devoir* that far from being indifferent to the situation they were seeking to remedy it by pursuing original research with the aim of enriching their history courses. Bourassa congratulated them, but returned to the charge by calling for the establishment of Chairs of Canadian History at the University. In 1915, Thomas Chapais inaugurated his courses in Canadian history at Laval University in Quebec, and Lionel Groulx became the first occupant of a Chair of National History at what was then the Montreal campus of Laval University. A half-century had elapsed between the death of Jean-Baptiste Ferland and the first courses given by his successors at the University. What can the state of a discipline be which has not been taught at university level for such a long period? Those people who today express such astonishment that several fields open to historical research have not yet been explored, should remember these facts before pronouncing their rash judgments.

The new Professor's responsibility was to give five public lectures a year. The first was scheduled for November 3, 1915, and Groulx had only been told about his appointment the preceding summer. With only a few weeks notice, he was asked to prepare a book! For this undertaking, he received a fee of $50.00 a year, or $10.00 a lecture. In order to acquire the necessary books and to cover his transportation costs when he went to pursue research in Ottawa, Quebec or London, he had to rely on the generosity of a few friends and benefactors. Philippe Perrier, *curé* of the parish of Saint-Enfant-Jésus-du-Mile-End, gave him free bed and board at his vicarage. A few courses, paid by the hour, at the Faculty of Letters and the School for Higher Commercial Studies, where he taught universal history and the history of commerce, brought him an income of less than $800.00 a year. Such was the fate of an academic in the humanities in French Canada during the years 1915-1926! Yet, according to the official mythology, were French Canadians not supposed to maintain a humanist tradition? They certainly did not support it financially! Still, we must acknowledge the untiring devotion and absolute faithfulness of a small elite of men and women who understood, long before anyone else, the role played by this avant-garde intellectual and researcher. Among the collaborators who supported him without fail, we cannot forget his niece, Mme. Juliette Rémillard, who served as his unpaid secretary and research assistant for thirty years. The Lionel Groulx Foundation, set up through the initiative of Maxime Raymond, Groulx's student at Valleyfield, and a few other admirers and friends, today continues this tradition.

As a member of the group which organized the first Faculties in the University of Montreal when it obtained its independence in 1920, Groulx experienced all the difficulties which would have to be overcome by the men who tried to establish higher learning in French Canada. Having realized that he could not carry on his career as a writer and researcher while still an hourly-paid professor, Groulx requested, after much hesitation, a reasonable annual salary – only to be asked by the University authorities to sign a declaration pledging his loyalty to the institutions and political leaders of the country. Was he not the editor of *L'Action française*? Had he not, in that capacity, directed the inquiry into *Our Political Future* (1922) which foresaw the possibility of a break-up of Confederation? His ideas, his frankness, his intellectual independence, his search for new working hypotheses, his rejection of official clichés, his anxiety that his Quebec compatriots should have justice and social progress, his questioning of the political institutions inherited from the past, his concern for economics – all these disturbed vested interests, and provoked the men with power who had no reason to complain of the established order since it was profitable to them.

This kind, indulgent man discovered, to his sorrow, that he

had aroused a great deal of envy and even enmity. His opponents wished to reduce him to silence. With the counsel and support of his friends and disciples, he resisted the pressures exerted upon him and silenced those people who cast doubt on the value of his teaching and on the scientific nature of his historical work, among whom was a certain contributor to the *Canadian Historical Review* who swooped like a bird of prey upon each of his publications and tore it to strips. Firmly and proudly, Groulx won the cause of academic freedom, of the right of an academic to pursue his own research, to intervene in public debates, and to judge men and institutions whose behaviour and evolution he has watched. Contemporary French Canadian academics who at the present time enjoy a degree of freedom which compares very favourably with that of their colleagues in other North American universities, and whose status is closer to that of the European professor than to the Anglo-American "College teacher," owe a great debt of gratitude to Lionel Groulx, this pioneer of intellectual commitment and action within the university community, beyond the bounds set down and imposed by the "Establishment". His example and that of his successors opened the way for the new charter of the University of Montreal, the most protective of academic freedom and one of the most democratic in the Atlantic world.

A few narrow minds seeking simplistic explanations and incapable of grasping the multiple dimensions and various stages of the distinguished career of this constantly vigilant researcher, this particularly gifted writer, this hard worker, this eloquent speaker – a veritable generator of energy – this master of thought, wanted to dismiss him with a few catch phrases. They accused him of racism, because he used the word "race" at a time when it meant a collectivity, a nationality, an ethnic or cultural group, a nation. Did anyone contend that André Siegfried was a racist because he published a book in 1906 called: *Le Canada: les deux races (The Race Question in Canada)*? Many people are also determined to see in Groulx a doctrinaire disciple of Maurras. Have they even read his work and that of Maurras? It never occurs to them that a French Canadian thinker could pursue an independent intellectual path simply by casting a novel and penetrating eye on the Canadian and North American situation. Just because they parrot ideas derived from foreign authors whom they have largely misunderstood, and just because they are unable to adapt such ideas to a pan-Canadian setting, they imagine that other researchers suffer from the same kind of mimicry, the same kind of intellectual colonialism.

Finally, the great accusation was made, the supreme

condemnation: Lionel Groulx was an Anglophobe. In fact neither hatred nor envy ever clouded the vision of this man whose ideas were large and generous, whose convictions were democratic because he believed in the innate good sense of the people if politicians would only attempt to inform them rather than deceive them, who respected opinions expressed by honest opponents, and who always exhibited the most refined politeness, an indication of his self-control. However, if every French Canadian who refuses to espouse the opinions and concepts of the Anglo-Canadian majority, who refuses to submit himself in a servile way to its leadership, who recognizes his solidarity with his own ethnic group and who wishes to work for its advancement, – if every such man suffers from Anglophobia then we might as well say straight away that all *Canadiens* who are not entirely assimilated by Canadians are Anglophobes. Given such a view, there must be some 5,000,000 anglophobic *Canadiens* in Canada. Applying the same criteria to English Canada, we would have some 15,000,000 Canadians who are Francophobes. At the dawning of Confederation's second century, has the time not come to abandon these puerile debates which belong to a past era in which Canada had not yet attained its political maturity?

All these erroneous myths rest upon the tragic blindness of accusers pretending to be judges, upon their ignorance of the intellectually liberating work accomplished by the man who, after François-Xavier Garneau, had the role and thus the heavy responsibilities of being the national historian of French Canada. Groulx will be the last historian to merit the title, for a collectivity cannot have several national historians. In the United States, George Bancroft did not have a successor, and English Canada, because of particular circumstances, among which must figure a prolonged colonial mentality, has never had a national historian. Such a historian usually appears in societies which have been subjugated and have had to struggle to liberate themselves. Every tiny nation of central or southern Europe which detached itself from the former Ottoman and Austro-Hungarian Empires has had its national historian. A few historians have played a similar role in a Germany which had been parcelled out in turn to the imperialist ambitions of Spain, France, Sweden, and the Austro-Hungarian Empire. In the United States, the work of Bancroft justified the Revolution of 1776 and consolidated the unity of a democratic nation which was determined to gain recognition in the face of a hostile and monarchic Europe. By reading their national historian, Americans of the nineteenth century gained confidence in themselves and their destiny. A study of the historiography and the political evolution of most of the former colonies which have become independent nations in Latin America, Africa and Asia reveals the same phenomenon.

In French Canada, Lionel Groulx was the master craftsman of a global emancipation. The humble rural environment in which he grew up, unlike that of the traditional elites, had not undergone the slow assimilation or de-culturalization experienced by French-Canadian families who, over two or three generations, had raised themselves to the higher echelons of society. Take, for example, the case of Thomas Chapais. Through his family and his psychological inheritance, he was linked with the Establishment. His view of the past and the present remained on the whole, that of the winning team, a "Whig interpretation", as Herbert Butterfield has called it. Groulx came to the study of history with a rather different outlook, even though his first works do reveal that he had partly absorbed the official interpretation of the past which had hitherto been generally accepted in well-heeled and right-thinking circles; this can be seen in his excessive severity for the France of Louis XV, his unjust opinion of the men administering Canada during the last years of the French regime, the argument that the British occupation had been a stimulating challenge to the *Canadiens*, the thesis that the latter had consolidated their nationality as they saw themselves cut off from France and forced to abandon their continental adventures, the idea of the benefits derived from British institutions and the material prosperity resulting from the enterprise and initiative of British capitalists, and other such hackneyed commonplaces.

His research, his reading, his observations, his reflections, his intimate contact with the ordinary people of Quebec – people who have been in a state of passive resistance from the very beginning of the British occupation immediately following the Conquest and have remained least affected by the process of assimilation – made him aware of, and thus rapidly free himself from, certain assumptions which had been uncritically transmitted by the leaders and spokesmen of previous generations. Even as a young schoolboy, he had felt the popular passion both at home and in his village against the execution of Louis Riel. The Boer War shocked him. Like the majority of French Canadians, he saw in it a brutal manifestation of British imperialism directed against a small defenceless people. Many people in Great Britain had the same reaction. The passionate and chauvinistic attitude of British Americans was a revelation to him of the racism and Anglo-Saxon nationalism of English Canada. The foul war presently waged by the United States in Vietnam has had a similar impact on the conscience of nations who resist domination by powerful countries or alliances. The educational persecutions in Manitoba and Ontario moved Groulx profoundly. The difficult destiny of his compatriots obliged to emigrate to the United States awakened within him a particular interest in our community's economic and social problems. The large-scale transformation of urban French Canadians into a proletarian class shocked him. He widened his view of the past and took care to introduce socio-economic aspects into his historical studies. The history of ideas equally retained his attention. He was one of the first to see the weakness of history written exclusively about political and constitutional problems. He did not fear to question the Constitution of 1867 or to ask whether it had to be considered the final phase in the historical evolution of Canada. He exploded the myth that Providence had permitted the British Conquest in order to protect French Canadians from the "wicked" French Revolution. All his work and all his activities have helped to de-assimilate French Canadians who now see themselves as members of a distinct collectivity in the valley of the Saint Lawrence, associated through history with the English Canadian nation.

A pioneer and precursor in many fields nowadays explored by the historians, sociologists, economists and political scientists of French Canada, Groulx often shocked the men who profited by the established order and drew their angry fire. At the French Language Congress in 1937, he brutally declared them to be the "generation of the dead", and that the French State, an ideal pursued by the collectivity since the foundation of New France in the seventeenth century, would be achieved by the "generation of the living". His opponents and critics at the time, with their facile popularity among assimilated French Canadians, among inveterate and invertebrate advocates of *bonne entente*, and among English Canadians, have suffered the humiliation of being buried and forgotten even before their death. When one thinks that they once considered themselves to be in the mainstream of history!

One of the great moments of Groulx's career occurred when the Canadian Historical Association, during its annual meeting in Montreal, in 1961, awarded a certificate of merit to the *Institut d'histoire de l'Amérique française* and to its journal which Groulx had founded fifteen years earlier and awarded him the title of Honourary Life Member. Although he had previously received many tokens of appreciation and many honours, the gesture of his colleagues throughout the country touched him deeply. Forgetting the malevolent criticism for which the *Canadian Historical Review* had occasionally been a medium, and the unfair judgments which badly-informed or hostile observers from English Canada had passed on him, Groulx had the great consolation of seeing, after spending almost half a century in historical research, that members of the historical profession had at last attained a sufficient degree of maturity and objectivity to engage in a veritable dialogue.

The last meeting of the Learned Societies in Ottawa, during which historians, economists and political scientists proved that they are henceforth able to analyze the problems of Canada without the emotions and prejudices which have paralyzed the progress of the social sciences, was an eloquent demonstration that the tribute paid to Groulx in 1961 had been only the first step in a pan-Canadian movement of intellectual and scientific development. We are rapidly approaching a meeting point, when people defining the two Canadas will use the same words to describe the phenomena of coexistence between *Canadiens* and Canadians, and will provide mutually acceptable definitions of the problems which we face in common. The solution of these problems will certainly then be much easier, or at least less difficult.

Lionel Groulx was fortunate to pursue his career long enough to realize that his vision had been an accurate one. His intellectual daring as well as his writings favoured the emergence in French Canada of a type of collective thought better adapted to our time and whose beneficial results we are just beginning to see in our daily undertakings. At his death, a unique and revealing phenomenon occurred in Quebec. At least three generations met to acknowledge their debt towards him. Even English Canada joined French Canada in this respect. Its principal newspapers printed tributes to Lionel Groulx which they would not have dreamed of doing twenty years ago. Another sign of the times.

The last national historian of French Canada, Lionel Groulx contributed as well to the advance of English Canadian historiography. His work, his novel hypotheses, the disciples he inspired in all fields of social science, the politicians who found useful information in his work – all these obliged the historians, sociologists, economists and political scientists of English Canada to realize that their reading of Canada's past, present and future could be questioned and that they had not received from God the privilege of always being right. The challenge of his work and that of his successors led them to a revision of their frame of reference, their assumptions, and their age-old prejudices. In this sense, Groulx has been doubly a national historian since his fertile career has served the two Canadas, that is, the whole of Canada.

# Lionel Groulx

André Laurendeau, "Lionel Groulx," Le Devoir, May 24, 1967. Reprinted by permission.

As I write I am far from his books, far from any reference, far from the documents I should no doubt consult. But I am near him. Nor am I quite willing to acknowledge that we must now speak of him in the past.

It was such a short time ago that we saw him on television. He was relating some of his memories, with which I was already familiar, by and large. A reporter, forced to mind the clock, occasionally interrupted him. We were furious with the reporter. We felt like saying to him: "Will you be quiet: he knows where he is going, and we are completely happy to follow him!" He was very old; he spoke rather laboriously, in a weak voice, but after the first thirty seconds, did anyone take any notice?

He was speaking of his background. He spoke of his mother, the only educated daughter in her family – and educated, at that, against the wishes of her own father. He spoke, and this was not just rhetoric for him, of the courage of country people; he remembered the misgivings they had about education. A world so near and yet so far! We thought: how distant his place of origin, how prodigiously far he has come, yet his simplicity and courage stamp him indisputably as someone from that world.

I first knew the historian in the Faculty of Letters at the University of Montreal, not so much through his early books, which are a trifle eloquent, but rather through his less formal seminars for groups of ten students. That was where he revealed the results of his research, and his very soul.

Everything which had hitherto seemed disconnected to me in the history of French Canada – dates, military chronicles, missionary annals – all these he gathered in his vigorous grasp. At last I thought I understood something of the history of my own people. The past – "the past, our master" – made sense.

Did it make the right sense? He would repeat that all historians write for their own generation. A passionate synthesis may catch the attention of the young but is soon shown to be vulnerable. In that sense, the work of any historian is soon dated. Yet it is this very quality which rescues the truly great works – the inspiration, the fundamental intention, the feeling for life and the power to recreate it.

He spoke of what he called a "race", which was becoming, in the vocabulary of that period, a "nationality", and is today a nation. But the expression which came most spontaneously to his lips was *ce petit peuple*, "this tiny people", the object of his love, his anxieties, his hope. I think that he was referring to the ordinary folk, the humble people from which he himself had emerged, as well as to an entire community relegated in North America to the role of the underdog.

His intention was to see that role in all its reality. When he was young, discussion centered on the language, the rights of the language, the value and qualities of the language. Without denying the importance of language, he wished both to extend and to fathom the problem. Thus it happened that along with others – Olivar Asselin and Edouard Montpetit for example – he began to explore the political, economic and social dimensions of his "tiny people". The issues soon took on a quite different dimension. That, I believe, is what he bequeathed to succeeding generations; he helped them move away from narrow views and to confront the entire problem.

He went forward, slowly. He had a sense of reality: while remaining very much himself, he was capable of evolving, annexing new ideas, listening to the young. His determination to be open to everything was remarkable. That, in any case, was the man as I knew him, pessimistic about short term progress, occasionally rude to his own people, hard-headed, sometimes gloomy, but always ready to spring back, always capable of hope.

People have stressed the fact that some of his views were rather idealistic: his concept of an "idyllic" New France, for example, or his delight in heroes to whom he perhaps contributed rather generously from his own imagination. Quite apart from this often exhilarating mythology, we should notice the realism of his demands, his instinctive rejection of empty formulas or solutions based principally on good intentions. In 1937, when he cried out: "We *shall* have our French State", I cannot tell whether he was thinking of full sovereignty for Quebec, but I know that he was concerned more with the internal structure of the building than with its façade, with a genuine utilization of institutions which would at last become active and creative – in short with everything we have come to know since 1959. For the quiet revolution was partly an eruption into reality of ideas which Groulx had nurtured and championed for more than a third of a century. Thus the tribute recently paid to him by the Legislative Assembly in Quebec takes on symbolic value.

Those who felt his influence and recognize it are not at all alike, and they often opt for contradictory things. Nothing, it seems to me, could show more clearly the great fertility of his work.

This was a man imbued with his priesthood, and his religious faith never ceased being the primary source of his inspiration.

On the other hand he also took part in the quarrels of the world, but without ever being narrowly partisan. I have met few men with such a virile spirit of independence. His convictions never deserted him; he knew how to distance himself from them, to adopt a detached attitude, yet nothing was more magnificent than his sense of loyalty, unless perhaps it was the youthful ardour with which he threw himself into life.

We loved him dearly.

# Suggested Reading

*L'Oeuvre du Chanoine Lionel Groulx, Témoignages Bio-Bibliographie.* Montreal, Les publications de l'Académie canadienne-française, 1964.

*Le Canada français: classes sociales, idéologies et infériorité economique. Recherches Sociographiques* VI, 1 (January-April 1965).

Cook, Ramsay. *Canada and the French Canadian Question.* Toronto, Macmillan, 1966.

Cook, Ramsay (ed.) *French Canadian Nationalism: An Anthology.* Toronto, Macmillan, 1969.

Fraser, Blair. "Crisis in Quebec," *Maclean's* 57 (August 15, 1944).

Hughes, E. C. *French Canada in Transition.* Chicago, University of Chicago Press, 1943.

Levitt, Joseph. *Henri Bourassa and the Golden Calf.* Ottawa, University of Ottawa Press, 1970.

*Lionel Groulx, ptre. L'Action nationale* LVII, 10 (June 1968).

Mudroch, V. "The Abbé Groulx – History as a Weapon," *Queen's Quarterly* LXIII (Summer 1956), pp. 179-187.

Oliver, Michael. "The Social and Political Ideas of French Canadian Nationalists, 1920-1945" McGill University, unpublished PhD thesis, 1956.

"Quebec Today," *University of Toronto Quarterly* (April 1958).

Robertson, Susan Mann (Trofimenkoff). "L'Action française: l'appel à la race," Université Laval, unpublished PhD thesis, 1970.

——."Variations on an nationalist theme: Henri Bourassa and abbé Groulx in the 1920's," *Canadian Historical Association Historical Papers* (1970), pp. 109-119.

Stanley, G.F.G. "Lionel-Adolphe Groulx: historian and prophet of French Canada," in L. Lapierre (ed.), *Four O'Clock Lectures. French Canadian Thinkers of the Nineteenth and Twentieth Centuries.* Montreal, McGill University Press, 1966.

Vadeboncoeur, Pierre. "A Break with Tradition? Political and Cultural Evolution in Quebec," *Queen's Quarterly* LXV (Spring 1958), pp. 92-103.

Wade, Mason. *The French Canadians.* 2 vols. rev. ed., Toronto, Macmillan, 1968.

1 2 3 4 5   #13300   78 77 76 75 74